The True Story of The
Maid of Orleans

MAURICE DAVID-DARNAC

The True Story of The Maid of Orleans

Translated by PETER de POLNAY
from the French 'Histoire véridique et
merveilleuse de la pucelle d'Orléans'

W. H. ALLEN · LONDON · 1969

HISTOIRE VÉRIDIQE ET MERVEILLEUSE
DE LA PUCELLE D'ORLÉANS
© EDITIONS DE LA TABLE RONDE, 1965
TRANSLATION © W. H. ALLEN AND CO. LTD., 1969
MADE AND PRINTED IN GREAT BRITAIN BY
THE GARDEN CITY PRESS LIMITED
LETCHWORTH, HERTFORDSHIRE
FOR THE PUBLISHERS
W. H. ALLEN AND CO. LTD.,
ESSEX STREET, LONDON W.C.2
491 00083 9

'A historian should be guided by one aim alone: the search for truth.'

LUDWIG VON PASTOR
History of the Popes

'NE QUID FALSI AUDEAT
NE QUID VERI NON AUDEAT'

POPE PIUS XI

'The Church has nothing to gain by the spreading of vain legends, nothing to lose by the manifestation of historical truth.'

POPE PIUS XII

'It is good to guard the secret of a King, but glorious to reveal the works of God.'

THE BOOK OF TOBIT, XII; 7

Introduction

Every French schoolboy knows that Jeanne d'Arc was born at Domrémy, liberated Orléans, took Charles VII to Reims to be crowned, was taken prisoner at Compiègne, burnt at the stake in Rouen, and remains the most popular and attractive figure in French history.

In 1429 two-thirds of French territory was occupied by the English and the country seemed lost. Jeanne appeared, kindled the flames of hope, stimulated the nation and forced victory to change sides. The defeated enemy was struck by panic, and, put to flight, was soon chased out of the Kingdom of the Fleur-de-Lys. This complete reversal of the situation in less than two years sharply strikes the imagination; however one is even more astonished by the vivid contrasts one finds throughout her heroic career.

The national heroine of France is a shepherdess who dictates the king's conduct, a young girl whom great captains obey, an innocent pious victim condemned by an ecclesiastical court, abandoned by a king who owes his throne to her, a saint who has to wait for centuries before Rome accepts her. She rose suddenly out of obscurity, gloriously held the stage for some months, then disappeared in the infamous flames of the stake, and hardly was she burnt before her executioners hid their faces, trembling. How deeply moving, how worthy of admiration and full of marvels are the great moments of Jeanne's life!

Understandably an immense number of books of all varieties, historical studies, poems, plays and other literary works were written about her in France and throughout the world. With a few exceptions, which only showed up their dismal authors, all and sundry who wrote of her sang her praise and bowed to the purity of her soul. Her exploits inspired many painters who depicted her in different moments of her life, and her statue, invariably decorated with flowers in May, can be found in every French church.

Everything seems to have been said about her, everything is known about her, except the truth, perhaps. Precisely because of her immense importance in French history many historians have tried to solve the mystery of some of the episodes in that extraordinary and marvellous life which strangely have remained in obscurity. Patient research by learned men, ingenious theories put forward by seekers of truth, untramelled by accepted tradition and encouraged by unexpected discoveries, have succeeded in slightly lifting the veil which five hundred years ago was drawn over the origins and life of one who was to become the great saint of France.

Today there are several who, drawn by the epic poem that was her life, cannot help asking themselves whether the real Maid of Orléans was truly the humble peasant girl who, according to school books and all approved biographies, was born in Domrémy and died in Rouen.

We believe that the truth is quite different.

A number of readers will first be astonished by this Life which is so different from all they learnt at school, but if they are willing, as it were, to shake off what they heard in their youth, they will be surprised that such a work was not written before and by a more competent hand. As regards those who will shout "Sacrilege!", may we be allowed to point out that what matters most in the study of history is the search for truth whatever the result? And that as that exceptional woman appears under her real name and true personality she becomes greater, more beautiful and even worthier of our admiration.

One

At the beginning of the fifteenth century France was overrun by complete anarchy. The tenacity of Charles V and Du Guesclin's victories had almost restored the unity of the kingdom. Of all the provinces handed over to the English by the disastrous Treaty of Brétigny in 1360, only Calais and a part of Guyenne near Bordeaux remained in English hands.

But the kings of England had by no means renounced their claim to the throne of France; in the other camp, the French monarchs were waiting for the first auspicious occasion to re-unite the lost provinces with France. In fact, the truce lasting for thirty-five years was caused as much by the exhaustion of the two belligerents as by the troubles inside their kingdoms.

Since 1392 France had been stricken by the fits of madness from which Charles VI suffered, for they brought in their wake a ferocious struggle among those who wanted to gain real power in the land. By consent the old councillors of the king, who had administered the country with wisdom and sagacity, were elimin-ated without any rewards for their past services, and were replaced by a Regency Council, the members of which were the four uncles of the king, who in a short time fell under the influence and rule of the most brazen of them, the powerful Philippe, Duke of Burgundy.

The unfortunate Charles VI in his moments of lucidity saw the dangers his dynasty was exposed to by Philippe, who did not succeed in hiding his ambition to become king of France, and tried his best to hand over the government of the country to his brother, Louis d'Orléans. However, when he relapsed into mad-ness it became easy for the Burgundian again to be entrusted with the direction of public affairs.

With great cunning the Duke of Burgundy dazzled his

nephew Louis, Duc d'Orléans,* who by his marriage to Valentine Visconti had become the son-in-law of Giovanni Galeazzo, one of the most powerful lords in Northern Italy, with prospects of glorious victories and a second crown beyond the Alps.

In 1394 the Duc d'Orléans' troops, commanded by Enguerrand de Coucy, occupied Liguria, taking twenty fortified localities including Savonna. However the occupation, which was the first phase in the plan to establish a kingdom in Italy to be called Adria, bore no fruit and was of short duration. Indeed, in 1396 the cream of French knighthood, answering the anguished appeal of King Sigismund of Hungary, hastened to join his forces under the orders of the future King Jean sans Peur, and was crushed by the Sultan Bajazet. Thus d'Orléans' best soldiers found heroic deaths under the walls of Nicopolis.

Moreover, the personal ambitions of Giovanni Galeazzo, newly created Duke of Milan with the help of the Holy Roman Emperor; the indecision of the French Court and the influence of the Duke of Burgundy; added to the difficulties begotten by the Great Schism which opposed the Pope in Rome in his struggle against the supporters of the second Pope in Avignon, quickly brought to an end the aims of the Duc d'Orléans in Italy.

As a result the intrigues of the Burgundian became weapons turned against himself; for his nephew, disappointed in his hopes, never ceased opposing him whenever the opportunity presented itself. In every field the two men now were in open rivalry.

Valentine Visconti was the only person who retained a constant influence over the unfortunate Charles VI. In order to rid himself of her the Duke of Burgundy cleverly brought on the scene Isabeau of Bavaria whose grandfather, Bernabo, had been assassinated in Milan on the orders of Giovanni Galeazzo. Accused of having practised magic on the king, the Duchesse d'Orléans had to leave the Court in September 1396, and her enraged husband had to accept this humiliation. In the same

* *Translator's Note: Princes who were rulers of their own lands or provinces are referred to throughout the work in the English style— e.g. the Duke of Burgundy while ducal subjects of the King of France are styled in the French manner—e.g. Duc d'Orléans.*

year Philippe le Hardi, who sought the English alliance, succeeded in marrying off Isabelle, daughter of Charles VI, to King Richard II of England. Immediately Louis d'Orléans hastened to support Henry of Lancaster who unthroned Richard in 1399, a success of short duration, as the Duke of Burgundy soon came to an understanding with the new sovereign in London.

The conflict in Brittany was handled in a similar manner, Louis wanting the guardianship of young Jean V but Philippe obtaining it.

The deposing of the Emperor Wenceslas of Luxembourg by the Diet of Oberlahnstein in August 1400 and his replacement by the Elector Palatine Robert of Bavaria once again divided the Regency Council, Louis wishing to support the deposed Emperor, whereas Philippe declared himself in favour of the new scheme of things. Here also the Burgundian succeeded, because in the end Wenceslas himself acknowledged the new Emperor.

More and more infuriated by his uncle, Louis d'Orléans nevertheless achieved an important advantage. On August 18, 1402 he bought the Duchy of Luxembourg from Josse, first cousin of Wenceslas, for the sum of one hundred thousand *ducats*. By securing for himself that corner of land between Flanders and Burgundy he dealt Philippe a heavy blow.

Armed conflict seemed inevitable between the two rivals; and the two adversaries were preparing themselves for it by looking for outside help when suddenly Philippe le Hardi died on April 27, 1404. Owing to his death the Duc d'Orléans became master of the situation, helped by the fact that Isabeau of Bavaria, having at last understood that she was but a pawn in the hands of the Burgundian, now took the part of her brother-in-law.

At the time the Queen of France was thirty-three years old. Daughter of Etienne II, Duke of Bavaria, she was married to Charles VI when she was fourteen years old and he seventeen. Of that union, a happy one till 1392, five children were born before the king fell ill: Charles, born in 1386, who died two months after; Jeanne born in 1388, who died in infancy; Isabelle born in 1399 who was intended for Richard II; Jeanne again who was to marry Jean VI, Duke of Brittany; and another Charles born in 1392, heir to the throne till his death in 1401.

During the first phase of the King's mental illness the marriage ties remained more or less constant and five more children were born. Marie, in 1393 who died as a nun in 1438; in 1395 Michelle, the future wife of Philippe le Bon, Duke of Burgundy; Louis in 1397, who married Marguerite, daughter of Jean sans Peur, and died in 1415; Jean born in 1398, future husband of Jacqueline of Bavaria, who died in 1417; finally Catherine born in 1401, who was to marry King Henry V of England.

Because Charles VI's brainstorms became more frequent, and more and more violent, from 1402 the marriage of the royal couple ceased to function. When he was seized by violent madness which petrified all the people round him, the King rushed along the passages of the palace and struck anybody he found in his way with his sword. On several occasions the Queen herself narrowly missed becoming her unfortunate husband's victim. After the attacks the King fell dazed into a sort of coma, spending his entire days in the Hôtel Saint-Pol (the royal palace in Paris) stretched out on his bed, refusing to be nursed by his servants. During the lulls in which he partially recovered his reason the queen left the Hôtel Barbette, which she bought in 1401 and where she resided most of the time, and resumed conjugal relations. In such circumstances she gave birth to her eleventh child, the future Charles VII, on February 21, 1403. But the King's madness became more and more violent, those around him only approached him trembling, the unhappy monarch, covered in filth and vermin, was but a lamentable wreck.

By the beginning of 1404 Isabeau, perceiving at last that the real ambition of the Duke of Burgundy was to get rid of Charles VI and to mount the throne himself, decided to enter into an alliance with her brother-in-law, the Duc d'Orléans, who was then thirty-three years old. He was one of the most magnificent noblemen in the kingdom. Tall, slim, elegant and cultured, he attracted everyone by the charm that practically oozed from him, and was a great lady killer. Isabeau, who had tired of a husband who illtreated her during his periods of insanity, could not for long resist the spell of such a seducer. To the great shock of the people of Paris, who reproached the Duc d'Orléans with his excessive prodigality and the Queen for leading a festive life in the midst of a debauched court, the two lovers publicly flaunted their relationship.

Louis and Isabeau had another reason for making public their love affair: several of the eleven children the King had sired died at an early age, and Louis, the heir to the throne, was in poor health like his brother Jean, while Charles, the youngest boy, was such a puny child that everybody was of the opinion that he would not live long. Consequently, if the male descendants of Charles VI were to die, the crown would come to the Duc d'Orléans. In this far from unlikely event Isabeau's position would be assured at Court, even without entertaining the possibility of the Duc d'Orléans marrying her after repudiating Valentine, who since 1396 had been exiled to the Château d'Asnières, from where he was in no hurry to recall her to Paris.

The Regency Council spent the whole year of 1404 in preparation for the renewal of hostilities with England. The Duc d'Orléans had himself appointed Lieutenant-General in Normandy and Picardy by his brother, and obtained from the King of Navarre the retrocession of the port of Cherbourg and the town of Evreux. Moreover, he was given the fortified places which protected Paris from the north, Soissons, Ham and Coucy; already in possession of Orléans, Dreux and Château-Thierry he controlled a solid belt enabling him to protect the capital equally from the English and from the Burgundians. And while in Guyenne and in the Limousin the King's troops skirmished with the English garrisons and the soldiers of the Constable d'Albret, a fleet was being hastily prepared at Brest, its goal the invasion of Wales.

The money needed for all these enterprises was collected through a special tax, and the sums thus obtained were stacked in a tower of the Louvre, whence it was forbidden to remove them without permission of the Regency Council. However, in the face of the opposition shown by the Duc de Berry, who was more or less in agreement with Jean sans Peur, the Duc d'Orléans, armed with a permit he had wrung from Charles VI in a moment of the King's weakness, got hold of that treasure and with it himself financed the preparations for war.

However those resources proved inadequate, and in the month of March 1405, the Regency Council was obliged to raise new levies for the purpose of "resisting the ventures of Henry of Lancaster, so-called King of England."

Skilfully the new Duke of Burgundy chose that propitious occasion to make his entry on the scene. After the death of Philippe le Hardi, Jean sans Peur had hurried back to his states in order to claim his inheritance. Back in Paris at the beginning of the year 1405, he came to an agreement of sorts with Isabeau, in which they promised each other mutual friendship, though Isabeau had not forgotten that while his father was still alive Jean sans Peur had several times hinted at favouring the murder of the Duc d'Orléans and the dethronement of Charles VI. Furthermore, she was well aware that the new head of the House of Burgundy would do his utmost to put his threats into execution so as to gain the kingdom of France for himself.

The general levy ordered by the Council hit not only the usual taxpayers, but also the clergy who in normal conditions were exempt. Jean sans Peur immediately let it be known that the order to levy the tax was illegal, since the Council had not decided on it unanimously, both he and the Duc de Berry opposing it. He declared that he would forbid the collecting of this tax in his Burgundian and Flemish states, adding that before any new levy was decided on it was indispensable to have an inquiry into the uses made of previously collected funds. His demagogic language went straight to the hearts of those on whom the taxes had been levied.

To counteract Jean sans Peur's declaration, the Royal Council had to resort to devaluation, which at once raised a great outcry and vigorous protests. As the Parisians did not fail to take advantage of the confused situation by abstaining from paying the new tax, the Council reacted by having a certain number of tax dodgers thrown into prison; and to the sound of trumpets the recalcitrant populace was warned at every crossroads in the capital that carrying daggers or swords was henceforth forbidden. All those authoritarian measures only helped to increase the general malaise, especially as rumours originating from the Duke of Burgundy, made people believe that the Queen had sent six waggons laden with gold to Bavaria. On top of all this, the Burgundian faction assured the people that a reasonable tax levied on "1,700,000 towns and villages" was ample to obtain the funds necessary for the national expenses and the pursuit of the war against England. This handsome reform plan, though without any serious foundation, immediately brought Jean sans Peur enormous popularity.

In the month of July 1405 the Duke of Burgundy asked the Royal Council for credits he considered necessary to raise an army with which he proposed to recapture Calais from the English. On the pretext that the royal coffers were empty, thanks to the Duke of Burgundy's actions, the Duc d'Orléans saw to it that the Council rejected his demand. Besides, Orléans was far from convinced of his cousin's sincerity when he declared his intention to fight the King of England with whom the Flemish cities had entered into a very advantageous commercial treaty.

At last Jean sans Peur perceived that only through the use of force could he achieve his aims; and on August 15, 1405, he left Arras with an army of six thousand lances, declaring that he was resolved to occupy Paris and take into his own hands the reins of the government of the kingdom.

Realising that all resistance would be useless since the capital was entirely on his adversary's side, Louis d'Orléans left Paris precipitately on August 18, accompanied by Isabeau and followed a few hours later by a large troop which included Louis, the Dauphin, and other royal children. Crossing Paris quickly on August 19 the Duke of Burgundy caught up in Juvisy with the convoy that was taking the Dauphin away, and took the Dauphin back to the capital. Thus he held in the person of the heir to the throne a most valuable hostage and had no qualms in making use of him in furthering his ambitions.

The following day Louis d'Orléans sent a protest to the Parliament of Paris, complaining of his cousin's conduct, but the Parliament, which was entirely won over by Jean sans Peur, restricted itself to registering the protest but doing nothing else.

On August 26 the Duke of Burgundy staged a great scene at the Hôtel Saint-Pol, presenting Charles VI with a long petition in which he attacked the administration of the Duc d'Orléans, and swore not to disband his army before serious reforms were undertaken and accomplished in the kingdom, especially where finance and justice were concerned. In his semi-coma the King approved all the Burgundian asked for, and agreed to the text of the petition to be read in every town in every province.

At once Louis d'Orléans reacted by making public his indignation caused by his cousin's behaviour in having separated the Queen from her children, by force, particularly from the Dauphin who was held as a prisoner in the Louvre. Jean sans Peur replied by stating in simple terms his loyalty to the crown. However, these exchanges did not stop the two adversaries from preparing to join battle. While the Flemish and the Burgundians occupied the valley of the Oise the Duc d'Orléans massed the bulk of his troops in the district of Melun.

Civil war seemed inevitable, but the old Duc de Bourbon, who plotted the ruin of Jean sans Peur, was cunning enough to make Charles VI sign an ordnance forbidding his subjects without any exception to resort to arms in the defence of any cause whatever. Then one after the other the Kings of Sicily and Navarre and the Duc de Berry intervened to bring about peace between the two enemies.

With hatred in his heart the Duke of Burgundy was compelled on September 20 to sign an agreement with the Duc d'Orléans. The two cousins faithfully promised to live in friendship with one another and to work jointly for the common weal. A few days later, escorted by the members of the Regency Council, Isabeau of Bavaria took up residence again in the Hôtel Saint-Pol.

Nonetheless the crisis was far from over. Instigated by the Duke of Burgundy, the University of Paris demanded reforms in the administration of the kingdom. The Regency Council confined itself to a few savings by dismissing a number of officials. But nothing drastic was done as evidently Louis d'Orléans did not wish to lose the presence of those he had put into different government jobs. Jean sans Peur was careful not to insist, as by not doing so he retained the advantage of an excellent position when the time came to be able to say that in spite of his proposals no serious reforms had been carried out.

Soon their partisans began provoking each other anew. They were encouraged by their leaders who showed their hostility in public. In answer to the Duc d'Orléans who took as his emblem a knotty staff with the motto "Je l'ennuie," the Duke of Burgundy riposted by choosing one with a plane tree. "Je le tiens," was the inscription surrounding it.

Jean sans Peur had on his side the town of Paris with its

Parliament, the University and the well-organised, powerful guilds. But Louis d'Orléans had succeeded in winning to his side the provinces, in particular the Midi, which were envious of the corporations and other organised bodies of the capital. Also many joined forces with him because of their mounting fear of the authoritarian methods of the Burgundian. Yet neither of the two cousins was strong enough to carry it off inasmuch as a large bulk of people were undecided on which faction to join. It was, therefore, most necessary for one as for the other to improve his position before new hostilities could break out between them.

On January 27, 1406 Jean sans Peur succeeded in getting the King to sign an ordnance conferring on him all the powers that his father had exercised in the Council. The Duc d'Orléans tried in vain to parry that blow by finding some counter-measure. The most he achieved was to marry his son Charles to Isabelle, widow of Richard II and daughter of Charles VI and Isabeau of Bavaria. However, that momentary advantage was immediately rendered void by the Duke of Burgundy who persuaded the Council to agree to the marriage of his niece Jacqueline of Bavaria, daughter of Marguerite of Burgundy, with the Dauphin's younger brother, Jean Duc de Touraine. At the double wedding on June 24, 1406 which took place at Compiègne, the two rivals made an effort to show a bold front and exchanged presents and honeyed words, though nobody was gullible enough to believe that their mutual politeness had a sincere basis. Jean sans Peur had especially to exercise immense control in not showing the anger within him, for as a retort to the treaty of alliance between the Dukes of Burgundy and Lorraine his adversary did not hesitate to support the Liégeois in their revolt against their bishop, who was the brother-in-law of his cousin. In this way, being already master of Luxembourg, Louis d'Orléans' influence spread into that region and could thus turn from the north the Flemish possessions of his rival.

At the beginning of 1407 members of the Duke of Burgundy's household let it be publicly known that the year would not pass without Jean sans Peur executing the Duc d'Orléans and all his descendants. Those words much alarmed Isabeau of Bavaria who was expecting to give birth to a child in the autumn.

For many years Louis d'Orléans had been in the habit of

going to the Monastery of the Celestins to see aged Philippe de Maizières who had in the old days been one of the most prudent advisers of Charles V and with whom he enjoyed discussing matters of state. One morning in the month of May in 1407, after having passed a night in the monastery, where he shared the life of the monks and assisted at all offices night and day, Louis d'Orléans had a vision: his death was at hand. He then hurried home, and told Isabeau of his vision. Isabeau was overcome. Together they decided on the course to follow in case he died. Independently from all the other plans they made to safeguard their personal interests they discussed the future of the child Isabeau was carrying, their one aim to protect it from the hatred of the Duke of Burgundy. The Queen was convinced that it would be a boy who in time would become his father's avenger if the Duc d'Orléans were to perish fighting Jean sans Peur.

By the middle of the summer it was evident that the first incident would spark off the war between the two antagonists. The Duke of Burgundy did not cease uttering threats of the most violent kinds against the Duc d'Orléans and all his progeny, but dared not take the initiative in plunging the entire kingdom automatically into civil war. On November 10, 1407, Isabeau of Bavaria gave birth to her twelfth child in the Hôtel Barbette, a girl named Jeanne, who, according to the plan adopted by the parents, was replaced by a still-born boy to whom the name of Philippe was given.

A few days later—in fact on November 20—the old Duc de Berry, who once again was trying to reconcile his two nephews, reunited the Duke of Burgundy and the Duc d'Orléans in his mansion, the Hôtel de Nesle. On November 22, the two dukes together attended the Regency Council which gathered in the Hôtel Saint-Pol, and Jean sans Peur chatted cordially with his cousin.

The next night, supping with the Queen in the Hôtel Barbette, celebrating the birth of Jeanne, the Duc d'Orléans assured Isabeau that the Duke of Burgundy's intentions now were altogether friendly towards them.

Towards the end of the meal, one of the male servants in the Hôtel de Saint-Pol, who was in the pay of the Duke of Burgundy, appeared with the message that the King urgently wanted to talk with the Duc d'Orléans. Without harbouring any suspicions, in fact leaving most of his body-guard with Isabeau, and followed only by a page and two horsemen mounted on the same horse and four lackeys carrying torches, he left the Hôtel Barbette in answer to the supposed summons of his brother the King. Hardly had he entered the rue Vieille-du-Temple when out of the darkness emerged about fifteen armed men who had been hiding in doorways. Pulled off his horse, felled by axes and beaten with clubs the Duc d'Orléans was at once killed. When his corpse was lifted they found that his left arm had been cut off, the body literally pierced through in several places, the skull cleft open and the pavement splashed with his brains.

The monstrous murder shocked the entire city. An inquest was held by Guillaume de Tignonville, Provost of Paris. He was a courageous man who did not hesitate to accuse the Duke of Burgundy of the murder of the Duc d'Orléans.

Jean sans Peur, who had the impertinence to be present at the funeral of the man for whose assassination he was responsible, was forced to admit before the Council that the murder was of his doing. Then before the censure mounting on all sides he quickly left Paris and put himself out of harm's way in Flanders, not without taking the precaution of having, after he had crossed it, the bridge spanning the Oise at Sainte-Maxence destroyed to avoid being caught and killed by the hundred Orléanist knights who were in pursuit of him.

Two

The assassination of the Duc d'Orléans plunged Isabeau into despair and terror. No longer feeling safe at the Hôtel Barbette she rejoined the King who at the time was going through a period of lucidity at the Hôtel Saint-Pol.

In her deep pain, for she had sworn eternal love to d'Orléans, the Queen had but one consolation, namely that even if her, the Dauphin's and her other sons' lives were in jeopardy, at least little Jeanne was safe from the machinations of the Duke of Burgundy. Already at birth the child had been put into the care of one of her ladies-in-waiting called Jeanne d'Arc, whose family, due to their devotion to the House of Orléans, had been given high official positions at Court.

The extremely cold weather that gripped Paris, beginning on November 25 and lasting for a whole month, the like of which had not been seen for a century, held up the child's departure to the country, because a long journey in such difficult conditions could have been dangerous for a newborn babe. It was only towards the end of December 1407—the Dauphin and his young brothers Jean and Charles were already in safety at Tours—that the trusted lady-in-waiting left Paris discreetly, accompanied by a wet nurse for little Jeanne, and escorted by some heavily armed servants in case they met with a band of cut-throats, always a possibility in such troubled times.

After a journey lasting about ten days, and without incident, the small procession reached Domrémy, where lived one of the branches of the d'Arc family, into whose care the child was to be put.

Moreover, that small locality offered many important advantages. Firstly, it was situated on the border of Lorraine and Champagne, in the Barrois, personal fief of Queen Yolande, wife of Louis d'Anjou, King of Sicily, a resolute adversary of Jean sans Peur. Also, as it was situated on the direct road between

Paris and the German States, it had the advantage, in case the necessity arose, of evacuating the child swiftly either to a town in the Holy Roman Empire or to Luxembourg, which had belonged to Jeanne's father since 1402. Finally, the village itself was part of the domain of Vaucouleurs, joined to the realm in 1365 when King Charles V, having acquired it from the Sire de Joinville incorporated it in his possessions.

The small convoy arrived in Domrémy on the night of Epiphany 1408, their arrival not going unobserved by the happy groups wandering through every street of the village, celebrating that great Christian feast. But nobody was astonished to see those strangers knocking on the door of their lord, for Jacques d'Arc, a pious and charitable man, kept open house, even at night, for travellers or monks who came to ask for alms or a roof.

The trusted confidante of Isabeau of Bavaria confined herself to the story that the child she brought to them was the daughter of a great lord belonging to the Orléans party, the Orléans family being the protectors of the d'Arc clan. Jacques d'Arc and his wife did not ask for any details since they were well aware that in such circumstances it was preferable to know as little as possible. They took the handsome sum given them as payment for the upbringing of the child and for the stilling of their tongues, and undertook to look after the babe in arms and bring it up as their own.

In the course of the next few days the Abbé Guillaume Front, vicar of the parish, baptised little Jeanne in the Church of Saint-Rémi. In accordance with the customs of the period, she was given several godparents, Jeanne Thévenin and Béatrice Estellin, both of the parish of Domrémy, Jeanne Tiescelin and Jeanne Roze, who lived at Neufchâteau were the godmothers, and Jean Moreau, farmer of Dreux, Jean Barre of Neufchâteau, and two inhabitants of Domrémy, Jean de Langart and Jean Rainguesson were the godfathers. But, as a matter of fact, only Jean Moreau whom the d'Arc family entirely trusted and Jeanne Tiescelin, assisted at the ceremony. The latter's husband was a clerk employed by the Domain of Vaucouleurs which was surely the reason why the choice of the d'Arcs fell on her.

Jacques d'Arc's roots were in Champagne—his ancestors hailed from Moutiers-en-Der—and belonged to an old family of the minor but authentic nobility which was ruined by the Hundred Years War, his coat of arms was "azure to a bow put in fesse, charged with three interlocked arrows, the points mounted with iron, two of them in mounted gold and argent, the third of argent and gold with argent shield charged with a lion of gules." He came to Domrémy and settled there around 1404. He was considered a man of standing; not only did he farm twenty hectares of pasture and arable land, but also he was the owner of fine herds which he sent grazing on the village common, an old custom in that part of France dedicated to cattle raising. Moreover, he lived in one of the largest houses in the village, part manor, part farm house, which had four rooms on the ground floor, two more rooms on the floor above, and above them a vast attic.

His wife, Isabelle de Vouthon, brought him as dowry several acres of forest land situated in the parish where she was born. She belonged to a deeply pious family—one of her surnames being Romée which indicated that she had been on a pilgrimage to Rome (in fact she was more often referred to as Romée than Isabelle). She belonged to a social class which had managed to rise above the level of ordinary peasants. Several brothers were in religious orders, and one of them, who was to play a particularly important part in Jeanne's life, was the vicar of Sermaise. It was well known in the region that the d'Arc family was under the protection of the House of Orléans, a number of them holding the office of counsellor or chamberlain at the Court of France.

Such were the foster parents into whose care the daughter of Louis d'Orléans and Isabeau of Bavaria was put. Brought up in the same fashion as the d'Arcs' own children, three sons and one daughter, little Jeanne grew up watched over by Jacques and Isabelle d'Arc. When she reached the age of twelve she was allowed now and then to go with the other children of the village to the common and watch the herd. On such occasions her great joy was to jump on a horse, so that in no time she became an excellent horsewoman. But more often, while the father laboured in the field in the company of his sons Jacquemin, Jean and Pierre, and from time to time with his daughter Catherine too, Jeanne stayed behind with Isabelle, doing household chores or weaving. Isabelle, whom Jeanne treated as her mother, could not teach her writing and reading because she herself could neither write nor read, and it was out of the question to confide her education to a schoolmaster as such a different treatment—the other d'Arc children were illiterate too—would have given rise to suspicion among the neighbours, especially as at that time even girls belonging to the upper classes were rarely given any education whatever. On the other hand, devout Isabelle missed no opportunity to teach the child the many prayers she knew by heart. Already as a very small child Jeanne took to going regularly to church, and daily kneeling in front of the altar of the village church she fervently prayed to God for her family, that is the d'Arcs, the defeat of the Burgundians and the return of peace to France. All the travellers who came to ask Jacques d'Arc's hospitality which was never refused, and the large number of mendicant friars who were always sure of being given generous alms by Isabelle, brought the latest news from France, where the war with the English was pursued with varying fortunes and where the Orléans party, now known under the name of the Armagnacs, continued to oppose the partisans of the Duke of Burgundy.

Unceasingly Jeanne listened to talk about the war and the terrible ravages it caused from one end of the Kingdom of France to the other. Brought up in a family devoted to the House of Orléans, living in a village where the sympathies of all the villagers were on the Armagnac side, naturally she grew up to detest the English and the Burgundians. Besides, now and then hostilities took place in the vicinity of Domrémy. In the course of the year 1421 the village was on the verge of being invaded. The inhabitants on those occasions took refuge on an island in the River Meuse, where they had put their cattle for safety.

One day to the villagers' alarm a strong contingent of armed men were seen approaching the village. The d'Arc family fled to Neufchâteau, where they remained for four days, staying with a woman called la Rousse. When the danger appeared to be over the family went back to Domrémy, finding it completely sacked, their house pillaged and part of the church burnt down. There was a similar alarm in 1424, but on that occasion the garrison of Vaucouleurs succeeded in pushing back the enemy.

The sight of all that havoc and misery profoundly impressed

the girl Jeanne. Full of compassion she cried often over those who suffered from the horrors of that endless war. However, in her deep devotion and faith in God not for a moment did she doubt that taking pity on the poor kingdom of France He would force the English to go back to their own country. Her conviction grew in strength as she listened to the talk in the home whenever the d'Arcs sheltered a traveller; and often she heard allusions to the saying that "the Kingdom of Fleurs-de-lys, lost by a woman would be saved by another woman."

Seated beside the hearth, attending to her weaving, and wrapt in silence Jeanne sent up her fervent prayers to God, begging Him to send that other woman who was to give back the throne of France to the lawful king and put an end to the trials and tribulations of the poor, cruelly suffering nation. To forget the pain in her heart Jeanne took more and more refuge in prayer. Morning and evening she took herself to the church, where she stayed for a long while, praying with all the fervour of her soul. Her piety greatly pleased the preaching brothers who so frequently came to ask for alms or hospitality from Isabelle-Romée. They were almost invariably Franciscan monks who were bound by many ties to the Celestin Brothers whose grand protector Louis d'Orléans had been. The Franciscans like the Celestins were on the side of the Armagnacs, whereas the Dominicans were supporters of the Burgundian faction. Thus it was quite natural for Jeanne to join the Third Order of St Francis. The Franciscans spoke of the misfortunes of the kingdom, cursing the English and the Duke of Burgundy and everyone else who was allied with the enemies of France.

A nobleman who had estates in the vicinity, Bertrand de Poulengy, often took part in those conversations. Jeanne knew him well since from her childhood onward he came regularly to the house, and took much interest in her, always inquiring after her health, showing her every form of kindness. He did not hesitate on every possible occasion to declare his complete faith in the English being defeated and Charles VII acknowledged by the whole French nation as their sovereign king. Now and then the evening discussion ended with one or other of the guests of the moment singing one of the many laments that were written on the murder of Louis d'Orléans. When the company withdrew

Jeanne meditated on all she had heard; then prayed for a long time before falling asleep.

Every week she went on a pilgrimage to Notre-Dame-de-Belmont which was only at a short distance from Domrémy. Belmont drew many pilgrims and visitors. It stood on a hillside overlooking the River Meuse, in the midst of a little wood, known as Bois-Chesnu. A spring near the chapel was famed for the curative quality of its water and a large concourse of sick people flocked there to drink it. The spring was canopied by a century-old beech tree, and on certain days, but especially on the Sunday in Mid-Lent, the young folk of the whole neighbour-hood came to sit under it, and eat white bread spread with honey. The feast ended with dancing to the sound of pipes.

Old wives swore that in the cover of the night fairies emerged from the forest of Bois-Chesnu and danced in a circle round the beech, which, because of their nightly visits, was known locally as the Arbre-aux-Dames, Ladies' Tree. The young people laughed at the tale. While the girls made wreaths of flowers to hang on the branches the young men pressed round them, teas-ing and joking with them. Those gatherings that often led to betrothals belonged to local tradition; which did not however prevent the Vicar of Domrémy, who celebrated open-air Mass on those days, from referring disapprovingly to their behaviour in the course of his sermon.

Jeanne crowned the tree with garlands like all the other girls, but she refused to dance, considering dancing too frivolous. Any-how, the youths were self-conscious in her presence and did not dare to joke with her as they joked with the others. Nevertheless, there was a young peasant belonging to the district who, struck by her physical beauty and virtuous behaviour, did have the courage to ask her to marry him. Jeanne gently replied that she hadn't yet decided to marry. Her smile took the sting out of her words. For several years the suitor continued to renew his offer, though with no more luck than on the first occasion. So as to bring her to heel, so to speak, he hit on the capital idea of suing her for breach of promise.

The case came up in Toul in the year 1427. Mounted on a horse Jacques d'Arc had lent her she rode the twenty-five miles between Domrémy and Toul in one go, and stepped into court all alone—she had come of age a few months before—to conduct her own defence. The judge, who probably had heard of her from her well-wisher, Bertrand de Poulengy, ruled that as she promised nothing there could be no breach of promise, therefore she owed nothing to the peasant.

The news of the Dauphin's catastrophic defeat at Verneuil-sur-Avre, where he lost over seven thousand men, reached Domrémy towards the end of August 1424. In the Barrois, as in all other parts of the kingdom, the followers of the Armagnacs were in dismay. Alone Louis d'Estouteville's heroic resistance at Mont Saint-Michel stopped them from plunging into utter despair. The monks of the Abbey, who owned land in the vicinity of Domrémy, asked the faithful to invoke their patron saint's help to deliver France from her enemies. Jeanne did not fail to go on a pilgrimage to Moncel where was a sanctuary dedicated to the Archangel Michael.

An extraordinary event took place in 1425 which was to upset Jeanne's present existence. She fasted each week on several non-fast days, believing that her fasting gave added strength to her prayers. One day towards noon in full sunshine she was in her adopted father's garden, walking about as she meditated on the pitiful state of the Kingdom of France. Suddenly a vision appeared to her. In front of her stood a resplendent angel whom she recognised as the Archangel St Michael before whose statue she so often prayed. Simultaneously she heard a voice coming from the direction of the church, saying, "Jeanne, be a good and wise girl, go often to church."

Petrified, Jeanne fell on her knees and with all her strength recited all the prayers she knew. Then great peace descended on her, and she went into the house, though without mentioning what had happened lest they laughed at her.

A few days later travellers reached Domrémy, bringing tidings that gave the followers of the Armagnacs intense joy: having lost all hope of taking Mont Saint-Michel the English had lifted the siege. From that moment onward Jeanne lost all doubt she could have had, and hurried to the church in Moncel, where she prayed for a long time in front of the statue of the glorious

Archangel, thanking him for giving victory to the defenders of Mont Saint-Michel.*

After the first apparition Jeanne threw herself into prayer with even more fervour than before. Her two best friends, Mengette, who helped her frequently in household work, and Hauviette, whom she kept back to spend the night with her if their evenings together lasted too far into the night, became alarmed by all this excess of piety. Her answer was to beg them not to worry on her behalf, and she continued her life of devotion, kneeling for hours at the foot of the altar.

In the course of the year 1426 she again had visions. With dazzling clarity St Michael appeared several times to her, either in Jacques d'Arc's garden or beside the chapel of Notre-Dame-de-Belmont. The Archangel was accompanied by two saints whom Jeanne recognised as St Catherine, patron saint of the church of Saint-Maxey, where she often heard Mass, and St Marguerite whose statue stood in the church of Domrémy. Once again the Voices enjoined her to remain pure and continue to pray.

She became accustomed to the visions, and was no longer frightened by them, was in fact, happy and filled with joy when they appeared. When they had vanished she broke down in tears, for the saints did not take her with them to Paradise.

In time the Voices gave more precise orders:

* *This is not the place to discuss Jeanne's sincerity in the matter of the Voices. Without mentioning the position the Church takes, nowadays science itself admits that in exceptional cases certain persons finding themselves in special circumstances are capable of perceiving things out of the common run that are invisible to ordinary men. We know of several cases of premonition, the authenticity of which cannot be doubted. Of course, there is no rational explanation. One is limited to recording them as does each year the Office of Verification in Lourdes, when it registers the cures which one is bound to call miraculous considering that the medical profession is unable to explain them.*

As regards Jeanne, the truth about her visions is even less debatable if one remembers that her father, Louis d'Orléans, also had a vision a short time before his death and which has been already mentioned in this book. In that field which reason cannot explain such gifts are often hereditary.

"Go to the help of the King of France and you will give him back his kingdom!"

Terror-stricken she burst into tears and cried,

"I am only a poor girl. I do not know how to ride a horse and lead men at arms!"

The Voices calmed her saying,

"St Catherine and St Marguerite will come to your aid."

Jeanne prayed for long hours after the saints left her. Then she went back to her adopted father's house, carrying within her the heavy treasure of her vision, convinced that now she had a mission which would be fulfilled with the help of the saints.

Three

The Treaty of Troyes, signed on May 21, 1421, disinherited the Dauphin Charles, and the inheritance, namely the Kingdom of France, was to go to King Henry V of England after the death of Charles VI who thus became the heir to the throne.

There is no doubt that Isabeau was for the double monarchy, a principle also accepted by the Duke of Burgundy and ratified by the Parliament of Paris. But all the provinces south of the Loire, with the exception of Guyenne and part of Limousin, continued to support the Dauphin. Moreover, the territorial ambitions of the English king rightly alarmed the great lords whose lands were inside the "Kingdom of Bourges" as Article 14 of the Treaty of Troyes stipulated the return to the royal estates of all lands reconquered from rebels.

Among those great rulers who feared confiscation of lands they held outside their fiefs, Queen Yolande of Anjou was one who had most to lose. Not unreasonably, that princess became convinced that once finally established in the provinces north of the Loire the new kings of France and England would not hesitate to annex Anjou and Poitou in order to reunite their possessions in Normandy with their fief of Guyenne. Queen Yolande was the widow of Louis II, Duc d'Anjou and King of Sicily, who died in 1417. She was an energetic and remarkably intelligent woman who almost all alone brought up the Dauphin Charles whom his mother abandoned when still of tender years because his presence reminded her too harshly of the painful married years she led with his poor, insane father.

Yolande of Anjou could count on the Dauphin's gratitude; but she even went one better in attaching him to the House of Anjou by giving him her daughter Marie in marriage. Their wedding took place in 1413. Having thus become the mother-in-law of the lawful heir to the throne of France, her influence was considerable in the Dauphin's councils. During the years 1420–1422 Queen Yolande worked zealously in whipping up enthusiams among the Dauphin's followers. At her suggestion Charles went on a long propaganda tour which took him from Lyons to Toulouse, taking in the Massif Central on his way. It made a deep impression on his supporters who now began personally to approve of him.

Using the fervour of the friendly provinces south of the Loire to his own advantage the Dauphin attacked the English strongpoints. On March 22, 1421 at Baugé-en-Poitou his army, consisting almost entirely of Scotsmen, heavily defeated an English army led by the Duke of Clarence who fell in the battle. In his hurry to exploit the victory the Dauphin laid siege to Chartres. Frightened by his enemy's successes Henry V promptly left England for France, bringing strong reinforcements with him. On Yolande of Anjou's advice Charles, whose forces were very inferior to those of his rival, prudently refused battle and raised the siege of Chartres. That policy was doubly wise considering that the Duke of Burgundy, irritated by the audacious attacks in which the Armagnacs excelled, and which reached the frontiers of his own states, joined forces with the English.

On August 31, 1422 Henry V, King of England, died in Vincennes, preceding Charles VI of France to the tomb by nine weeks or so (Charles died on October 21). Whereas in Paris little Henry VI was proclaimed King of France and England, in Mehun-sur-Yèvre the Dauphin was acclaimed by his supporters as Charles VII, King of France. As the Duke of Burgundy refused to act as regent during Henry VI's minority the Duke of Bedford, who was the young king's uncle, was coerced into accepting the title of Regent of the Kingdom.

The year 1423 was distinguished by the defeat of the troops of Charles VII at Cravant in the Yonne (on July 30), which was soon outweighed by the brilliant victory of the Comte d'Aumale at Gravelle over an English army led by Suffolk (September 26). Exploiting their success with energy the army of the lawful king took Compiègne and Creil from the English and threatened even Paris. During that time small skirmishes broke out in Champagne, Lorraine, Perche and Vexin.

Bedford riposted by attacking the troops of the Dauphin in

Low-Normandy which he defeated at Verneuil (August 17, 1424). That heavy defeat cost Charles VII so many soldiers that for a long while he could not resume the offensive. On their side the English, who were continuously harrassed by partisans whenever they left their strongholds, were also paralysed by the difficult situation in London, and therefore could not take substantial advantage of their victory. For those reasons the two belligerents took little action during the next two years. Meanwhile Yolande of Anjou worked hard and cleverly in trying to heal the breech between Charles VII and Philippe III,* doing all she could, too, to bring in the Duke of Brittany on Charles's side. Her tenacity brought about happy results. On March 7, 1425, the Comte de Richemont, brother of the Duke of Brittany and brother-in-law of the Duke of Burgundy, was named Constable of the King's army. A few months earlier a truce was arranged at Chambery between the armies of Charles and those of Philippe of Burgundy.

No important military event took place in the course of 1426. The Duke of Bedford was kept in London by the machinations of the Duke of Gloucester while Philippe of Burgundy had to deal with a revolt in the Low Countries, and Charles VII was busy reorganising his army. But in 1427 Bedford came back from England, resolved definitely to destroy Charles VII and his forces. The English took Pontorson and Vendôme from the French, then took by assault Montargis on July 1. However, Dunois reconquered them after two months' effort.

The war between England and France now took a decisive turn. The Duke of Bedford increased the strength of his army; Charles VII sent emissaries to Dordrecht, asking Philippe le Bon's help to push back the English. But the Duke of Burgundy refused to take sides, waiting to enter the conflict only at the moment it suited his interests. In fact, he soon recognised the sovereignty of Henry VI over his own lands in France. The Duke of Brittany was not loath to follow his example in taking the English side.

With the balance of power thus gone the cause of Charles VII began to look desperate. Though with the remaining forces at his

---

* *Philippe le Bon, Duke of Burgundy, son of Jean sans Peur.*

disposal the Dauphin could continue resisting for some months, there was no possibility left for him to renew the offensive. And if the fortifications of Orléans were overcome by the English the conquest of the South would be but a matter of time. The situation seemed hopeless. France was tired of the long war that heaped ruin on ruin and cost so many lives. In spite of the sympathy shown the lawful king by the large majority of the people, the exhausted country was ready to accept the foreign ruler willing to give it peace. In spite too of the courage of the remaining stalwarts attached to the cause of Charles VII, who continued to hold out inside the occupied provinces, there remained practically no hope of driving out the English. Sad and in despair, doubting his own claim to the throne and having no faith left in his military prowess, Charles VII spoke openly of entrenching himself in the Viennois or exiling himself to Scotland.

While almost the entire royal circle gave in to despair Yolande of Anjou persisted in trying to find a way out. What with the king's army compelled by its number to take no initiative and the Dukes of Burgundy and Brittany in the enemy camp, she could think of no better solution to redress the balance of power and appeal to the imagination of the people than to bring on to the scene a virgin who would fulfil the famous promise made to Charles VI by a fortune teller, Ermine of Reims, that "the Kingdom of France, lost by one woman would be saved by another woman." Although unconvinced and sceptical about such a move Charles VII dared not to oppose his mother-in-law's plans, and allowed her to do so in her own fashion.

Towards the end of the year 1426 Colette de Corbie had visited Domrémy, and according to the instructions she was given by Queen Yolande, that great inspirer of the Third Order of St. Francis, she told Jeanne, without giving the names of her parents, that she was not the daughter of the Arcs but the descendant of a noble house. Though overwhelmed at first by the revelation Jeanne soon became accustomed to the idea that it was her destiny to live in a world very different from the one she hitherto knew. She kept her word to keep silent about this ginn to her visitor who conferred on her the dignity of *Grande Dame Discrète* of the Third Order, and who gave her a ring with the device of the Franciscans' Jhésus-Maria engraved on it. As to Colette de Corbie she was deeply moved by the fervent faith and purity of heart of one who was the daughter of as dissolute a woman as Isabeau of Bavaria.

In the beginning of 1427 Yolande of Anjou ensured that Jeanne was taught such rudiments of education as she would need when circumstances were propitious to unveil the secret of her origin. It certainly was the Queen of Sicily's intention in time to marry her either into the family of the Duke of Burgundy or the Duke of Brittany thus to strengthen the king's cause in his fight against the English. Jeanne learnt to read and write and, one imagines, was given some lessons in general culture. Jean de Novelempont, a fierce supporter of the Armagnacs, gave her riding lessons and Bertrand de Poulengy taught her the manners and customs of society.

Before undertaking the risky move Yolande of Anjou found herself in duty bound to acquaint Charles d'Orléans, who was prisoner in England since the French defeat at Agincourt, with her plans. So she sent one of her trustworthy followers, Guillaume Bellier, over to England. The head of the House of Orléans, in the same manner as Charles VII, confined himself to saying, let Yolande do as she wished.

Queen Yolande started to prepare the ground for the coming of the virgin who was to save the Kingdom of France. Following her instructions, Gérard Machet, the king's confessor, who entirely agreed with her views, had the rumour spread by the wandering friars that soon a virgin would come to France who would put Charles VII on his throne. In the Barrois the monks let it be known that God's new messenger who would put the English archers to flight would come from the wood called Bois-Chesnu, situated on the border of Lorraine, swearing that that prophecy was made by Merlin himself.

Jeanne was aware of all those rumours and could not help trembling as she contemplated the enormous task that was assigned her and which she would have to accomplish. The Voices spoke to her more and more frequently and commanded her, "Go, Jeanne, go to the rescue of the King of France!" Profoundly shaken she fell on her knees and after long meditation she submitted to the Divine Will, and she became calm and regained her peace of mind.

She continued to study while waiting to start out for France. She learnt the French language which she hardly knew as in Domrémy a Germanic dialect was chiefly spoken. Bertrand de Poulengy, who was in close touch with Gérard Machet and had been so for a considerable time, little by little acquainted her with the history of their time, explaining the reasons of the war which ruined the kingdom, and talked to her in detail of all the members of the d'Orléans family who, as she had heard from Colette de Corbie, were the close allies of her real parents.

After occupying the Maine and the country between the Loire and the Seine, the English, taking Montargis, Fargeau, Meung, Beaugency and Olivet on the way, began to lay siege to the town of Orléans on October 12, 1427. That fortified city was the gateway to all the provinces south of the Loire. Its conquest would swiftly have brought about the total invasion of Charles VII's possessions which would have meant the end of the Capetian dynasty its replacement by the House of Lancaster.

The town's inhabitants numbered thirty thousand, large for those times. It was protected by a powerful enceinte flanked by thirty-four towers. At their feet deep trenches were dug which spread to the river. Beside the five thousand burghers and artisans who were allowed to bear arms the garrison included between four and five thousand *routiers* (mercenaries) drawn from many nations, and commanded by La Hire, Xaintrailles and Dunois. Finally, the artillery possessed seventy-one pieces which could throw stone balls weighing between two hundred and three hundred pounds as far as eight hundred metres.

The English army, about twelve thousand men strong, made the first assault on October 21; after three days of heavy fighting the attackers were forced to withdraw. Realising that he could not carry the town by direct assault—the outlying parts were destroyed by the Orléanais themselves—Suffolk, who succeeded Salisbury killed in combat, decided to dig a trench strengthened with heavy fortifications round the town. Winter and early spring were spent by both belligerents in fortification work, the monotony of which was now and then interrupted by skirmishes in the front line.

34

The siege was expected to last a long while. From time to time food and small reinforcements managed to penetrate the town, but soon food began to run out. Nonetheless the townfolk preferred to die of starvation than surrender to the English. The resistance of Orléans was to become as much a symbol of heroism as Verdun during the First World War. The cities south of the Loire showed their admiration by sending the defenders money, arms, gunpowder and food. Charles VII, shaken from his apathy by the Queen of Sicily, at last decided to assemble a few thousand soldiers, most of them Scotsmen, who under the command of the Comte de Clermont took the road to Orléans. On February 12, 1428, when they were thirty kilometres away from Orléans, they tried to intercept an English convoy of three hundred wagons loaded with victuals. Badly executed, that military operation ended in total failure. After that poor show, known as the Day of the Herrings, Clermont was compelled to reach Orléans as quickly as possible with what was left to him of the reinforcements the town so eagerly awaited.

Furious with his soldiers for not having executed his commands the Comte de Clermont left Orléans eight days later, taking with him his remaining two thousand men, and leaving the townsfolk on the verge of despair.

Alone Dunois, a bastard of the House of Orléans, refused to leave, and in order to raise the morale of the besieged he declared that "a maid from the borders of Lorraine would soon appear to deliver Orléans."

Four

The heroic resistance of the city of Orléans became a byword in all the French provinces.

At Domrémy, thanks to passing travellers, all the details of the defence became public property; and the death of Salisbury, who had sacked the church of Cléry, and who was hit on the forehead by a stone ball fired from a cannon installed in the steeple of Notre-Dame, did not fail to impress Jeanne deeply. Since she knew that it was her mission to go to the help of the King of France, the young girl, normally so quiet, was devoured by impatience. The visions became more and more frequent, and two or three times a week the Voices, more and more precise in their meaning, exhorted her to go to France. On several occasions when the family was together by the fire Jeanne expressed her feelings for the cause of the Armagnacs, and spoke of the joy that going to France and taking part in the battle for Orléans would give her. Listening to her plans which she often repeated to him, Jacques d'Arc, who first simply shrugged it off, became worried and told her that he would prefer to drown her with his own hands than letting her go off in the company of soldiers.

Jeanne remembered that Colette de Corbie suggested that if the need arose she could apply for help to Robert de Baudricourt who represented Charles VII in Vaucouleurs. She did not want to quarrel with the man, whom now she knew to be but her foster-father, so she spoke no more of her intentions while she waited for the first opportunity to go to Vaucouleurs.

At the beginning of May 1428, Jacques d'Arc, convinced that the young girl, who seemed sensible and obedient once more, had chased from her mind the extravagant ideas of becoming mixed up in matters of war, gave her permission to go to Burey-en-Vaux, a village near Domrémy, to visit her uncle Durant-Laxart whose wife was expecting a child. After having assisted at the laying-in Jeanne asked Durant-Laxart to take her to Vaucouleurs. She pleaded her case so well that the uncle, after trying in vain to dissuade her from embarking on such a strange adventure, preferred to take her there himself rather than let her face the dangers of the road alone.

On May 23, 1428 Jeanne presented herself before Robert de Baudricourt whom she found in the midst of his men at arms, and boldly declared that "she came to him sent by the Lord for him to send word to the Dauphin to hold fast but not to give battle because the Lord would come to his aid in mid-Lent." In assured tones she added that in spite of his enemies the Dauphin would become King of France and she herself would conduct him to Reims to be crowned. First stunned by such a declaration the Captain of Vaucouleurs recovered enough to burst into loud laughter, and his soldiers, giving vent to their mirth, derided her and scoffed at everything she had said. Robert de Baudricourt, who knew well Jacques d'Arc with whom he often discussed matters concerning the parish of Domrémy, put an end to the scene by ordering Durant-Laxart to take her back to her father and box her ears.

Back in Domrémy, where she received the full blast of her adopted father's anger, Jeanne resumed her former life. She was not in the slightest discouraged by her failure, and remained resolved to fulfil the mission which the Voices ceaselessly urged her to accomplish.

A few weeks after Jeanne's fruitless journey to Vaucouleurs, grave events shook the entire district. The Burgundians, who were allies of the English, occupied most of the fortresses of the Armagnacs one after the other. With its customary horrors and ruins the war again came near to Domrémy whose inhabitants now lived in anguish. The town of Vaucouleurs itself was invested on July 16. To save it from the vicissitudes of a siege Robert de Baudricourt had to agree, as was the rule of war at the time, to surrender the town if within a year Charles VII did not give proof of his intentions to keep it by sending him reinforcements.

Early in 1429, Bertrand de Poulengy, who had received precise instructions from Gérard Machet, had a long conversation with Jacques d'Arc, letting him understand that in future he should not oppose Jeanne if she evinced the desire to leave.

Though he undoubtedly was astonished Jacques d'Arc, whose responsibility, as it were, was lifted by the nobleman's decision—de Poulengy always had shown Jeanne his affection from her early teens—could do naught else than to bow before his decision.

Becoming even more impatient because of the military situation in the Barrois, Jeanne only thought of leaving for France. One day she could not hold herself back from calling to a Domrémy farmer named Gérardin d'Epinal, "Friend, if you weren't Bourguignon I would have a lot to say to you!" The farmer thought that she had some plan to get married, so did not ask her exactly what she meant.

In February 1429 without saying a word to her adopted parents, without even taking leave of Mengette, the friend she loved best, embracing only Hauviette whom she met on the road, Jeanne left Domrémy never again to return.

When she reached Burey she succeeded in persuading Durant-Laxart to escort her once more to Vaucouleurs, where they both went to the wife of a cartwright, Catherine Le Royer, who had some relations in Domrémy. On her repeated insistence Jeanne managed to be received by de Baudricourt to whom she repeated what she had already said to him eight months ago. This time the Governor of Vaucouleurs did not sneer at her, but replied, saying he would attend to the matter and asked her to wait patiently for a little while. Jeanne returned to her landlady with whom she remained for three weeks.

Rising early, continuing with the routine she acquired in Domrémy Jeanne went every morning to the church of Notre-Dame-de-Vaucouleurs, where, at the foot of the altar, she prayed fervently, begging her saints to help her to achieve her tremendous task. She openly told anyone who asked her what she was doing in Vaucouleurs that it was her intention to go to France to liberate Orléans, chase out the English and take Charles VII to Reims to be crowned there. The story of the girl who wanted to save France spread through the town.

One day she met Jean de Metz who addressed her rudely. "Pray, what are you doing here, sweetheart? Do you want the King to be chased from France and all of us to become English?"

Jeanne answered that she came to the town to ask Robert de Baudricourt to help her to go to the King, but he seemed to show interest neither in her nor in her mission. "Yet before mid-Lent," she said, "I must reach the King even if it means going to him on foot!" Remembering all Bertrand de Poulengy had explained about the affairs of the realm in general and the plans for the Dauphin's son to make a good match, she added, "Nobody in this world be he king, duke or daughter of Scotland or anybody else can save the Kingdom of France. I am the only one who can."

Moved by her declaration Jean de Metz promised to join her as soon as she received permission to leave for France. Then he asked her whether she intended to travel in the dress she was wearing. They were not suitable, he thought, for the long journey she intended to undertake. Jeanne replied, saying she herself had given the matter thought and decided to follow St Catherine's example who in the course of her existence had to cut her hair and dress like a man. After she had spoken Jean de Metz lent her a coat and a pair of breeches which belonged to one of his sergeants, and Jeanne took off her heavy red dress made of coarse wool and donned the soldier's garments.

A few days later at her landlady's Jeanne received a visit from Bertrand de Poulengy, who soothed her by assuring her that soon she would be sent to the Dauphin. He did not disclose that he had seen Robert de Baudricourt with whom he had a long talk, in the course of which he told him, in accordance with the instructions he had received from Yolande of Anjou, that Jeanne was of high birth and the Court of France looked forward to her coming, in fact expected her.

Not wanting to do something that might cause him trouble and have annoying consequences the Captain of Vaucouleurs first let Jeanne know that he intended to treat her case favourably, then in secret sent a messenger to the Queen of Sicily, asking for precise instructions.

To give thanks to her saints who were beginning to make things easier for her Jeanne went on a pilgrimage in the company of Durant-Laxart to Saint-Nicolas-de-Sept-Fonts, where she spent her time in prayer. Hardly had she returned to Catherine Le Royer when she saw the Vicar of Vaucouleurs approaching. He wore his vestments, was accompanied by the choir-boys and followed at some distance by Robert de Baudricourt. The priest made the sign of the Cross, adjured her to cast out the Devil if she were possessed by him, then sprinkled her with holy water. The saintly girl fell on her knees and made reply, reproaching him in a sweet and quiet voice for wanting to exorcise her when in fact he knew her sentiments and all her thoughts since he confessed to him two or three times a week. Then Baudricourt took her aside and questioned her for a long while without being able to get more out of her than what she had said on previous occasions. He had already been impressed by what Bertrand de Poulengy revealed to him. Now he went back to his castle. Though not yet completely convinced, he was struck by the moving sincerity of the girl's convictions.

In the meantime Jeanne's fame spread throughout the countryside. The old Duke of Lorraine, when he heard of the young girl who pretended to be sent by God to save the Kingdom of France, expressed the wish to meet her, as his only daughter, having married Yolande of Anjou's son, was Charles VII's sister-in-law. So Jeanne journeyed to Nancy accompanied by Durant-Laxart and Jean de Novelempont who travelled with her as far as Toul, where he put an armed escort at her disposal to protect her during the journey. She was dressed in an elegant new suit, wearing coat, breeches and leggings, and riding a horse valued at sixteen francs, all that paid for by the inhabitants of Vaucouleurs who had banded together to offer her the outfit.

Charles of Lorraine who had for a long time led a dissipated existence asked her to cure the gout which made him suffer cruelly. Jeanne advised him to eat and drink more moderately for the sake of his body and to take back his wife, for the sake of his soul. Her words greatly pleased the old rake who, on the advice of his mistress Alizon du May who was devoted to the Queen of Sicily and was her secret agent at the Court of Lorraine, presented Jeanne with a fine horse and a purse full of money.

The manner in which she was received by the duke and the presents he gave her made the entire town of Vaucouleurs speak up in her favour. On February 12, 1429 Jeanne went to see Robert de Baudricourt to insist on being sent into France. The

Governor, who had not yet received a reply to his message from the Court of Charles VII, asked her to have patience a little longer. Disappointed by his answer, and showing signs of irritation, Jeanne thus spoke to him:

"God's truth, you do take long in sending me! For today the gentle Dauphin has had big trouble near Orléans, and he is in danger of having far worse trouble if you do not send me quickly to him."

A week after that prophecy a royal messenger by name Colet de Vienne brought Robert de Baudricourt a letter from Yolande of Anjou, ordering him at once to send the young girl of whom he had spoken in his message to the King of France. The messenger also brought the news of a heavy defeat of Charles VII's troops at Rouvray near Orléans. The news of that defeat which Jeanne had predicted galvanised the population of Vaucouleurs, everybody in the little town now becoming convinced of Jeanne's ultimate success.

Jeanne took the road to France on February 24. She wore her new suit: a black doublet made of strong cloth tied with twenty aiguillettes to tight fitting breeches, a grey cloak falling from shoulders to knees, her head covered by a black hat with raised brim and laced leather boots. Mounted on the handsome horse the Duke of Lorraine gave her, riding between Bertrand de Poulengy and Jean de Metz, preceded by Colet de Vienne, the royal messenger, and followed by the archer Richard and two men at arms, Julien and Jean de Honecourt, she rode out of Vaucouleurs cheered by the inhabitants.

Before her departure she asked Robert de Baudricourt to let Jacques d'Arc and Isabelle-Romée know that she was going to France. They had been to see her in Vaucouleurs at the time she was at Nancy. Robert de Baudricourt promised to reassure them on her fate, then made each member of her escort solemnly to swear even at the peril of his life to conduct her to the King, and turning to her of whom he had no more doubts he presented her with a sword, and said,

"Go! Go! What is to happen will happen!"

Five

Between Vaucouleurs and Chinon, where Colet de Vienne had orders to take Jeanne, the distance was over one hundred and fifty leagues, and they had to cross hostile country as far as Gien, held by the Burgundians or the English; moreover, it was infested with brigands.

As a matter of security the small group travelled at night, avoiding the main roads, cutting across fields, fording rivers so as not to be noticed by the sentries guarding bridges. They slept during the day. Jeanne rested fully dressed either on straw in a deserted barn or at the foot of a bank watched over by Poulengy and Jean de Metz. They made the journey at a feverish pace, covering from sixteen to eighteen miles from one halting-place to the next. Frequently danger loomed ahead. The frightened escort spoke of turning back, but with a calm smile Jeanne restored their courage and confidence.

"Be not afraid," she said. "God mapped my road!"

The young girl's endurance, good humour, simplicity and deep piety filled her companions with admiration, and during the entire journey they treated her with respect and affection. On February 27 the small group reached Auxerre where Jeanne heard Mass and went to Communion. On March 4 the travellers were at Gien, where Jeanne dictated to Poulengy a message to Dunois, the Bastard of Orléans, who still held out in invested Orléans, and charged one of the soldiers to take it to him.

After going three times to Mass at Fierbois, and praying before the statue of St Catherine, Jeanne dictated another letter, this time to Charles VII, in which she inquired whether she would find him at Chinon, where the Court was at the moment. Colet de Vienne took it along to Chinon. But Jeanne had not the patience to wait for the answer. Hardly had the royal messenger disappeared at a fast gallop than already she decided to follow him. It turned out to be a happy inspiration.

In fact, next morning the little troop ran into a group of soldiers who were preparing to lay an ambush for Jeanne and all who travelled with her, their aim to massacre them, but as they believed that Jeanne was still at Fierbois waiting for Charles VII's reply, the wretches had not yet finished their preparations. When the cortege appeared they dared not attack it. They were afraid that if anyone escaped their misdeed would come to light. Some days later Jeanne found out that the ambush was conceived and prepared by order of the Sire de La Trémouille, one of the most powerful lords at Court and in the Royal Council, who had acquired his positions thanks to the Queen of Sicily. To repay her for her protection he wickedly opposed all her designs. His heart was filled with fierce hatred of her.

On March 5 towards noon Jeanne entered the town of Chinon with the remainder of her retinue. Her entry caused great excitement in the entire city. In accordance with the wishes of the Queen of Sicily, she took lodgings in an inn run by the widow Régnier de La Barre, where the wife of Guillaume Bellier, one of the lieutenants of Raoul de Gaucourt, Governor of Orléans, was waiting for her.

While she spent most of her time praying to her saints, beseeching them not to abandon her, her companions were hardly able to prevent the crowd from forcing its way into her room. Some agents of de La Trémouille, who was in a constant state of fury since the ambush had failed, succeeded in meeting Jeanne because of their position at Court, and tried to find out what her intentions were. With good grace, and probably amused by their insistence, she did not answer their questions but assured them that the King would be the first person to receive her declaration.

On the evening of her arrival, due to the widow Régnier, Jeanne received an unexpected secret call from Gérard Machet, sent by the Queen of Sicily. During their long meeting the King's confessor confirmed all Colette de Corbie had revealed to her, then told her what even Colette de Corbie probably did not know, namely that she was the daughter of Isabeau of Bavaria and the late Duc d'Orléans. Then the King's confessor called in Bertrand de Poulengy, and ordered him to hand to Jeanne the small sealed chest he had been entrusted with twenty-two years ago on the night of Epiphany of 1407. The sealed chest contained several letters and a ring. Two letters signed by Isabeau and Charles established her royal descent. The third, signed by Jacques d'Arc, related the reasons and circumstances that brought the Queen's trusted confidante to Domrémy with the child to arrange for the child to be brought up there. In the fourth and last letter Yolande of Anjou exhorted Bertrand de Poulengy to watch over the child and named him keeper of the small chest containing the documents. The ring was a gold signet ring with the arms of the House of Orléans engraved on it and which the Duc d'Orléans wore on his finger when he was assassinated.

Finally, Gérard Machet spoke in detail of the intrigues that divided the Court into two rival sections. Then he gave her a description of the different members of her family, especially of Charles VII, her half-brother, of whom he drew a detailed portrait.

The next morning, March 6, probably on the advice of Yolande of Anjou, who wanted to rid the girl of the crowds that literally invaded the inn, the King issued orders for Jeanne to go to stay at Coudray in a tower guarded by soldiers and watched over by the wife of Guillaume Bellier.

The Royal Council debated for two days without reaching any conclusions on the attitude it should adopt towards the girl.

De La Trémouille, who suspected Yolande of Anjou of inciting the Maid in order to regain her ascendancy over the King, assured the King in most vehement tones that they were dealing with an adventuress and the King would lose all respect if he had anything to do with her. His councillors went one better, declaring that if she were inspired, which they doubted, it could only be by the Devil. On the other side, the Angevins maintained that the King could not send away the girl who said she was sent by God to take him to be crowned in Reims after lifting the siege of Orléans, and who had without meeting any obstacles travelled one hundred and fifty leagues through enemy country, which could be considered a miracle in itself.

The Astrologer Royal, who in secret was a partisan of the Queen of Sicily, in grave tones let it be known that Jeanne was truly the one whose mission was inscribed in the stars, and

44

Monseigneur de Vendôme, a faithful ally of Yolande of Anjou, assured the King that he could receive her without any danger to the faith, as in any case if she were an impostor she would give herself away. Undecided, as was his wont, the King veered between the two contrary opinions. At the age of twenty-six the King of France, whose health had always been fragile, was still a puny fellow. Of indifferent height, with definitely ugly features, small worried eyes, a bulbous nose, too large a mouth, thin, sickly legs, and a staggering gait, he did not cut much of a figure. But, on the other hand, Charles VII balanced his physical imperfections with intellectual strength and moral qualities which, unfortunately, were often hidden by his natural timidity. Though intelligent and cultured he did not shine in conversation. His gentleness and kindness were often taken for weakness, for he feared that by imposing his will he might cause pain. His horror of seeing new faces led him to putting matters of state into the hands of intriguers or useless men, and taking no decision without the full approval of those who were around him. Scrupulous in every sense, Charles VII was tortured by doubts of his legitimacy. For a long time he had been aware of his mother's debauches. Besides, she had officially disowned him at the signing of the Treaty of Troyes. Considering himself unworthy of sitting on the throne if he were not his father's son, every night he prayed with all his strength, begging God to give him a sign as to his legitimacy and thus save him from his terrible doubts.

As the Royal Council was divided on the subject of Jeanne, the King was in the embarrassing position of having himself to take a decision. After long reflection and rereading Poulengy's letter which Jeanne had dictated at Fierbois, and taking into consideration Dunois's urgent message in which he let him know that the entire population of Orléans was waiting for the arrival of the envoy of God who would deliver the town to Charles VII, on March 8 he decided that he would receive the young girl that very evening.

After dinner the Comte de Vendôme went in person to the Tower of Coudray to fetch Jeanne and take her to the royal castle. A large crowd gathered to watch them on their way to the King.

To confound the young girl de La Trémouille persuaded the weak King to receive her in the midst of a large circle of courtiers. To put her second sight to the test the King would stay in the circle while the Comte de Clermont would take his place beside the throne. To the surprise of the adherents of de La Trémouille the Queen of Sicily did not oppose those unusual arrangements as they could not know that she discreetly sent Gérard Machet to Jeanne to apprise her of the conditions in which she was to be received in audience.

Led by Vendôme, Jeanne entered the great hall of the castle which was illuminated by fifty torches held by guardsmen and filled with over three hundred noblemen and noble ladies.

Silence was complete.

The glittering assembly beheld a beautiful young girl of over medium height, her man's attire perfectly fitting her body, the doublet showing up her large bosom, her brown hair close-cropped, and clear eyes that lit up her long, oval face. The Comte de Bourbon, who was waiting for her, began to guide her towards the Comte de Clermont who stood at the foot of the throne, but after taking a few steps forward Jeanne stopped for a second, then went towards the end of the hall; and after the courtesies etiquette demanded she genuflected in front of a simply dressed knight and to the stupefaction of everyone present she said,

"God grant you long life, gentle Dauphin."

"I am not the king," Charles answered. Then showing her the Comte de Clermont he added, "There he is."

Still on her knees Jeanne said simply, "In the name of God, gentle Prince, you are the king and nobody else." She embraced his knees.

Though profoundly moved Charles VII yet managed to ask, "Who are you and what is it you want?"

Raising her eyes, shining with zeal, Jeanne replied,

"I am called Jeanne la Pucelle, and through me God lets you know that you will be consecrated and crowned at Reims and become the lieutenant of the King of Heaven, that is the King of France."

The King bade her to rise and led her to a window recess, and ordered the guard to push back the guests. And while that was done one could still hear her speaking to the King. "I tell you in the name of God that you are the lawful heir of France and the son of the King! "

His face wet with tears caused by the deep emotion he felt, Charles appealed to her to show him the sign he had asked from God. She handed him the ring and the letters that stated without a doubt that the fruit of Isabeau's and the Duc d'Orléans's love was she and not he.

Their meeting lasted for over two hours. Jeanne told him her story, speaking for a long while of her visions, explaining that the Voices gave her a fivefold mission: deliver Orléans, take the King to be anointed in Reims, bring back Paris into the royal fief, obtain the release of the head of the House of Orléans who was kept prisoner in England since the defeat at Agincourt, and finally to lead a crusade to the Holy Land to wrest the Tomb of Christ from the infidel.

On his side Charles related the awful difficulties he had had since his childhood, promised his aid, but enjoined her to keep the strictest silence on everything she had revealed to him. When the King rose at the end of the audience he was like one transfigured. His eyes shone with joy such as nobody had seen before and deeply impressed all who were around him. Immediately, with that inconstancy that is the trade mark of courtiers, a large number of his counsellors who so far had kept aloof, openly declared themselves in Jeanne's favour.

A small incident occurred which also added to her popularity. On her way to the castle a soldier showed her the ardour her physical beauty inspired in him as she went by, with some loud, vulgar, obscene oaths.

. "How unfortunate you are," Jeanne simply said. "You deny God, you who are so near to death."

An hour later the man fell into the Vienne and drowned. From then on the inhabitants of Chinon had not a single doubt left of Jeanne being truly inspired by God, and that prediction which came true in such a brief time impressed the people far more than all they had heard about her Divine mission.

Already on the day following her reception by the King a large crowd of great lords and noble ladies, with the entire Orléans family at their head, invaded her apartments. Among other visitors the Maid (Pucelle)—she had presented herself as Jeanne la Pucelle to the King—received several visits from the Duc d'Alençon who became one of her most fervent partisans. That nephew of Charles d'Orléans burnt with the desire to avenge the defeat at Verneuil, the consequence of which had been his imprisonment in England for three years. He was set free only after the payment of a huge ransom.

Jeanne met the young duke for the first time in the royal castle, where she was daily received by Charles VII; on meeting the King's cousin she said, "I welcome you. The more we are together, we of the blood royal of France, the better for us all."

Due to the explanations and details Gérard Machet gave her the Maid came to know by heart the names of every member of her real family. The handsome Duc d'Alençon had long ago been told by Yolande of Anjou the truth about her origin.

After their first surprise had worn off Yolande of Anjou's furious enemies, particularly Georges de La Trémouille and Régnault de Chartres, made two different moves. On the pretext of it being imperative to collect all possible information on the life Jeanne led in Domrémy, they received the Royal Council's approval to send into the Barrois an envoy to make investigations. They also agreed to have Jeanne questioned by five members of the clergy in order to find out for themselves whether she were inspired by God or possessed by the Devil.

These manoeuvres hung fire for a long while. Yolande of Anjou obtained permission from the King that the investigation be handled by the preaching orders who were all devoted to her; and, as for the prelates who were to interrogate Jeanne, they took care not to compromise themselves. On the proposal of one of their members, the Franciscan Raphaël, Yolande of Anjou's confessor, they decided to send the Maid to Poitiers to be heard there by a commission consisting of theologians and experts in canon law who then would judge her case.

All those delays exasperated Jeanne who took her complaints to Charles VII, asking him among other things to dedicate his kingdom to God.

"Gentle Dauphin, I assure you that God has pity on you, your kingdom and your people, for St Louis and Charlemagne are on their knees before Him, praying for you."

Trying to calm her impatience the King did his best to make her appreciate his own difficulties, not only because the Duke of Burgundy had supporters in the Royal Council whom one had to treat gently lest they went over to him, but also because her wish to lead the King's armies was strongly opposed by the captains of the mercenaries, men little disciplined by nature, who categorically refused to obey orders given by a woman. Deaf to all the arguments she heard, Jeanne continued to hope that Charles VII would end up in granting her request and would give her the command of an army to relieve Orléans.

Torn between Jeanne and de La Trémouille the King found a third solution, namely that on the pretext of not wasting time the Maid should be taken to Poitiers without waiting for the results of the investigations in Domrémy. De La Trémouille flattered himself on having gained an important point, for he was persuaded that the theologians of Poitiers would swiftly make a public laughing stock of the girl who pretended that she could command an army successfully when not even professional warriors were able to resist English might; and who believed that she could take the King of Reims to be crowned there at the risk of falling out with the Duke of Burgundy, who in the long run would become the arbiter in the conflict between the King and the English.

On her side, Yolande of Anjou reckoned that Jeanne's sole chance to get the Royal Council's agreement to her mission rested on the highest prelates in the kingdom recognising the sincerity of her sentiments. Therefore, she busied herself in getting appointed as members of the commission which was to judge the Maid a certain number of prelates who were supporters of the Angevin cause.

Preparations for the departure began during Holy Week. Three days after Easter, the King, the Court and the high officials left the castle. Nobody dared to tell Jeanne of the real reason behind the journey. All she was told was that they were going to supervise military manoeuvres with the intention of finding out whether the troops were ready to undertake a campaign on the Loire. But when she saw that they were heading south instead of going towards Orléans she became so apprehensive that she had to be told that they were on their way to Poitiers. Considering herself deceived she waxed furious and uttered loud reproaches; but then she calmed down, and simply said, "Then let us go in God's name!"

In Poitiers Jeanne was accommodated at the Hôtel de la Rose, a beautiful mansion belonging to the Royal Advocate General, Jean Rabateau. In that house she had to submit for three weeks to the interrogations of the Commission appointed to examine her. It consisted of one archbishop, one bishop, several canons and monks belonging to the Carmelite and Dominican orders, also doctors of civil and canon law, not to mention several members of the Royal Council.

Already at the beginning one of the investigators, Guillaume Aymeri, tried to embarrass her by reminding her that according to her declarations God did reveal to her that He wanted "to save France from the misfortunes that overtook it"; or that "God who is almighty did not need the help of armies to discomfit the English." To all that Jeanne's reply was, "In God's name, the armed men will fight and God will grant them victory!"

Brother Guillaume Aymeri admitted that she defeated him. The admission gave him secret pleasure as he, like many of the preaching brothers, was a supporter of Yolande of Anjou. Another monk, Brother Seguin de Seguin, a Dominican from the Limousin who had retained the hard pronunciation of his native dialect put the question to her, "What language were your Voices speaking?"

To the merriment of the audience Jeanne gave this witty answer, "A better one than yours."

The Dominican wanting to regain lost ground put this insidious question to her, "Do you believe in God?"

"More than you," came the answer, and again the members of the tribunal laughed.

Without a doubt Yolande of Anjou had, through the agency of Gérard Machet, explained to Jeanne the line to take to carry favour with the learned commission, many members of which were in any case on her side from the very start; yet her prompt answers certainly show an admirable finesse of mind.

Brother Seguin made another attempt to embarrass her. He asked her "whether she could show them by a sign that one could believe in her" as the commission, "could not advise the King to give her armed men solely on her affirmation, and expose them to danger."

Jeanne very intelligently avoided the trap by saying, "In God's name, I did not come to Poitiers to show you signs, but if you take me to Orléans I will show you signs which will prove why I am sent." Then to press home the advantage her skilful answer to the loaded question gave her, she predicted before the tribunal that the siege of Orléans would be raised and the English defeated after her sending them a challenge, and the King would be anointed in Reims, the city of Paris would return to obedience to the King, and, finally, that the Duc d'Orléans would return to France.

If Jeanne had again to aver without the slightest ambiguity her intention to chase the English out of the kingdom of the fleur-de-lys, yet, following the advice given by Gérard Machet who wanted to appease some of the members of the tribunal, she was careful not to show hostility to the Burgundians but to treat them like misguided Frenchmen. On that subject she declared that it was her fervent wish that "the King and Duke generously forgive each other as befits loyal Christians."

On March 22 when several examiners had come to question her in Jean Rabateau's mansion Jeanne took the decision to send the English the challenge she spoke of. Addressing herself to Master Jean Ernault she said, "Have you paper and ink? Then write down what I say."

She dictated this beautiful letter:

✠ Jhésus   ✠ Maria

"King of England and you, Duke of Bedford, who call yourself Regent of France; you Guillaume de la Poule,* Earl of Sulford, Jehan, Sire de Talbot; and you Thomas, Sire d'Escoles, who call yourself lieutenant of the said Duke of Bedford, give the King of Heaven His due, hand to the Maid, who is sent by God, the King of Heaven, the keys of all the good cities you took and sacked in France. She has come on behalf of God to

---

* *We give in this text the exact faulty orthography of some names. It should be Guillaume de Pole, Earl of Suffolk, John de Talbot and Thomas de Scales.*

claim blood royal. She is ready to make peace if you want to see reason and return to France and pay for what you hold. And, before everything else, archers, companions at arms, foreigners and others encamped before the good city of Orléans, go back to your country in the name of God, but if you do not do so wait for news of the Maid who will shortly come to see you to your very great loss.

"King of England, if you do not go, I am chief of the army, and wherever I reach your people in France I will make them go whether they want or no; and if they do not want to obey, I will have all of them slain, but if they want to obey I will have mercy on them. I came here sent by God, the King of Heaven, to fight you hand-to-hand to push you out of the whole of France; against every one who betrays, cheats and damages the Kingdom of France. And have no illusion on being able to keep France, which belongs to God, the King of Heaven, Son of St Mary; therefore, King Charles, the true heir will keep it; for God, the King of Heaven, wants it, and it will be revealed by the Maid, and he will enter Paris in good company.

"If you do not want to believe the tidings the Maid brings from God, wherever we find you we shall hit you, strike blows and there will be a huge massacre, such as France has not seen in thousand years, if you refuse to see reason.

"And you can firmly believe that the King of Heaven will send the brave Maid more strength than you could muster in attacking her and her companions at arms and then we shall see who has right on his side, God in Heaven or you.

"Duke of Bedford, the Maid asks and requests you not to destroy yourself. If you see reason you can come in her company to the place where the French will show the finest deeds that were ever seen in Christendom. Give your answer to the city of Orléans if you want to make peace; but if you do not then a lot of harm will shortly come to you.

"Written on the Tuesday of Holy Week.

On behalf of the Maid."

The missive was addressed to "The Duke of Bedford, so-called Regent of the Kingdom of France or to his lieutenants who find themselves before the town of Orléans."

Jeanne's letter was a real masterpiece of skill. Firstly, by stating clearly her intentions the Maid forced her examiners' hand since in the letter she took it for granted that their decision would be favourable; secondly, she asserted with great force before a tribunal that consisted in a large number of churchmen that she was acting but "on behalf of God, the King of Heaven."

While giving the English a choice between peace and war she prudently refrained from sending a similar summons to the Burgundians, who were only indirectly included in the passage about "every one who betrays, cheats and damages the Kingdom of France."

Finally, she offered general reconciliation under the aegis of a new crusade against the infidel. In this she precisely followed the instructions given by Yolande of Anjou from whom the idea of the letter originated, and who always dreamed of founding a Christian kingdom in the East with a member of the Orléans family as its king.

Gérard Machet saw to it that the letter's contents became public property. It left a deep impression on everybody. Cleverly the Maid let it be known that she would send it to the Duke of Bedford only when she was already on her way to Orléans with the tribunal's approval. Those of the examiners who were on de La Trémouille's side found themselves in an embarrassing position, especially as the commission sent to Domrémy, duly influenced by de Baudricourt and the vicar of Sermaize—the brother of Isabelle-Romée—brought back a report which was completely in the Maid's favour. And to give the report even more weight Jean and Pierre d'Arc joined the members of the commission on the journey back and had just arrived in Chinon, where they found those members of their family who were attached to the Court. Moreover, Yolande of Anjou suggested to the King that he seek the opinion of two distinguished high prelates, Jacques Gelu, Archbishop of Embrun, and the retired Chancellor of the University of Paris, Jean Gerson, on why Jeanne had found herself compelled to dress as a man.

The first who belonged to the Angevin party answered that "it was more decent to do these things in a man's attire since she had to do them in the company of other men." The archbishop added that often God revealed to virgins matters that he wanted to keep from men. The second, who lived in Lyons retired from the world in a monastery of the Celestins whose benefactors were the Orléans family, wrote to say that "it was meet and proper for her to dress as befitted her state," adding that "even if the Maid did not accomplish all she promised one must not conclude that she was pushed by an evil spirit and not by God, but to blame our own ingratitude and our own sins which often hinder the Lord in the fulfilment of His acts of mercy." Thus the famous doctor gave her absolution in case she were to make any mistakes.

The town of Orléans did not cease asking for help, and the emissaries used every opportunity to insist on the Maid being sent to them.

The tide ran irresistibly in her favour.

To satisfy the wish expressed by the Archbishop of Ebrun the Queen of Sicily, assisted by the wife of Robert Le Maçon and Jeanne de Preuilly, wife of the Sire de Gaucourt, examined Jeanne to make sure that she was still a virgin. That unnecessary and ridiculous examination of course proved that she who called herself the Maid was untouched by men.

It remained only for the tribunal to publish its conclusions. After reiterating in detail all the precautions they took to reach no hasty judgment the examiners declared to have found in Jeanne "nothing bad, but only good, humility, purity, devotion, honesty and artlessness," and concluded that "the King, given the results of the examination, and of the steadfastness and constancy of purpose of the Maid, and her insistent request to go to Orléans with men at arms, should in honesty have her taken there, putting his trust in God. For to mistrust her or to forsake her with no reason would be repugnant to the Holy Ghost and unworthy of the help of God."

Pushed by the sentiments of the people, beseeched by the inhabitants of Orléans, covered by the tribunal's decision, approved by the Royal Council, the King, who believed in her ever since the revelations she made him, on April 15, 1429, put her officially in charge of the military operations against the English.

Thus thanks to the help of occult powers and the sensible advice given her by Yolande of Anjou, Jeanne won the day.

Six

On March 24, 1429 Jeanne left Poitiers for Chinon in the company of King and Court. They travelled through Châtellerault. The Orléanais were acquainted by Jean Langlois that soon they would see their deliverer, the Maid, riding at the head of an army, and bringing supplies for them offered by the Queen of Sicily.

The army to succour Orléans was to assemble at Blois. Towards the end of April the Maid arrived in Tours, where she was lodged in the house of Jean du Puy, privy counsellor of Yolande of Anjou. While waiting for military preparations to be completed, Charles VII decided to provide her with equipment and a staff. Her armour was white and of hardened steel, which still weighed at least twenty kilograms after it had been lightened as much as possible; and cost a hundred *livres tournois*. She was also given several horses in addition to those she had received before. When the question of a sword was raised Jeanne declared that she wanted to carry the sword which was kept in a box behind the altar in the Chapel of St Catherine in Fierbois. When on March 5 she passed through that locality the chaplain in charge of the sanctuary revealed to her the existence of that sword which had a deep symbolic meaning to her; for it was the sword of Charles Martel who left it as a thanks offering when he came on a pilgrimage to Fierbois after defeating the Saracens at Poitiers in 732.

An armourer urgently sent to Fierbois returned with that precious relic. The blade, only slightly rusty, had five crosses engraved on it. To that gift the priests of Fierbois had added a scabbard embroidered in gold; the people of Tours had one made for her in bright red velvet; and Jeanne had a third made in thick leather for use in battle.

At the same time in Tours she had a standard woven in white silk, sprinkled with fleurs-de-lys and fringed. For the fee of

55

twenty-five *livres tournois* a Scottish painter called James Power painted on one side God on His throne above the clouds, holding the orb in His hand, near Him kneeling Michael and Gabriel, each archangel holding a fleur-de-lys, and above them in gold letters the device of the Franciscans "Jhésus-Maria." On the other side the royal arms of France held by two angels.

She also ordered a pennant on which was painted the image of the Blessed Virgin with an angel holding up a fleur-de-lys.

Her wishes were consulted in the choice of her staff, the King paying for the equipment of those who were to serve her. Beside Bertrand de Poulengy and Jean de Metz, her two faithful companions, Jean and Pierre d'Arc were appointed, the special duty of the four of them to act as her bodyguard. Two pages, Louis de Coutes and Raymond, two heralds, Guyenne and Ambleville, and one confessor, Brother Pasquerel of the Eremites of St Augustine completed her military establishment. Soon they were joined by a relation of Jacques d'Arc's wife, Nicolas-Romée of the Benedictine monastery of Cîteaux. All of them were placed under the orders of the Chevalier Jean d'Aulon, a mature, experienced man whom Dunois had recommended to Jeanne, and who was charged to teach her in a few days the essentials of military skill. She showed herself an extraordinarily gifted pupil.

Thus well equipped and ready for battle Jeanne left for Blois, where she arrived on April 24. Yolande of Anjou had arrived there a week before, and sold or pawned most of her silver to allow the King, who had run short of money, to pay his soldiers and buy provisions for the defenders and inhabitants of Orléans. Due to her, Charles VII stored up a large enough quantity of food to fill sixty heavy waggons, also an imposing hoard consisting of four hundred and thirty-five head of cattle, and many pigs and sheep. As for the army that was to raise the siege of Orléans it was truly but a collection of eight to ten thousand looters and plunderers, most of them deserving the gallows, who were drawn into the King's service because of the good pay, and saw in military service their opportunity to redeem the misdeeds and crimes committed in ordinary life.

That fine crowd was encamped outside the town, living in complete anarchy, roistering with the camp followers whom one always found in the wake of mercenaries.

Jeanne was very disappointed by her first impression of the unedifying mob she was to command. But then she remembered that Du Guesclin, whose widow was related to the House of Orléans, and who a few days later sent her a messenger with a letter and a ring, had succeeded in his time in disciplining the big armies and making them fight for Charles V. The mercenaries here were by no means different from the bands of ruffians whom the great Constable had trained to obedience. But on top of this she was faced with an even more difficult task: before her the men swore loud, horrible oaths, refusing to serve under a woman.

Their leaders were no better than they. One of them was Etienne de Vignolles, known as La Hire because of his violent bouts of anger whenever things did not go according to his liking. At the siege of Montargis the chaplain refused to absolve him of his sins because he would not first confess. In front of the troops, pretending he was making penance he called out, "Lord, I beg you to do for La Hire today what La Hire would do for you if La Hire were God and you a captain!"

Even so Jeanne refused to be upset. She had the companies lined up and appeared before them on a black horse, wearing her white armour, her head covered by a felt hat, a red cloak floating from her shoulders, her sword buckled on, and bearing a lance. She was followed by a page, carrying her new banner on which was painted Christ crucified. Startled by the apparition of the graceful young girl who yet looked every inch a warrior and leader of men, the mercenaries were struck dumb with astonishment and admiration.

La Hire was conquered. (Yolande of Anjou helped therein in so far as she had given him a substantial sum of money to support Jeanne's cause.) Leaving the ranks he nobly saluted the Maid whom he assured in a loud voice of his and his company's loyalty, and promised to follow her wherever she took them. The spectacular change of mind of the man whom all the army feared made a strong impression on the mercenaries.

The Marshal de Rais came to pay homage to the Maid and put himself under her command. In time he came to commit the foulest crimes and acquired notoriety under the name of Bluebeard, but in those days he was a young and handsome knight,

57

related to the highest families in Brittany and renowned for his unfailing courage in battle.

Now that she could rely on the support of these two men Jeanne at once started teaching the mob a minimum of discipline and manners. Her first move was to order all loose women out of the camp. Then on her orders every morning and evening the priests who had rallied to her banner had to celebrate open-air Mass and sing hymns in honour of the Virgin Mary. The King, his household and the great captains assisted at these pious services to which only those who had confessed previously were admitted. The mercenaries could not resist the temptation to see for themselves what it was like and what the Maid, who was to lead them to Orléans, looked like. Within a few days she achieved the miracle of giving a kind of moral cohesion to that horde of tough soldiers and imparting her faith in victory to them.

On April 26 the army chiefs held a council to decide on the itinerary to take and to plan the advance of the troops and of the food column. With the ardour of the neophyte whom nothing can hamper Jeanne wanted at once to cross the Loire, cut the English to pieces and then enter Orléans. Theoretically her plan was not impossible since in numbers the armies were equal; however, in the heat of battle the food convoy would be in danger of an enemy onslaught. Furthermore, the fate of the besieged town and of France itself would in such circumstances be settled in one single battle. But the captains of the mercenaries, men accustomed to the vagaries of war and bearing in mind the favourable position of the English, who, supported by the artillery in their fortresses, could cause them enormous losses, were of the opinion that the army should move along the left bank of the river which was free of the enemy. Their plan was to take the food convoy as far as Chécy, situated three leagues upstream from Orléans, where a flotilla of small vessels would transport the cargo to the town.

In the Council of the King de La Trémouille ardently desired that the expedition ended in disaster which would rid him of the Maid and give him back the influence over the King that he lost to Yolande of Anjou. As regards Régnault de Chartres, he hoped that the enterprise would have no practical result, as that would give him the chance officially to call in Philippe of Burgundy, with whom he was in secret correspondence.

The army chiefs' plan perfectly suited Jeanne's enemies because it seemed unlikely that it could succeed, for even if the convoy managed to reach Chécy that did not mean that the food would reach Orléans. And the King's soldiers could achieve no more odd victories for the excellent reason that the main English army was on the other bank of the river.

Tired out by the strong opposition to her plan, anxious to go to the aid of Orléans as quickly as possible, and totally unacquainted with the topography of the region, Jeanne in the end gave in.

On the evening of the 26th she dispatched to the English the letter she had dictated in Poitiers, in which she told them to raise the siege of Orléans. When the English received the missive they were livid with anger, called her vile names, and kept back the messenger, whom they threatened, against all rules of warfare, to burn alive as an accomplice of the sorceress.

On the 27th the army marched out from Blois in the early morning, led by the priests intoning *Veni Creator* grouped round Jeanne's standard, which had been blessed at Saint-Sauveur by the Archbishop of Reims. Jeanne followed surrounded by her staff, the great captains, La Hire, Marshal de Boussac, Marshal de Saint-Sevère, Admiral de Culand, Sires de Rais, Xaintrailles, Florent d'Illiers and many others, behind them the mercenaries, to their rear the waggons and the cattle, protected by a strong rearguard.

When night fell they camped in the fields. After praying for a long while Jeanne lay down fully dressed on straw. She awoke bruised by her heavy armour. At the crack of dawn the army was on the march again. In the afternoon from the heights of Olivet the Maid saw for the first time the town she was to deliver from the English. In accordance with the plan the waggons and the cattle continued as far as Chécy while the fighting army approached the Loire.

Only then did Jeanne perceive that the town was on the other bank of the river. Now she realised that the military chiefs and the Royal Council deceived her, and either did not dare to or did not want to measure themselves against the English.

Moreover, the situation as it was was pretty dangerous. Masters of the fortifications on the left bank—Les Tourelles, the fort of the Augustins, the fort Saint-Pryvé and the Watch-Tower of Saint-Jean—supported by their artillery, the English could easily stop the convoy from penetrating into the town. On top of that, the Loire was low, and the ships could not sail up-stream as the wind was unfavourable.

Some of the chiefs thought of throwing a bridge across the river; others spoke of forcing the passage with the help of ligh-ters. There was great confusion. In spite of her disappointment and deception Jeanne tried to keep her temper. Late in the afternoon Dunois, the commander of the beleaguered garrison of Orléans, with courage bordering on madness, crossed over under English fire. The Maid rode up to him and said before he had time to step out of the boat, "Are you the bastard of the House of Orléans?"

Hurt by the brutal words of welcome Dunois answered, "I am." Then he added, "I rejoice to see you here."

In the same bitter tone Jeanne asked, "Is it you who sug-gested that I should come here instead of marching straight against Talbot and the English?"

Dunois endeavoured to explain that the reason why he and the other military leaders gave her that advice was because the army's safety was at stake.

Jeanne flared up, "In God's name, the councils of God our Lord are wiser than yours! You believed that you were harming me, but you did yourselves far more harm; for I bring you the greatest help that any captain or city ever received: the help of the King of Heaven."

She added that God on the intercession of St Louis and Charlemagne took pity on Orléans and would no longer allow the English to hold the Duc d'Orléans as their prisoner. After utter-ing those words her anger abated, and Dunois's irritation van-ished. For a long moment the two bastards of Louis d'Orléans, who now met for the first time, contemplated each other almost moved to tears. Jeanne broke the silence, saying to her brother, "Have patience, the wind will change and the ships will arrive without mishap."

Hardly had she spoken the words than the wind veered to the

west, gathering strength. The vessels, which until then were becalmed, raised their sails, and without any effort sailed upstream, much to the surprise of the English. Dunois jumped into a boat and escorted the flotilla as far as Chécy, where Jeanne and her escort, who followed them along the river bank, joined them. Accompanied by two hundred lances the Maid crossed the Loire in a ship, and spent the night as guest of the Duc de Cailly in the castle of Reuilly.

At dawn the barges laden with supplies, protected upstream by Jeanne and downstream by the main body of the army which was encamped near the port of Bouchet, sailed down the river and one after the other tied up beside the Porte de Bourgogne. Stricken by a sort of superstitious paralysis from which they had been suffering ever since the arrival of the Maid, the English did not even try to stop them.

That first success was of great importance, for the people of Orléans now saw that hers were no vain promises. Their enthusiasm was immense.

But Jeanne wanted more than that. All her thoughts were concentrated on raising the siege. However, the bridges were either held by the English or had been destroyed by them. Therefore, the only solution was for the army to return to Blois and cross the river there.

Dunois insisted on Jeanne immediately entering Orléans, but she refused because she feared that in her absence the captains would find some excuse not to cross to the right bank and thus waste time. But then on the request of a delegation of burghers and soldiers she gave in, handing one of her standards to Brother Pasquerel who was to accompany the main army.

Towards eight o'clock in the evening of Friday, April 29, Jeanne made her entry into Orléans amidst enormous enthusiasm. Mounted on a magnificent white horse, wearing her white armour which shone in the light of thousands of torches that lit up the street, her standard bearer in front of her, Dunois and de La Hire at her side, she rode through the town to the frantic acclamations of the population.

Jeanne stopped first at the Cathedral of Sainte-Croix, where she gave thanks to God for having helped the food barges to reach port. As she came out of the cathedral the continuously swelling thick crowd, comforted by her presence, pressed round her, shouting with delirious joy, everyone wanting to touch her armour or her sword, even the trappings of her horse. In his enthusiasm a torch bearer approached so near to Jeanne that he set fire to her standard. Accomplished horsewoman that she was, Jeanne turned her horse round and put out the blaze herself. It had wellnigh started a panic. Graceful and smiling at everybody she advanced but slowly, as her escort could scarcely clear a way for her through the acclaiming multitude. Eventually she did succeed in reaching the apartment near the Porte Renard, to the west of the town, prepared for her in the house of Jacques Boucher, treasurer to the Duc d'Orléans.

Though a sumptuous banquet awaited her Jeanne, who had fasted for twenty-four hours, contented herself as on every Friday with five small slices of bread soaked in wine. Then she went to the room that had been made ready for her. After long prayers addressed to her saints she fell into quiet sleep, sharing on her special demand the same bed as Charlotte, the eldest daughter of her host.

Next day, which was April 30, the military leaders met in Dunois's quarters. Wishing to exploit her first success, Jeanne wanted to attack the English at once, counting on the enthusiasm of the Orléans militia and on the four hundred lances sent as reinforcements from Châteaudun, commanded by Florent d'Illiers.

Raoul de Gaucourt, the Governor of Orléans, who was in the confidence of de La Trémouille and carried on a secret correspondence with the Duke of Burgundy, opposed the plan, declaring that first they ought to wait for the arrival of the royal army. He had good reasons for hoping that the mercenaries would not be in a hurry to see the town walls again. Most of the captains agreed with the governor, for they did not want the campaign brought to a quick end since that would bring about the disbanding of their troops. Dunois pretended to share their views, thus obtaining the council's agreement to sending Marshal de Boussac to Blois to press the King for the return of the royal army with a convoy of fresh supplies and ammunition.

However, de La Hire and a few other captains who were equally impatient to measure themselves against the English, agreed with Jeanne's plan. Their attitude caused a sharp incident which was an example of the difficulties the Maid encountered. The Sire de Gamache, who was member of the royal household, shouted in a voice trembling with fury that "as the captains sided with a hussy of low origin, preferring her advice to that of a knight" he would resign his command and right there he handed his banner to Dunois. Only after a lot of soothing did Dunois succeed in calming the enraged nobleman to whom he could not reveal the illustrious lineage of the girl he treated so disdainfully, and make him embrace her as a symbol of their reconciliation.

In the course of the afternoon, ignoring the council's decision, de La Hire skirmished with the English though without any particular success.

Jeanne took no part in the engagement as she did not want to alienate the other military chiefs. She restrained herself to renewing her summons to the English to raise the siege of Orléans, and demanded the immediate liberation of her messenger whom they had imprisoned against the rules of war. Then, without waiting for a reply, she went to the Boulevard de la Belle-Croix in front of the Port of Tourelles, and calling to William Glansdale, commander of the English garrison, she summoned him to surrender, in which case she would spare his life.

Glansdale's sole answer and that of his soldiers, was to jeer at her, treating her as a cowherd and an Armagnac whore, and promising to burn her as a witch. The foul insults brought tears to her eyes, but she quickly mastered herself and in calm tones she predicted that the English would be chased from Orléans in less than a week, and Glansdale would find his death in battle before long.

On the next day, followed by the people who continued to support her, the Maid inspected the English fortifications. When she came near to the Fort of Croix-Morin she invited Granville, the commander of the fort, at once to lay down his arms. Granville only laughed, grossly insulting her, as he assured her that if he ever surrendered it certainly would not be to a woman surrounded by "wretched whoremongers."

On Sunday, May 1, during a meeting in the morning, it was decided, in spite of the opposition of Raoul de Gaucourt, Governor of Orléans, that Dunois would leave immediately for Blois in the company of the Chevalier d'Aulon to hasten the coming of the royal army. Meanwhile Jeanne would remain in Orléans to reassure the population. To protect the sortie of Dunois and his small troop, the Maid at the head of several companies of the Orléanist militia took up position in front of the English forts, but the English showed no bellicose intentions: they just observed the movements of the troops.

Jeanne spent almost the entire day of May 2 in prayer. During that time in Blois de La Trémouille and Chancellor Régnault de Chartres, in order to paralyse Jeanne's efforts, exerted themselves in persuading the Royal Council that new reinforcements were needed before the army could march to Orléans. Yolande of Anjou fought vigorously against this proposition, observing that it was indispensable to liberate the city before the English had time to send the forces they were assembling in Normandy to Talbot's relief. Then the arrival of Dunois tipped the scales, and the King issued orders for the army to march to Orléans.

On Tuesday, May 3, Jeanne took part in the solemn procession with which the Feast of the Holy Cross ended.

Next morning a messenger brought news from Dunois: the royal army was approaching Orléans on the road to Sologne. Escorted by de La Hire and five hundred soldiers the Maid went out to meet it. The army and the food column entered the city with no difficulty as the English were so demoralised that they did not even try to oppose them. For a second time Jeanne's prophecy was fulfilled.

Soon after the midday meal Jeanne received Dunois's visit. He announced that an English army, commanded by Falstaff, was less than a day's march from the town. That news filled her with joy.

"In the name of God," she said to her brother, "I command you to let me know when Falstaff is coming, for if you do not I will have you beheaded."

"Do not worry on that score," Dunois replied goodhumouredly. "I will let you have the news the very moment I receive it."

Reassured on that score Jeanne, who had spent part of the night deep in prayer and had risen early, now went to her room, where she lay down to sleep beside little Charlotte.

64

While she slept several captains of the mercenaries, who on that particular day were in a specially bellicose mood, resolved to attack the fortress of Saint-Loup east of the town which Talbot had provided with a strong garrison. As Dunois failed to dissuade them he decided to sally forth with them.

When battle was joined Jeanne awoke with a start, crying out, "My people are fighting! Blood is flowing . . . 'tis all wrong! Why did they not warn me?"

She called for her armour, her squire helped her into it, then seizing her sword and banner she rode out to the battle, followed at a distance by the Chevalier d'Aulon, and her small page Louis de Coutes. When he saw her ride past at a furious pace one of the look-out men rang the alarm-bell in the belfry, and soon about six thousand fully armed militia men took the road leading to the fortress of Saint-Loup.

When Jeanne reached the scene the mercenaries, who had foolishly mounted a wholesale attack against a heavily fortified redoubt and were received with a salvo of cannon balls and showers of arrows and bolts, were in disorderly retreat, reeling under the blows received from the English. But her presence alone sufficed to restore order. Once the mercenaries were regrouped Jeanne ordered a fresh attack. With an immense shout the militiamen hurled themselves against the fortress, while Marshal de Saint-Sévère, at the head of five hundred men at arms, prevented Talbot, who was in the Fort of Saint-Pouair, from taking part in the battle.

After three hours of fierce fighting the Fort of Saint-Loup was taken and soon devoured by flames. When the battle was over Jeanne cried over all the blood that was shed. Later she rode back to Orléans, where the people in their frenzy of joy saluted her as the victor of the battle. Before returning to her apartment, she went, followed by the crowd, to the cathedral and prayed for a long while. The church bells were ringing joyfully when she reappeared. She announced that within five days every fort would be taken and not an Englishman left in the vicinity of Orléans.

Jeanne's striking victory only increased the animosity of those who for various reasons had always tried to oppose her plans. Moreover, several captains of the mercenaries felt humiliated by the young girl's decisive influence on the battle. As for the Sire de Gaucourt, he hardly managed to hide his resentment. Because of her success he was compelled to wait with the appeal for help which, with the approval of de La Trémouille and Régnault de Chartres, he wanted to send to the Duke of Burgundy.

For all these reasons Jeanne was not invited to attend the council which was held on Ascension Day in the house of Gousinot, chancellor of the town. Presided over by the governor, it included most of the mercenary captains, the aldermen and the chiefs of the militia. Annoyed with himself for not having notified the Maid of the impending assault on the Fort of Saint-Loup, also desirous not to be suspected of being in league with her, Dunois thought it was preferable for their common cause to be present at the meeting.

After a long discussion it was decided to make a sham attack on the Fort of Saint-Laurent. Then while the English were thus tied down the main body of the army would be transported to the left bank, where it would invest the Fort of Saint-Jean, and lay siege to the fortresses des Augustins and des Tourelles. As the meeting was coming to an end, Jeanne, whom Dunois kept informed of what was going on, burst into the room. She began by asking the reasons why she was not invited. The Governor of the City answered that they wished to keep secret their operational plans.

"Tell me what you decided to do," Jeanne said, adding, "I can keep bigger secrets than this one."

Gaucourt then said, the Council decided to attack next day the Fort of Saint-Laurent.

"Is that all?" Jeanne insisted. With long strides she paced the council room, making no effort to hide her displeasure.

The others in their embarrassment kept their council, afraid of annoying her more. Then Dunois intervened, saying, "Do not get angry, Jeanne. One cannot relate everything in one sentence." Pretending to be unaware of the disapproving looks of most of the mercenary captains he explained to Jeanne the plan the council decided on.

"That is a good plan," she said when Dunois finished. As she was leaving she added, "On the condition that all is done accordingly." She said that to make them understand that she would not let herself be duped.

Late in the afternoon she dictated to Brother Pasquerel another letter to the English.

"You men of England, who have no lawful right to the Kingdom of France, the King of Heaven orders and commands you through me, Jeanne the Maid, to leave your forts and retire to your homes. If not I will cause you so much damage that you shall remember it for ever. This is the third and last time that I write to you."

Under the Franciscan device of "Jhésus-Maria" and the signature of "Jeanne la Pucelle" she had the following postscript added,

"I should have preferred to send you a more polite letter, but you still retain my herald Guyenne: send him back to me, and I will return some of your people taken in the battle of Saint-Loup, for not all of them are dead."

The letter was tied to an arrow which an archer sent into the Fort des Tourelles. Jeanne in person approached the fort, shouting, "Read it, it is a message!" Low insults were the only answer she received from the English.

Back in the town she issued a proclamation to the men-at-arms, which read, "Tomorrow nobody should be so foolhardy as to go to the attack of the fortresses before going to confession; and all men-at-arms should behave properly, for to punish men for their sins God allows battles to be lost."

Early in the morning of Friday May 6, Jeanne heard Mass and went to communion. Many of the soldiers followed her example. When the appointed hour for the start of the operation had passed without any intelligence reaching her, the Maid realised that the Sire de Gaucourt wanted to deceive her.

Without bothering about the plans the Council had adopted she decided to join battle with the English. Besides, all she had promised was that she would follow the plan adopted in her absence on the condition "that all is done accordingly." Placing herself at the head of the militia Jeanne left the town through the Porte de Bourgogne. Archambault de Villars with the troops he raised at Montargis, Gilles de Rais with his Bretons, La Hire with his mercenaries and Dunois, who commanded nearly four thousand soldiers of the royal army, hastened to follow her.

Soon they reached the river. However, the operation had been badly prepared by the Council. The pontoon-bridge put in place in the course of the night was too narrow to allow the rapid passage of an army that was swollen by the unexepected arrival of the militia. On reaching the other bank the advance-guard occupied the Fort Saint-Jean, evacuated by the English who withdrew to the Fort Saint-Augustin. After setting fire to the fort the militiamen, drunk with easy victory, ran to attack the Fort Saint-Augustin, a fortified monastery, where the English speedily repulsed them, and many militiamen were killed in the engagement.

Panic followed, and soon the men of Orléans were surging back to the pontoon-bridge and getting in the way of the soldiers of the royal army who were pressing forward. The confusion was indescribable in spite of the superhuman efforts of the Chevalier d'Aulon in trying to protect the militia's rearguard.

But Jeanne saw the danger. Followed by de La Hire, whom her courage had deeply impressed, she charged the English, her lance forward, thrusting with her sword and encouraging her troops to fight. Before that counter-attack, as violent as it was unexpected, it was the turn of the English troops to run from the enemy. They retired to their fort. In the meantime the royal army had reached the left bank of the river, then marched on the fortified monastery. Jean de Lorrain, the famous artilleryman, smashed the fort's door with one cannonball. Jeanne dismounted at the foot of the fort, stuck her standard on the parapet and shouted with all her strength, "Forward in God's name!"

A loud shout was the answer; and with an irresistible rush knights, squires, militiamen, mercenaries and regular soldiers threw themselves against the fort. Practically submerged by them the defenders were all massacred.

With the Fort des Augustins taken Jeanne ordered it to be burnt down. Then, since night was approaching, she decided to encircle the Fort des Tourelles with a strong cordon of troops. She had plenty of food brought out for them from Orléans.

The Maid would have liked to stay with her men the whole night, but she had been seriously wounded in a trap during the final attack. De La Hire and Dunois insisted on her going back to her lodging and having the wound attended to. So she returned to Orléans, and contrary to her wont—it was a Friday—she did not fast, for she felt the necessity of feeding herself so as to gain the strength she would need next day for the hard battles ahead.

While she supped a messenger arrived from de Gaucourt, informing her that the council of the military chiefs had met and having considered the far superior number of the English troops, decided "not to send out the men-at-arms tomorrow." He added that the cordon of troops thrown round the redoubt of Tourelles would permit them to await the reinforcements the King would not fail to send to his dear town of Orléans. Therefore, it was unnecessary for her to cross over to the left bank of the Loire tomorrow.

Jeanne calmly answered, "You went to your council, and I went to mine. Now, believe me that the council of the Lord will hold, whereas yours will perish!"

Then she turned to Brother Pasquerel who was present in the room. "Do not fail to rise early in the morning. Do your best to stay all the time at my side—tomorrow I have a lot to do, greater things than I did hitherto. Tomorrow I shall be wounded and blood will spurt above my breast."

That prophecy was new to those who were at her side. However, already in Poitiers she warned the King that SS Catherine and Marguerite had announced that she would be wounded at the siege of Orléans. Nobody had time to ask Jeanne to explain the words she uttered as a delegation of aldermen and burghers of the town asked to be received by her.

The delegates unfolded a plan very different from the one the military chiefs had evolved: they requested that the Fort of Tourelles be taken by assault as soon as the next day dawned, because not only would the upkeep of so many armed men cost a lot of money, without mentioning the disadvantages of keeping a strong contingent of troops in the midst of a civilian population, but they also feared that such a strong fort, with plenty of food and ammunition, would hold out easily against a blockade till such time as an English army arrived to relieve it.

Jeanne reassured the aldermen and burghers, promising to

attack the Fort of Tourelles the next day with every soul that was willing to fight at her side.

During the night the English evacuated the Fort of Saint-Privé, one part of the garrison to strengthen the defences of the Fort of Saint-Laurent, the rest as reinforcement to the Fort of Tourelles, whose defenders now numbered over twelve hundred men.

On Saturday, May 7, Jeanne rose at three in the morning, then went to Mass. Before she left, her host's daughter tried to persuade her to partake of a fine shad which an Orléans fisherman had given her.

"In God's name," Jeanne said, "keep it for tonight, for I will bring along a Godon (a name given to the English by the populace because Goddam was their favourite swear-word) who will eat his share of the fish."

She mounted a horse, then placed herself at the head of a large column of militia, and took the road leading to the Porte de Bourgogne, where the Governor surrounded by a detachment of soldiers wanted to stop her progress. In vain the Governor tried to justify his action by repeating what the Council had decided in the evening and with which she was well acquainted. Jeanne stopped him, and expressed her feelings in this sentence:

"You are a wicked man, preventing my people from leaving!" And indicating the growling crowd she added, "But they will leave whether you want it or not." That was no empty threat. Then turning to the militiamen, she said, "In God's name, I am going! He who loves me will follow me!"

The Governor, fearing for his life, thought it safest to give in, and to the cheers of the crowd the militiamen followed Jeanne through the city gate.

Jeanne and her men crossed the Loire in boats, and joined the royal army which was investing the Fort of Tourelles. The chiefs of the mercenaries were not loth to exploit her determination to fight, insofar as they did not want to lose the occasion to take prisoners who would pay high ransom; so they too crossed the river.

At sunrise the battle began. The English, whose number was twelve hundred or thereabouts, had the immense advantage of fighting behind the fortifications, and sent showers of arrows and cannon balls on the besiegers, forcing them to retreat. Three times the fort was attacked in the course of the morning; the English repulsed each attack. The exhausted attackers withdrew towards noon, so as to rest and eat a meal. Afterwards there followed the fourth assault which also was repulsed with great loss to the attackers; again a devastating failure.

In vain Jeanne encouraged her troops, "Do not hesitate! The fort is yours." However, the soldiers were at the end of their tether, had lost hope and began to give way.

At one o'clock in the afternoon Jeanne went down into the trench, a ladder was put against the wall, and waving her standard she tried to climb to the top. At that moment an arrow from a crossbow hit her between the breastplate and her neck. She fell off the ladder and collapsed in the trench—she was carried from the battlefield. It was a serious wound. The arrow had pierced her shoulder and the point stuck out of her back. Bravely Jeanne pulled out the arrow herself, then the sight of her blood moved her to tears. But soon she overcame her weakness, allowed her men to put fresh fat and olive oil on the wound. She had already refused a soldier's offer to cure her by casting a spell over her.

"I would rather die than sin. Thy will be done!"

After confessing to Brother Pasquerel she mounted her horse to show the troops that she was still alive, for the English claimed that they had killed her.

On the battlefield no progress was being made, and night was not far off. The captains decided to stop all further attack, take their siege guns back to the town, and wait till next morning. They went to tell Jeanne of the decision they had made. Dunois had already issued the order to retreat. But the Maid would not hear of it; in the end they listened to her. While the troops were given the fresh order to continue fighting Jeanne on horseback rode into a vineyard, and there in the middle of the vineyard she prayed to her saints, begging them not to abandon her at such a crucial moment.

She was radiant when she returned to the battlefield. Addressing herself to Guy de Cailly and all those near him, she said, "Return to the assault in God's name! The English shall not have the strength to defend themselves if we make no mistake. The Tourelles will be taken and the bastions too! "

Jean d'Aulon, the Maid's squire, had handed her banner to a Basque soldier. When Jeanne saw it held by a stranger she rushed up to him to tear it from his hand and shook it so vigorously that the fighting men took that for a signal and with a loud shout threw themselves against the fort. Taking immediate advantage of the misunderstanding caused by the waving banner Jeanne called out, "Forward! It is yours! Go for it! "

With an irresistible dash mercenaries, militiamen and regular soldiers advanced to a last assault while the English, beginning to panic, crossed back over the drawbridge.

The Orléanais, who the whole day long had not ceased bombarding the fort, contrived to knock together several planks which were then placed on the bridge, where the English had destroyed part of it, so as to make crossing over again possible. Without hesitating even for a second an old knight of Rhodes, the Commander Nicole de Giresme, got on the fragile foot-bridge and followed by a number of courageous men took the English, who were busy repulsing Jeanne's attack, in the rear. Moreover, the soldiers brought over a large barge full of inflammable material which was pushed under the bridge spanning the culvert between the fort and the bridgehead. The big fire-ship soon devoured the beams with its flames.

Then Jeanne shouted to Glasdale, "Glassidas! Glassidas! Surrender to the King of Heaven! You called me a whore, but I take pity on you and yours! "

Shortly after, the fired bulwark collapsed under the weight of the escaping English soldiers, and Glasdale and every one of his men fell into the Loire, where all of them were drowned. Thus the prophecy Jeanne made on the preceding Saturday was fulfilled. It was seven o'clock in the evening. After thirteen hours of fighting the Fort of Tourelles was taken.

In the light of the flames rising from the burning fort the Maid returned to Orléans, cheered by the population, and assisted at a solemn *Te Deum* sung in the cathedral. Her wound was again attended to, and she supped on a few slices of bread soaked in a glass of wine.

On Sunday May 8 she was up at dawn and crossed over to

the left bank of the Loire. As her wound hurt her cruelly she did not wear armour but a simple coat of mail. Soon after, the English came out of their forts and took up their positions in battle order in front of the town. The tocsin was rung in the city, calling every militiaman to the walls. Jeanne had an altar erected in a field where she and her troops were. She heard Mass and took communion. At the end of the Mass she received information that the English were deploying their troops, and the mercenaries' cavalry was preparing to charge them.

"Do they turn their faces or their backs to us?" she asked.

"Their backs," was the answer.

"In that case let them go! It does not please the Lord to fight them today. You will beat them another time. Let us go to give thanks to God."

On that evening of May 8, 1429 the town of Orléans which had been besieged for over seven months was at last liberated.

The first part of Jeanne's mission was accomplished.

Seven

While Jeanne was acclaimed in Orléans by the happy populace, and a messenger, called Fleur de Lys, was at once dispatched to the King with the good news, de La Hire and his lieutenants did not miss the opportunity to go out and pillage the forts which the English had evacuated so precipitately and bring back everything they found there, arms, ammunition, clothes and a lot of victuals.

On the afternoon of Sunday, May 8, the Maid organised a solemn procession which moved across the town, visiting all the churches and chapels of Orléans to give thanks to God for the quick and brilliant victory.

Next day, while most of the mercenary captains left the town, a number of them following the Loire in the direction of Meung, searching for English stragglers, the guilds and corporations of Orléans came officially to thank their deliverer, whom they offered many presents including a beautifully ornamented saddle, cloth for a fine dress, a large chest covered with delicately worked leather, several barrels containing the best wines of the district, and a lot of foodstuffs.

On Tuesday May 10, Jeanne tore herself away from the gratitude of the people of Orléans who had not ceased showing it, and left the town, followed by the royal troops and accompanied by Dunois, their destination the town of Chinon, where the Court was assembled. In spite of the terrible pain her wound caused her she reached Blois on the same evening, and left it next day for Tours, where she spent Thursday. In the afternoon of Friday, May 13, she met the Dauphin who had come out to meet her on the road to Chinon. As she reached her sovereign she grasped her banner and bowed low over her horse's neck.

The Dauphin raised his hood, beamed with joy as he saluted her, asked her to dismount, then embraced her and spoke to her affectionately. They rode side by side, the Dauphin, as always, wearing a threadbare green tunic, Jeanne resplendent in her golden armour. They took the road to the town, and when they arrived there the crowds loudly cheered them.

The entire country already knew that Orléans was liberated. On the advice of Yolande of Anjou Charles VII had sent messengers everywhere in the kingdom, his aim to whip up the enthusiasm of his partisans, with official letters in which after thanking God for the great victory, he declared that "the Maid was present in person the whole time when all this was accomplished."

From all the provinces loyal addresses were sent to the Dauphin, congratulating him on the victory. Each contained praise of Jeanne. In any case it was decided to take immediate advantage of the favourable situation brought about by the raising of the siege of Orléans. Already on May 10, even before he saw Jeanne, he wrote to the inhabitants of Narbonne, telling them that he would "make haste to pursue our good luck," and added, "our affairs will come to a happy conclusion."

In the royal household, as everywhere else in France, everybody was waiting for the launching of a new offensive against the English troops. The Royal Council was unanimous as regards the necessity of attacking the English anew, but there were many different opinions on the tactics to be adopted.

The Duc d'Alençon was of the opinion that they should advance boldly, going without delay into Normandy and chasing out the occupying troops before they had time to receive reinforcements. He did not mention it, though everybody knew, that an advance into Normandy would be to his benefit, enabling him to take possession of his duchy again. On the other hand, Dunois and all the other military men were of the opinion that the first move should be the retaking of all the fortresses the English were still holding along the Loire, which would give them easy victories followed, of course, by profitable looting.

Jeanne herself, who was not present at the meetings of the Royal Council, repeatedly insisted that the Dauphin should as soon as possible march on Reims to be crowned there, thus outstripping the English who had made the big blunder of not having yet crowned Henry VI as King of France.

Wavering as always, Charles VII did not know which plan to

adopt. Besides, de La Trémouille, who more than ever was careful to avoid trouble with the Duke of Burgundy, and taking advantage of the divisions in the Royal Council, advised him not to jeopardise, by being over hasty, the considerable advantage which the victory of Orléans gave him. Irritated by the many delays Dunois, who wanted to put a *fait accompli* before Charles, threw his troops against Jargeau, but was repulsed. He returned discomfited to Tours.

After ten days of fruitless discussions the Royal Council, influenced by de La Trémouille, decided that the Court should move to Loches, and stay there for the time being. The Court arrived on May 22.

Yolande of Anjou hesitated for a while about whose side to take, but eventually decided on backing those who advocated immediate opening of hostilities with a powerful force under Jeanne's command. Dunois's attempt at Jargeau showed her that isolated attacks without Jeanne's presence could only end in failure. Once the lines of communication were assured by the cleaning up of enemy-held forts on the Loire, the march to Reims seemed to her no longer a fanciful dream but a spectacular enterprise which, if successful, would have an immense effect on the Dauphin's subjects.

Shortly after this, the members of the Royal Council once again separated without taking any decision. Yolande of Anjou arrived, and on the same day took Jeanne to the Dauphin's chamber, where they found him in the company of Dunois and two faithful allies of the Queen of Sicily, Christophe d'Harcourt, Bishop of Castres and the Dauphin's confessor, and Robert le Maçon, ex-chancellor of the kingdom. Jeanne fell on her knees before the Dauphin and said,

"Noble Dauphin, stop holding those endless councils, but go as soon as possible to Reims to receive your worthy crown."

The Dauphin was astounded by the firmness of her voice. The Bishop of Castres tried to get the Dauphin's consent by asking her a question, the answer to which already he knew.

"Jeanne, was it your Voices who ordered you to say this?"

"Yes," she replied.

"Would you not mind telling here in the King's presence how your Voices speak to you?"

Jeanne blushed, then said, "Well, when I am upset by anyone who does not believe willingly in the things I announce in God's name, I withdraw and pray to Him and complain, asking Him why people are such unbelievers. When I finish praying I hear a voice that says to me, 'Daughter of God, go, go, go! I will help you, go!' And when I hear that voice joy fills me, and I should like to be always like that."

As she spoke those words the flame within her lit up her features.

Deeply moved the Dauphin raised her and promised to go to Reims and have himself anointed without further delay.

The Royal Council was obliged to bow to the King's decision. De La Trémouille made a last attempt to hold back the expedition by pointing out that the royal troops had dispersed, which was true, but he forgot to mention that he had made no effort to find the financial help that was needed to pay the soldiers. The Dauphin ignored his arguments and summoned his vassals for the feast of St John. The troops were to assemble at Gien, and the Duc d'Alençon was appointed commander-in-chief of the army on the understanding that he would strictly follow the instructions Jeanne received from her Voices.

This sort of double command could have had calamitous consequences if there had not existed complete harmony between Jeanne and d'Alençon whom she familiarly called her handsome duke, and who was the son-in-law of her half-brother Charles d'Orléans.

At the end of May the Maid had gone to the Abbey of Saint-Florent near Saumur, where lived, retired from the world, the mother and young wife of d'Alençon. She promised the two women, frightened by the prospect of another military campaign—the young duke had been for four years the prisoner of the English before ransom money was found—that she would bring him back from the war hale and hearty.

On her return to Loches on May 26 Jeanne received the Dauphin's permission to mount an attack against Jargeau immediately after the royal troops had been assembled. So that all should appreciate the high esteem in which he held her, and also because as a descendant of the Valois she was entitled to it, the Dauphin officially confirmed on June 2, 1429 that Jeanne might

77

bear the royal coat of arms of France, "azure with two golden fleurs-de-lys, a sword argent with a golden hilt charged with five fleurs-de-lys on the blade and above a golden crown."

On June 3 Jeanne was back in Selles, and sent a gold ring as a present to the ladies of Laval whose great-grandmother in her youth was the wife of the great Constable du Guesclin and was related to the House of Orléans. With that gesture, which she knew would be appreciated by the initiated, she wanted to signify that the Third Order of St Francis, of which she was one of the highest dignitaries, accepted the affiliation with the Knights Templar which order was officially suppressed in 1312, but which had been reconstituted in secret and had elected du Guesclin as its Grand Master at the time.

On June 9 Jeanne, with Marshal de Boussac riding at her side and followed by a strong escort, entered Orléans across the Pont-des-Tournelles. The inhabitants of Orléans gave their deliverer a huge ovation. She took up her temporary abode in Jacques Boucher's house, where all the important local people called on her. Next day the Duc d'Alençon, Dunois, de Gaucourt and an army of eight thousand men, strong in artillery, arrived in the town.

Jeanne was impatient to leave before de La Trémouille had time to change the Dauphin's mind. On her insistence the royal army marched out of Orléans, taking the road leading to the fortress of Jargeau which was held by seasoned English troops, seven hundred in number and provided with plenty of food and ammunition. Their commander was William de La Pole, Duke of Suffolk, who had a great military reputation. Simultaneously with the advance of the royal army forty watermen transported siege artillery in five barges, Jeanne having insisted on the cannons because she wanted to reduce the garrison before the army led by Falstaff could come to its rescue. Falstaff, so she heard, had already left Paris with his men.

When they were in sight of Jargeau a council of war was held. Several military leaders hesitated to attack the fort because in their considered opinion it was too well fortified for an assault to succeed. Jeanne was all in favour of an immediate powerful attack, and the Duc d'Alençon agreed with her, so it was decided to take Jargeau by assault.

Showing great military ability the Duke of Suffolk posted part of his army in battle order in front of the ramparts and round the fort that guarded the bridge. Imprudently the French army made its first attack, which was soon repulsed with many casualties on the French side. In the confusion of battle and the rout of the Dauphin's soldiers Jeanne did not lose her head, but raising her standard and holding it high she rallied the men and took the offensive again, succeeding in establishing a foothold on the outskirts; surprised by the violence of the counter-attack the English were forced to withdraw as fast as their legs could carry them.

At dawn next day Jeanne ordered the bombardment of the old castle of Jargeau. The towers were quickly destroyed by cannon balls, and Suffolk at once asked for a truce of fifteen days which La Hire and several other military leaders were willing to accept. However, Jeanne refused and gave the English the choice between "their and their horses' immediate departure" and the fate that awaited them after she took the town.

The English made no reply, so Jeanne ordered a general assault without listening to the Duc d'Alençon who thought such an attack premature.

"Forward, gentle duc," she said. "To the attack! God's hour has come. It is for the best! God helps those who help themselves." But as the young prince still hesitated she added, "Are you afraid, gentle duc? Do you not know that I promised your wife to take you back hale and hearty?"

During that time the English artillery countered with all its might against the French cannons. Showing the Duc d'Alençon a siege gun pointed in his direction she said, "Move back, for this engine will kill you!"

The young man followed her advice and took a few steps back. The next second a cannon ball dropped precisely where he had been standing and mortally wounded the Comte de Lude who had taken his place.

For four hours the royal troops tried unsuccessfully to scale the ramparts of Jargeau. Repulsed each time and suffering great losses, the French began to lose confidence. Putting a ladder against the wall and waving her standard to encourage the martial spirit of the assailants Jeanne decided to climb to the top of the rampart. Hardly had she climbed a few steps when a cannon ball hit her steel cape which made her lose her balance and she fell over and into the moat. There was a brief moment of panic among the French troops, but ignoring her pain Jeanne bravely rose to her feet, and waving her banner she shouted on the top of her voice, "Forward! Show your courage, climb up there bravely, go to it!"

A loud shout was the answer, and with irresistible dash the Dauphin's troops climbed the walls. They moved across the town, chasing the English and killing most of them. The Duke of Suffolk himself had to surrender to an Auvergnat squire called Guillaume Regnault whom he knighted before handing over his sword.

In the evening of that Sunday, June 12, Jeanne once again entered Orléans triumphantly.

On Monday morning after the artillery had been brought back to Orléans and the troops had rested and fed copiously, Jeanne declared her intention of continuing the military operations. "Tomorrow afternoon I want to go to see those who are at Meung," she said.

On Wednesday, June 15, Jeanne and the army left Orléans and followed the Loire downstream. The fortified bridge over the Loire at Meung was taken by onslaught; however the garrison entrenched itself in the town; so Jeanne restricted herself to throwing a cordon round the outskirts while with the main body she went to lay siege to the castle of Beaugency four miles downstream.

The Maid had received intelligence that Talbot had left the town to meet Falstaff, the victor of the Day of the Herrings, who at the head of five thousand first-class soldiers was marching towards the Loire to aid the English garrisons and above all to stop the different enemy forces joining up.

On the morning of June 16 the French were informed that the two English leaders were advancing swiftly towards the battleground. In those circumstances the Dauphin's troops risked being crushed between the relieving army and the castle of Beaugency which could be taken only after a long siege. Some of the French military chiefs already were talking of retreating fast to Orléans. But suddenly there appeared a completely unexpected reinforcement: Richemont, Constable of Brittany, who was in disgrace at Court since his one-time protégé, de La Trémouille, had supplanted him in the Royal Council, had come spontaneously with an army of four hundred lances, eight hundred archers and many knights to take part in the battle for Beaugency. While his troops crossed the Loire at Amboise the Constable received the visit of the Seigneur de la Jaille, sent by de La Trémouille, ordering him to return to Brittany. But Arthur de Richemont simply said that all he wanted was to serve the common cause, and ignoring de La Trémouille's orders he continued to march on Beaugency.

His arrival much embarrassed the Duc d'Alençon, who had also received orders from de La Trémouille to fight the Constable and his troops if he refused to return to Brittany. Much against his inclinations d'Alençon sent his own troops to bar him the road, and give battle if he refused to withdraw and continued marching on Beaugency. The two armies came face to face on June 16 at dawn. The many friends of the Constable, among them La Hire and the entire Breton nobility, were in utter misery and did not know whose side to take. Jeanne spoke to no one of her intentions, but when she arrived with the Duc d'Alençon and his gentlemen before the Constable she, who had kept her feelings to herself, jumped lightly off her horse, rushed up to the Constable and embraced his knees. The Constable got off his horse, lifted her, then said to her,

"I was told, Jeanne, that you wanted to fight me. I do not know whether you are sent by God or not. If you are sent by Him I need not fear you because God knows my good intentions. But if you are sent by the Devil I fear you even less!"

In front of this *fait accompli* the Duc d'Alençon had to give in, leaving the responsibility for what took place to Jeanne. So as to avoid a clash between the two armies Jeanne decided that the Constable and his fifteen hundred Bretons should take up positions before Beaugency while the Dauphin's men would try to stop the English reinforcing the garrison.

The English captains themselves were divided on what action to follow. Impressed by Jeanne's enormous successes John Falstaff thought it preferable to withdraw to some well-fortified town and there to await the fresh troops promised by the Duke of Bedford, and only then to take the offensive, with a far greater chance of success. On the other hand, Talbot, who had been in a rage ever since his defeats on the Loire, wanted at once to attack the Dauphin's forces. Most of the English captains were of his opinion, so it was decided to attack. Falstaff had to give in. He left with his army for Beaugency. One league from Meung he caught sight of the French army ranged in battle order. Immediately he decided to fight, and, in accordance with the customs of the time, he sent heralds to announce the battle. Jeanne received them on the highest hill in the neighbourhood.

"It is too late today," she said. "Go and find living quarters. Tomorrow if God and Our Lady wants it!"

Falstaff, whose troops were tired out by the long march, was pleased by the answer, and hurried into Meung to billet his men.

All that time the Dauphin's artillery did not cease pounding the walls of the castle of Beaugency. The Constable's Bretons were posted before it. When the defenders saw Falstaff and Talbot refuse combat and withdraw they thought they were abandoned. Cleverly Jeanne saw to the news being spread that the general assault would be mounted the next morning and no quarter would be given. In the course of the night emissaries from the besieged garrison arrived to ask her to negotiate a "treaty." Jeanne told them that she would let them go in peace and keep their weapons if they evacuated the fortress at once. Richard Guetin, the commandant of the fort, was only too pleased to accept her offer. In the morning of June 18, 1429, the Dauphin's troops took possession of Beaugency. The English had already left.

The Maid's excellent strategy upset all the English plans. The English troops were in an awkward position, and angry with Talbot, whose plan was the cause of it, Falstaff abandoned Meung, taking the garrison along. Then he ordered them to retreat towards Paris. They took the road through Yenville and Etampes. On Jeanne's order the French army went in pursuit of the English. She took that decision against the advice of some of the captains who in spite of their reverses still held the English troops in high esteem.

"In God's name, we must fight them, even if they lose themselves in the clouds!" Then she added, "The gentle king today will have his greatest victory. My voices tell me they will all be ours!"

Once again her assurance and the deep conviction with which she spoke carried the day. During the entire morning the French tried unsuccessfully to make contact with the English who had mysteriously vanished. Towards noon Jeanne ordered La Hire and Xaintrailles to take the advance-guard and some of the cavalry and cut the road leading to Paris. In their swift advance the mercenaries saw a stag chased by English hounds, and following them they discovered Falstaff's and Talbot's armies both hidden in copses near Patay. Scouts were sent back with the news of the enemy being near at hand.

The Duc d'Alençon, who was riding beside Jeanne, turned to her when they received the news and asked her, "Will we fight?"

"Are your spurs good?" Jeanne asked.

"What? Do you think we shall be obliged to run?"

"Not at all," replied Jeanne, "but the English won't defend themselves and good spurs will be needed to catch up with them. In God's name, go for them, for they will run away and never stop. They will be discomfited without our people suffering any loss."

Realising that he could not avoid battle Falstaff lined up his men in battle-order. His advance-guard was drawn up with the cannons, provisions and baggage on rising ground beside a wood stretching to Patay. The bulk of the army was placed behind two hedges as he expected the French to advance between them. Talbot with five hundred archers was given the task of impeding the French advance till the rear-guard reached the main body.

Those dispositions were probably excellent, but Falstaff did not reckon with the impetuosity of the overexcited French whom Jeanne loudly encouraged. With great dash they fought their way through Talbot's archers in spite of the strong defence they put up. From his vantage point Falstaff ordered part of his cavalry to go to the help of Talbot, but the archers when they saw the fast approaching horsemen thought that they were running from the French, and seized by panic they threw away their weapons and ran back to the woods. Falstaff had no time left to redress the balance, for into the gap wildly rode the entire French cavalry, sweeping everything aside. About three thousand English soldiers perished in the battle. Five hundred and fifty were taken prisoners, among them Talbot, Scales, Rameston and Hungerford. Falstaff owed his life to his very fast horse; however most of his men now understood what Jeanne had meant and harried by the French cavalry had to choose between death and surrender.

When the news of Jeanne's new victory reached Yenville it capitulated, and the English garrisons evacuated the forts of Montpipeau and Saint-Sigismond and took the road back to Normandy. Jeanne's resounding triumph at Patay made a deep impression on all the Dauphin's subjects. It was the first occasion since the Hundred Years' War that the French had succeeded in beating the English in open battle.

Eight

On June 18, 1429, Jeanne once more made a triumphal entry into Orléans. After giving thanks to God for the brilliant victory in the cathedral, she went to lodge with Jacques Boucher, while the entire population made feverish preparations for the arrival of the Dauphin, whose coming everybody eagerly awaited.

However, he was not too eager to come to Orléans. At the moment he was staying in the castle of Sully which belonged to de La Trémouille, who entertained him lavishly. The Dauphin again fell under the influence of his favourite. As de La Trémouille could no longer pretend that Jeanne was unable to win battles he minimised her part in them and tried to undermine her reputation in every conceivable manner. He succeeded, since the Dauphin had well-founded reasons to be irritated with her.

To begin with the Dauphin reproached Jeanne for having ignored the orders de La Trémouille gave, and for having forced the Duc d'Alençon to accept Richemont's aid instead of making him return to Brittany with his army. To that definite proof of disobedience, which was however mitigated by the glorious victory at Patay and the liberation of the forts along the Loire near Orléans which by no means touched the Dauphin's self-esteem, there was a far more serious charge against her.

The fact was that during the last battles Jeanne had carried a new banner which was no other than that of the Knights Templar. With that she proved in public that as a dignitary of the Third Order of St Francis she intended to pursue the ambitious political programme of the Templars for which the last of their grand masters, Jacques de Molay, had been burnt at the stake in Ile-aux-Juifs on March 18, 1314. Her use of that forbidden banner revealed her true intentions since the two colours of the banner symbolised the alliance between the low clergy (white) and the ordinary people (blue). As regards the famous motto

85

Non nobis, Domine, non nobis sed nomini tuo da gloriam (Give us not glory, Our Lord, but give it to your name) it suited the pious girl perfectly and could but encourage her in her schemes. For the true aim of the Templars was to unite all the Christian states of Europe into one kingdom in order to undertake a decisive crusade with all the might of such a powerful kingdom. Moreover, the Tomb of Christ and the liberation of the Holy Places could thus be assured against the onslaught of Islam.

The Templars had come to understand that the unnecessary rivalries which divided the monarchs of the West were the chief cause of the failure of successive crusades, in the same fashion as the intrigues between the high clergy at the Throne of St Peter prevented the Church from taking united action, without which it was impossible to achieve that noble end. And that was why the Templars, whose leaders were carefully chosen from the nobility, did not hesitate to rely on the lower ranks of the clergy whose members were still animated by apostolic ardour, often conspicuously absent from the high dignitaries of the Church; and to rely on the ordinary townsfolk and peasants who, generally speaking, were profoundly devout and always willing to take the road to Jerusalem with the ancient cry of *Dieu le veut*!

For the same reason the Templars had, either by conviction or necessity, tacitly to encourage the aspirations—more or less precisely defined—of the low clergy who wanted serious reforms inside the Church, also the aspirations of the better educated people, especially the world of clerks and merchants, who had sought more communal freedom ever since the feudal system had been riddled by far away adventures and by decay from within. And above all, after so many ruinous and bloody wars, the ordinary clergy and the people aspired to the unity of the West, in their eyes the only means of bringing about the peace for which they craved.

After a long war started in 1291 when the loss of Acre brought about the loss of the whole Holy Land, and followed by twenty-five years of the ups-and-downs of war known only to the initiated, the Templars were destroyed by the alliance of the two greatest European powers, the King of France on the temporal side and the Pope on the spiritual side, both considering themselves threatened by the Templars' aims. But their spirit survived

86

in the begging orders of the Church, especially among the Franciscans, who had a firm hold over the people.

Raised to the rank of *Dame très discrète* of the Third Order of St Francis long before leaving Domrémy, convinced that after the liberation of Orléans and her other military successes it was her duty to fulfil her mission completely of which the corner stone was the liberation of the Tomb of Christ, Jeanne did not hesitate to raise the banner of the Templars.

By doing so she gained the definite allegiance not only of the low clergy and the people south of the Loire, who being on the Dauphin's side applauded her victories, but also, which was far more important for her future schemes, the clerics, the peasants and the burghers of the provinces still under English rule.

Simultaneously, with the exception of the members of the powerful House of Orléans and the friends of Yolande of Anjou who appreciated that it was useless to oppose the reforms the times demanded, Jeanne became the target of the implacable hatred of the great noblemen and prelates, living on the fat of the land, who dreaded any change in the order of things. Undecided as always, the Dauphin wavered between the treacherous advice of his favourite and his private conviction that Jeanne was right. For the moment his strategy consisted of taking no action, refusing to return to Chinon as many near him wished, but refusing equally to make his solemn entry into Orléans.

Having waited in vain for him for three days Jeanne decided to join him in Sully, where he received her extremely well, and showered her, Dunois and all who came with her with praise: but she did not succeed in obtaining Richemont's pardon. Not only did the Dauphin refuse to give her satisfaction but issued orders for Richemont, who was staying in Beaugency, to go back at once to Brittany. De La Trémouille, who feared the return to Court of his erstwhile benefactor whom he had so wickedly betrayed, thought he had won the day. But Jeanne knew how to make sacrifices when in pursuit of the main aim, and obtained from the Dauphin a more important favour than Richemont's pardon, namely, the promise that he would go to Châteauneuf to consult the military chiefs.

They left together on June 22. On their way through Saint-Benoît-sur-Loire the Dauphin rode beside her and advised her to take a rest before she undertook further military operations. Jeanne perceived de La Trémouille's influence behind the advice, and for an instant she was so discouraged that she could not hold her tears back. Then taking hold of herself she said to him, "Gentle Dauphin, why do you doubt? You shall have your kingdom and very soon you will be crowned. Make use of me." She wanted him to understand that she was still willing to take him to Reims to be anointed King of France, but also to remind him that she had but little time to waste with the affairs of France since her final mission was the liberation of the tomb of Christ. She added, "I cannot wait longer than a year! "

The Dauphin did not reply; though his half-sister's tears and the perfect assurance with which she spoke profoundly touched him, as did even the threat she made.

At Châteauneuf several councils were held before a decision could be reached. The captains were divided in their advice. Some of them, thinking only of more loot, maintained that before everything else the enemy enclaves on the Loire should be cleaned up, and suggested laying siege to Cosne, La Charité, and other fortified towns still in the hands of the English. The Duc d'Alençon, who for evident reasons thought only of retaking Normandy, advocated a powerful offensive with Rouen as its aim. To every suggestion the Dauphin gave the same answer: he had not sufficient money to undertake any of them. As a matter of fact, he spoke the truth. Turning his own argument against him, Jeanne wrenched the promise from him that he would march on Reims.

While the Dauphin, pleased with Jeanne for having forced his hand, returned to Sully, Jeanne hastened to Orléans, where at once she assembled the men-at-arms, supplies and ammunition, without forgetting to unmount all the light guns she could find in the town. They were placed in waggons.

On June 24 Jeanne said to the Duc d'Alençon, "Have the trumpets blown and mount your horse. It is high time to join the gentle Dauphin and take him along the road to Reims for his coronation." Then she placed herself at the head of the troops to march to Gien to meet the other army.

Volunteers came from everywhere: noble lords who wished to assist at the anointing; noblemen who arrived at Yolande of

Anjou's bidding; mercenaries for whom war was always an occasion to enrich themselves; militiamen and ordinary men moved by the unflagging exhortations of the Franciscans, everybody full of immense enthusiasm, waiting for the order to move. The march on Reims appeared to them a prelude to the march on Jerusalem.

Nonetheless, de La Trémouille and Régnault de Chartres were still trying hard to postpone the date of departure. They obtained from the Dauphin the calling of one council after the other, where they argued that because of lack of money the army could not take the offensive. The noblemen who were too poor to follow the army at their own expense, signed up as squires, that is archers, or as paid men of their more fortunate equals. The mercenaries remained as well as the militiamen exhorted by the Franciscans not to abandon Jeanne's side.

Listening to his evil counsellors the Dauphin ostentatiously sent away the Comte Bernard d'Armagnac and all his men; and Jeanne had to submit to the elimination from the glorious expedition the head of a family she was devoted to. While the councils held by the Dauphin indulged in endless sterile discussions the troops waited in idleness. On June 25 de La Trémouille persuaded the Council to wait for the surrender of the garrisons of Bonny, Cosne and La Charité before marching on Reims. That astute creature had every hope that the garrisons would refuse to abandon their forts and thus the expedition could be indefinitely postponed on the pretext that the army could not be put to the risk of being taken in the rear.

In order to annoy him Jeanne, the very same day, took upon herself to address the following letter to the inhabitants of Tournai:

✠ Jhésus ✠ Maria

"Gentle and loyal Frenchmen of the town of Tournai,

"The Maid wants you to know that within eight days she chased the English from all the places they held along the Loire, where there were many killed and taken prisoner and discomfited in battle. Believe me that the Count of Suffolk, Lapoulle [La Pole] his brother, the Sire de Talbot, the Sire de Scales and Messire Jehan [Falstaff] and several knights and captains were taken, and the brother of the Count of Suffolk and Glacidas [Glasdale] were killed. Remain very loyal Frenchmen, I beg you; and I beg and request you to be all of you ready to go to the anointing of gentle King Charles in Reims, where we shall go very soon, and come out to meet us when you hear us approaching. I commend you to God. God keep you and give you grace so that you be able to keep up the good disputes of the Kingdom of France."

Brother Richard and Brother Didier, both of the mendicant orders, hastened to take this letter to its destination, and Brother Jean de Gand had it circulated in all the provinces.

Manoeuvred by his counsellors the Dauphin still hesitated to order the advance. On the 26th he took the decision to send his wife to Bourges on the pretext that her presence in Reims would entail the upkeep of an expensive retinue. However, on the next day he had not yet taken any decision about his own coronation. At Court the general impression was that de La Trémouille had won when he persuaded the King to send away the Queen who was Yolande of Anjou's own daughter, to Berry. In the city the army was still waiting to move. Whenever Jeanne appeared among the soldiers she was wildly cheered. Mounted on a handsome horse she kept up the troops' morale by her presence alone. With her male attire she wore a blue hat with large bands, raised both before and behind, embellished with fleurs-de-lys, the largest rising above the crown. The members of the Third Order of St Francis did not fail to observe that this unusual headgear, because of the insignia of royalty, was the symbol of the Dauphin's alliance with the districts whose colours she carried.

On the 26th Admiral de Culan took Bonny. However, the garrison of Marchenoir, which first decided to surrender, refused to do so when it heard that Richemont and his army had gone back to Brittany. De La Trémouille, who saw that his plan was succeeding, insisted in the Royal Council on postponing the march to Reims till all the forts held by the English along the Loire surrendered.

Jeanne was exasperated. To show her discontent she openly left the town on the 27th, and followed by a large part of the men-at-arms she camped with them in the fields on the road to Auxerre. The troops remaining in Gien began to grumble.

At long last the Dauphin understood where his duty and interests lay. In spite of de La Trémouille's objections, who for two days managed to restrain him from taking a decision, he finally gave the order for the departure for Reims. The soldiers' discontent at once disappeared, helped along by the three gold francs given to each of them.

On June 29 the small town of Saint-Fargeau surrendered. In the evening the army reached Auxerre. Summoned to open the city gates the leaders replied that they feared neither the Armagnacs nor the Maid. When the insolent answer was received Jeanne expressed the opinion that the town should be taken because that would be a salutary example to all large towns like Troyes, Châlons and Reims itself if they refused entry to the Dauphin's troops. She had complete faith in the army which numbered about twelve thousand eager and enthusiastic men, led by brave and circumspect captains like the Duc d'Alençon, the Comte de Clermont, Admiral de Culan, Gilles de Rais, La Hire, Xaintrailles, the young lords of Laval and many others. Moreover, the army was well equipped—a bold idea in those days—with pieces of artillery which were brought along in waggons. With them any siege could be considerably shortened.

But her plan was violently opposed in the council. Secretly de La Trémouille, who had been given the rank of King's Lieutenant in Burgundy and Governor of Auxerre, had pourparlers with the city authorities. After three days of laborious negotiations the burghers of Auxerre and de La Trémouille signed a compromise by which the city, keeping its neutrality would sell provisions to the Dauphin's troops without, however, opening the city gates to them, and would take no action to interfere with their march on Reims.

In spite of Jeanne's remonstrances—and she did not hide her dissatisfaction—the Dauphin accepted those humiliating conditions which made his army grumble again. The only winner in this business was de La Trémouille, who for his good offices, discreetly received the sum of two thousand gold ecus.

On July 3 the army moved on. Saint-Florentin and Brinon surrendered unhesitatingly to the Dauphin who wrote from

Brinon to the townsfolk of Reims to advise them that he "was on his way to their good town to be anointed and crowned there," and that he was "disposed to treat them in all matters as good and loyal subjects," adding that "if they desired to be better informed of his intentions he would with pleasure receive their representatives."

On Tuesday, July 4, Saint-Phal was reached, whence Jeanne sent a letter to the inhabitants of Troyes:

✠ Jhésus   ✠ Maria

"Very dear and good friends which is up to you to be, lords, burghers and people of Troies, Jeanne the Maid sends you the news and lets you know in the name of the King of Heaven, her Liege Lord and Soverign Master, in Whose royal service she is each day, that you give obedience to and recognise the gentle King of France who will soon be in Reims and in Paris, whatever happens, and in the other good towns of the Sacred Kingdom with the help of Jesus, the King. Faithful Frenchmen, come before King Charles, and there should be no mistake, if no, then watch out for your bodies and property if you do not do as told. And if you act like that, I promise and testify that with God's help we will enter all the towns which belong to the Holy Kingdom and we shall make good and firm peace against anybody. She commends you to God—God keep you if it pleases Him. Reply at once."

Jeanne received no reply from the town of Troyes, but their leaders hastened to write to the inhabitants of Reims to let them know that they "received from Jeanne the Maid, a real liar, mad and possessed by the devil, a letter which has neither rhyme nor reason, and after reading it and laughing at it they threw it into the fire without giving her an answer as it was but a piece of mockery."

Obviously they were encouraged to resist by the example of Auxerre.

The next day there was a sharp engagement between the Dauphin's advance guard and some of the garrison of Troyes who were imprudent enough to come out, but were forced to retreat swiftly. The incident so upset the people of Troyes that in haste they wrote to Bedford, Regent of Henry VI, King of England and France, and to the Duke of Burgundy, asking them to send help urgently, for the town was defended by five hundred Anglo-Burgundian soldiers only. Nevertheless, the thick walls of their fortifications must have reassured them, for they promised that "if the town were attacked they would hold out till death."

By the evening Troyes was invested from every side. The garrison attempted a sortie but was repulsed with heavy losses. In order to gain time the besieged asked to parley. It was accepted much against the Maid's will.

The negotiations lasted for five days. De La Trémouille let them drag on as long as possible as he was well aware that the soldiers' morale was at a low ebb. Bread was lacking and all they had to eat was tough beans which they picked in the fields, causing an epidemic of a kind of typhoid fever. It ravaged the camp.

The townsfolk did not share the opinions of their civil and military leaders. Many of the burghers feared an attack by the Dauphin's troops, for they had no doubts that if the defenders were defeated the town would be mercilessly sacked since the mercenaries gave no quarter. Moreover, Jeanne had warned them of the fate that awaited them if they refused to be loyal Frenchmen. The common people cordially detested the English but could not show their feelings.

Jean Laiguisé, Bishop of Troyes, was in secret a partisan of Yolande of Anjou, and thought of sending to Jeanne Brother Richard, a Franciscan famous for his oratorical gifts, who in Paris preached to vast crowds of five to six thousand people who came from everywhere to listen to his sermons. Travelling through Champagne he was at the moment staying in Troyes. On July 7 in the afternoon he went out of the town and was taken to Jeanne. When he came into her presence he crossed himself and sprinkled her with holy water.

"Approach without fear," said Jeanne, smiling. "I will not fly away."

The Franciscan came nearer, then suddenly fell on his knees. At once Jeanne knelt down too, and before he could say a word she invited him to recite the Rosary with her. After the prayers

Jeanne took Brother Richard aside and they talked for a long time. The Franciscan preacher and Jeanne, high dignitary of the Third Order of St Francis, came immediately to an understanding, especially as the monk wanted to join the Dauphin's side because in Paris, which he had to leave, the English had not treated him with the respect he considered his due. Returning to Troyes he went out of his way to let all and sundry know that Jeanne was "a good Christian in the royal service of her lord and sovereign master."

The following day, July 8, de La Trémouille, who was informed of the change of opinion in the invested town, quickly called the Royal Council together, and wanted to force the members to decide on raising the siege. Some of the counsellors suggested a retreat to Gien, where provisions could be found; others at the instigation of de La Trémouille and Régnault de Chartres, Archbishop of Reims, were of the opinion that the Dauphin's coronation should be abandoned for the moment and that he should return to Chinon. Alone Robert Le Masson, an old man over eighty, dared to speak in favour of remaining outside Troyes and following the original plan. After a lot of arguing he insisted on Jeanne being consulted because "when the Dauphin undertook the journey he did so on the Maid's advice who repeatedly said that she would have him anointed in Reims because that was the will of God." This request brought many protests from other members of the Royal Council who were aware that the former Chancellor of France belonged to Yolande of Anjou's party.

In the midst of the row the counsellors were interrupted by violent knocking on the door. It was Jeanne, who had been told by a squire in the service of Robert Le Masson of what was going on in the Royal Council, and had hurried there to give her own opinion.

Ungraciously Régnault de Chartres repeated in front of her all the arguments in favour of raising the siege and of retreating back to the Loire. While he spoke Jeanne, who refused to sit, paced the room without bothering to hide her irritation. After the Archbishop of Reims had spoken she did not deign to answer him but turning him her back she put a question directly to the Dauphin.

94

"Will you have faith in what I am going to tell you?" she asked.

Embarrassed the Dauphin answered, "Yes." But then regretting such a straightforward reply he quickly added, "That depends on what you say."

Then in a voice trembling with deep emotion, Jeanne said to the Dauphin, "Gentle King of France, if you wish to stay here before your town of Troyes it will submit to you within two days by force or from a sense of loyalty. Have no doubt of that!" And turning to the Chancellor of France she said, "And great will be the amazement of false Burgundy!"

Feeling directly attacked the Archbishop of Reims was forced to say, "He who will be assured that he can enter the town in six days will still have to wait . . ."

"I have not a single doubt," Jeanne answered. Turning again to the Dauphin, she said, "Noble Dauphin, order your people truly to besiege Troyes. Do not protract the meeting, and in God's name tomorrow Troyes will be yours!"

Since Jeanne asked only for a short delay, the Royal Council could not stick to its first decision, especially as it was running a far greater risk here than in front of Auxerre of antagonising the whole army if it found out, which easily it could, what had taken place in the Royal Council.

Believing that the decision was already taken, since the Dauphin had made no comment Jeanne left and mounting her horse she gave orders for the town to be attacked. Under her command the whole army got busy digging entrenchments and artillery emplacements, and carrying wooden beams, bundles of firewood and whatever timber they could find to fill the trenches surrounding the town. Waving a stick, hurrying from one spot to the other, encouraging soldiers here, scolding others there, her feverish activity lasted till the evening. By the dawn of July 9 everything was ready for the assault.

Inside the town the burghers, petrified by the imminence of the onslaught and fearing the terrible consequences of the entry of the army and above all of the mercenaries whose evil reputation they knew to be based on fact, hurried to their bishop, begging him to intervene with Jeanne on their behalf. The garrison had no confidence in being able to defend the town, for they were afraid of an insurrection of the common folk whom Brother Richard had convinced of Jeanne's sacred mission. In his zeal he even assured his audience that the Maid was perfectly capable of rising into the air and passing over the walls with her entire army.

After a brief discussion, in the course of which the bishop and the monk spoke in favour of the town submitting to the Dauphin, the Council decided to send a deputation to him urgently, especially as word came that the priests had already opened two of the city gates. The treaty of surrender was quickly signed. The Dauphin agreed to the garrison leaving unmolested, taking its baggage with it, and on Jeanne's advice he undertook to respect all the privileges conferred on the town by the English.

Already the townsfolk had moved out into the royal camp, fraternising with the troops. In the afternoon Jeanne made her entry into the town cheered and acclaimed by the populace, her task to make preparations for the Dauphin's arrival. When the garrison lined up ready to march out of Troyes the French prisoners threw themselves at her feet, begging her not to abandon them. Gripped by fury when she realised that the Anglo-Burgundians were taking advantage of the treaty of capitulation, she reared her horse and rode into their line and with her stick smote all the enemy soldiers she could reach and shouted, "In God's name they shall not take them away!"

In spite of the vehement protests of the Anglo-Burgundians she kept back those she had freed and the Dauphin paid their ransom on the spot.

On July 11 at nine in the morning riding beside Jeanne, the Dauphin made his solemn entry into the town, saluted by the happy crowds while all the church bells were ringing loudly. He had a magnificent reception. For the first time since the expeditionary force had set out, his face was aglow with joy. His thoughts must have gone back to the day of May 21, 1420 when in the cathedral of this town his mother signed the treaty in which after publicly repudiating him, she surrendered the Kingdom of France to Henry V of England whom she made her son-in-law. Today his entry into Troyes wiped out that shame.

The following day the town council, wanting to show its loyalty, sent letters to all the nearby towns, praising the Dauphin and the Maid. For their part, the Franciscans went everywhere in the region, praising Jeanne to all and sundry, thus making her task far easier. Before leaving Troyes she was asked to hold a newborn babe over the baptismal font; she willingly accepted to be its godmother; and the ceremony was considered by the entire population as proof of her taking the town under her protection.

On July 14 well provided with provisions the royal army marched out of Troyes and encamped at Bussy-Lettrè in the vicinity of Châlons-sur-Marne. The example of Troyes and the work of the preachers was bearing fruit: the bishop and the richest burghers of Châlons went out to meet Jeanne and offered the Dauphin the keys of the town. On July 15 the Dauphin and the army entered Châlons, where they spent the night. After the official ceremonies, to her great joy Jeanne received several inhabitants of Domrémy, who, having heard from the Franciscans that she would be passing through the district on her way to Reims to have the Dauphin crowned, had set out to meet her. She was delighted to see those friendly faces again, Jean Morel, who was one of her godparents, Girardin, a neighbour of her foster-parents and a number of others. They marvelled at the sight of the magnificent scarlet tunic which covered her shining armour, and were moved as they recognised in the heroic maid, whose exploits were known throughout the kingdom, the sweet and devout girl who left the village of Domrémy only a few months before. With great warmth Jeanne asked each for his news and gave them presents before they departed. Before leaving her, those kind folk, who shuddered at the thought of all the dangers that were in store for her, begged her to be constantly careful.

"I fear nothing except treason," she replied.

In the morning of July 16 the army moved on. This was the last stage on the march to Reims, where the authorities were in a cruelly embarrassing situation. Reims like all the other towns in the nearby provinces was in English hands and had been for a long time. However, the troops that defended it were far from strong enough to be able to resist the Dauphin's army.

The Duke of Bedford had at last understood what an enormous mistake he had made when he neglected to have little

Henry VI anointed as King of France. Immediately after the battle of Patay he sent envoys into all the French provinces held by the English to announce that heavy reinforcements would shortly arrive on the Continent.

Already on June 26 the Comte de Vermandois, a senior magistrate, came to Reims to acquaint the town with the Duke of Bedford's plans. He was accompanied by Pierre Cauchon, Bishop of Beauvais. While de Vermandois fulfilled his mission as well as he could, his deputy, though agreeing in public with him, did not hesitate in private and under the seal of secrecy to make observations in order to spread confusion in the minds of those who asked him for advice.

The point was that the Bishop of Beauvais had thought matters over after the lifting of the siege of Orléans. His public career began in 1413 when as a simple Master of Arts of the University of Paris he took up the political cause of the Cabochiens, partly because he sincerely believed that reforms were necessary, partly because he wanted to play an important rôle in politics. Excluded from the royal amnesty of August 23 which pardoned most of the trouble makers, Pierre Cauchon was taken into the service of Isabeau of Bavaria who needed someone renowned for his profound knowledge of law and legal procedure and who was also a talented negotiator. In March 1418 he took part as a representative of the Queen in the meetings that were held in the monastery of La Tombe with the plenipotentiaries of Charles VI. On that occasion Pierre Cauchon who was indirectly, yet wholeheartedly, a supporter of the Duke of Burgundy, in whose hands Isabeau had become a docile tool, came into close contact with many important personalities of the Armagnac faction, such as the Archbishop of Reims, Régnault de Chartres, and Robert Le Maçon, the Dauphin's Chancellor. Later he took part with other members of the University in drafting the Treaty of Troyes of 1420. As a reward for his good offices Isabeau gave him the revenues of several abbeys and supported his candidature to the bishopric of Beauvais.

Since those days he had rallied to the English cause, though his zeal for them somewhat cooled because they had not yet kept their promise to give him the episcopal seat of Rouen. Moreover, Pierre Cauchon was well acquainted with the ardent publicity the preacher monks were making in favour of Jeanne, and saw it bearing fruit as much among the Normans as in the low clergy of his own diocese. The advice he gave the civic dignitaries of Reims was not exactly what one would expect from one completely devoted to the English cause.

Torn between their oath of allegiance to Henry VI and the fear of seeing their fine town taken by assault and then devastated by the Maid's soldiers, the burghers, who had left unanswered the Dauphin's letter of July 4, hurriedly sent Hodierne, their magistrate, to Guillaume de Châtillon, Governor of the town, who at that moment was staying in Château-Thierry, to ask him to send reinforcements in haste. But at the same time they claimed that local custom forbade them to receive in the town more than fifty lances.

The Governor at once sent a reply, letting them know that he would come to Reims with six hundred men-at-arms, and insisted on holding as hostages in a fortified castle six members of the town council as guarantee of the loyalty of the townsfolk. Next day he appeared outside the wall with his men but the council refused to let them in because it was only too well known that the poorer neighbourhoods were on the side of the Dauphin and the Maid. Guillaume de Châtillon was obliged to withdraw, but not before announcing that eight thousand English soldiers had disembarked in Boulogne and that the Duke of Burgundy was preparing to raise troops. The two threats left the town council unimpressed, firstly, because they did not believe him—though the English landing was a fact—secondly, because the town council had no other alternative in saving the city from Jeanne's troops than to surrender it to the Dauphin.

On Saturday morning, July 16, a delegation of citizens went to the castle of Sept-Saulx, four leagues from Reims, where the Dauphin was staying, and offered him the keys of the town. The night before, the Dauphin did not believe that the town would surrender. Jeanne comforted him with these words: "Doubt not. They will come to you. Go, march, gentle Sire! If you are willing to act forcefully you will soon be master of the whole kingdom!"

In the same manner as in Troyes the Dauphin signed a treaty, giving full pardon for past action, and confirming the privileges the English had granted the city of Reims. The garrison was free to leave. However its captain had already disappeared.

In the course of the day Régnault de Chartres, preceded by the Chapter of the cathedral, went in procession to take possession of his archiepiscopal seat. Then he summoned all the local authorities so as to make the necessary arrangements for the coronation which, in deference to tradition, could take place only on a Sunday. On the insistence of Jeanne, who wanted to march on Paris as soon as possible and, therefore, did not want to lose a whole week by inaction, the Dauphin decided to be anointed the following day.

In the evening the Dauphin and Jeanne, followed by the army, made their entry into the town and were acclaimed by the population. The preparations for the coronation took up the entire night. In the morning everything was ready.

In the circumstances, some of the traditional details of the ceremony were left out, but in its essentials the rite was respected. The vestments used at the anointing of the Kings of France were kept in the Abbey of Saint-Denis, where were kept also the crown and sword of Charlemagne, the rod of justice and the clasp of St Louis. Needlewomen spent the night sewing and embroidering the finest materials to be found in the town, and from memory copying the traditional vestments they made resplendent robes for the Dauphin. It was decided to use a royal crown which, luckily, belonged to the treasure-house of the cathedral. They had to do without the rest.

On Sunday, July 17, 1429, in the early morning the Sires de Rais, de Boussac, de Graville and de Saint-Sévère, accompanied by Louis de Culan, Admiral of France, went in accordance with solemn custom to the Abbey of Saint-Rémy to fetch the Holy Ampulla to be used at the anointing. The ceremony began at nine o'clock in the morning. Of the twelve peers of France nine were absent. The Duke of Burgundy, premier lay peer, did not even bother to answer the invitation, but sent a delegation led by David de Brimeu. The young Duc d'Alençon was in his seat, and so were the Seigneurs de Clermont, de Vendôme, and de Laval as well as the Duc de La Trémouille who represented the absent peers. Among the lords spiritual only three were present: the Archbishop of Reims and the Bishops of Châlons and Laon.

To deputise for the three absent lords spiritual the Bishops of Orléans and Séez and a canon of the cathedral were chosen. Finally the Sire d'Albret acted as constable, holding in front of the King the handsomest sword they could find.

The lay peers, who escorted the Holy Ampulla, entered the cathedral on horseback. All the officials and some local citizens who managed to find their way in unnoticed already were present. The Duc d'Anjou had arrived from Nancy in the morning to assist at the anointing of his brother-in-law. Thus Queen Yolande was not altogether absent from the ceremony which was the outcome of her efforts, carried out with great intelligence and tenacity.

Charles VII, as the Dauphin had now officially become, made his solemn entry and was received by the peers present and the representatives of those absent who led him as far as the chancel. He knelt down at the foot of the altar. Though the ceremony was strictly limited both in number and rank of those admitted Jeanne entered the aisle followed by her little page, Louis de Coutes, who carried her standard displaying the colours of the Templars, which caused many a murmur in the noble assembly. Jeanne silenced the dignitaries in a loud, assured voice, "It was present in all the difficulties: it deserves to be honoured now! " Then she placed herself beside Charles in front of the altar.

The ceremony began. The ritual was scrupulously observed. After the monition of the Archbishop, "You want a position which mortals envy; but you should not forget that it is full of danger, toil and weariness. You are not king for your own benefit but for that of all your subjects'," Charles took the solemn oath with his hand on the Gospel, "In the name of Christ I promise. . . ."

Then the Duc d'Alençon dubbed him a knight and fastened on his boots the golden spurs. Four peers, the Bishops of Orléans and Séez as lords spiritual, and the Seigneurs de Clermont and Vendôme as lords temporal put the crown on his head. The Archbishop of Reims anointed him on the shoulder, the forearm and the forehead. Finally, the throne on which Charles sat was lifted so that the King of France should be seen by all present.

A loud ovation followed and outside the crowd shouted,

"Noël! Noël!" The trumpets sounded with such force that the vault of the cathedral seemed to be rent in two.

When the noise subsided Jeanne knelt before the King and shaking with sobs she said, "Gentle Sire, here and now is fulfilled God's will that I raise the siege of Orléans and bring you to this cathedral of Reims to be anointed so that all should see that you are the true king to whom the Kingdom of France belongs."

It was nearly two in the afternoon, and the crowd overexcited by the long wait shouted loudly for the King. He came out of the cathedral with Jeanne at his side and followed by his suite. When they appeared they received an enormous ovation, and in the midst of the almost delirious rapture of the people the new monarch went to the banqueting hall, where the town council awaited him with a magnificent meal. At the end of the meal the King was given the traditional presents, consisting of expensive robes and provisions, and should also have received a sword known as Brandelys (brandelys derives from *brant*, a heavy sword yielded with both hands, used by warriors in mediaeval times, and *lys*, the royal flower in French heraldry) which, in deference to tradition, ought to have been presented by a girl dressed as a man in black and white. Undoubtedly it was omitted because Jeanne's presence and her standard, Beauceant, were symbolic enough.

In the evening Jeanne wrote to Philippe le Bon the following letter:

✠ Jhésus   ✠ Maria

"High and mighty Prince, Duke of Burgundy, Jeanne the Maid requests you in the name of the King of Heaven, her Lord and Sovereign Master, that you and the King of France make decent peace that should last a long time. Forgive each other completely from the bottom of your hearts as befits faithful Christians; and if you want to make war then go against the Saracens. Prince of Burgundy, I beg, beseech and request you as humbly as I can, not to make war again in the Holy Kingdom of France, and withdraw at once and quickly your men who are in the ancient fortresses of the said Holy Kingdom; and as for the gentle King of France, he is ready to make peace with you, except for his honour, it all depends on you. And I let you know in the name of the King of Heaven, My Lord and Sovereign Master, for your and your honour's sake and on your life, that you shall not win any battle against loyal Frenchmen, and all who will make war on the said Holy Kingdom of France will be fighting against King Jhésus, King of Heaven, and of the entire world, my Lord and Sovereign Master. And I pray you not to battle and not to make war against us, you, your men or subjects; and you may well believe that however many the men are whom you lead against us, they will gain nothing, and then will be a great pity for the big battle and the blood shed by those who come against us.

"Three weeks ago I wrote and sent you a letter by a herald to warn you to be present at the King's anointing today Sunday, the XVII day of the present month of July, taking place in the city of Reims, but to which I had no reply or news of the herald.

"To God I commend you. May He keep you if it pleases Him, and pray God for a decent peace."

After despatching the letter Jeanne went to the inn of the Ane Rayé, where Isabelle, her foster-mother, her husband Jacques d'Arc, and one of her godparents, Jean Morel, as well as Dur-and-Laxart, who had taken her to de Baudricourt in Vaucouleurs, were staying. In their company were several inhabitants of Domrémy and Greux who had not hesitated to undertake the journey to see her again and be present at the coronation. The meeting was deeply moving. The good folk marvelled as they cast their eyes on her who, in spite of having accomplished her fabulous mission, of which the whole of France was speaking, had remained as simple as she was when she left them only a few months before. The most touched was certainly Isabelle because she saw at a glance that the handsome armour and superb tunic notwithstanding, her adopted daughter remained as pure and pious as in Domrémy. After she made them many presents Jeanne withdrew and issued orders that they should be fed and lodged for a month at the town's expense, and that when they left they were to be provided with victuals and good horses.

Nine

The triumphal march on Reims and the coronation of Charles VII coming in the wake of Jeanne's striking victories on the Loire caused deep anxiety among the English. Already on the day following the raising of the siege of Orléans the Duke of Bedford issued orders to the governors of the Norman ports, forbidding soldiers to embark for England. Now he had no doubts of Jeanne's intention to besiege Paris soon. Also, he was preoccupied not only with how to raise the morale of his soldiers who were beginning to desert in entire companies, but how to impress the Parisians, whose attitude did not inspire confidence.

At his request Philippe le Bon came to Paris on July 10. Bedford entertained him lavishly. A sermon with a strong political bias was preached in Notre-Dame by a priest who was a rabid foe of the Armagnacs. After a solemn assembly of the Parliament of Paris in the presence of the Doctors of the University, Bedford caused to be read out in public the treaty of alliance signed ten years before between the Duke of Burgundy and Philip of Lancaster. Then an orator reminded the audience of the circumstances of the murder of Montereau, and the Duke of Burgundy in his reply adjured the Parisians never to have dealings with his father's murderers. Bedford took advantage of the impression the Duke of Burgundy's declaration made on the audience, by making it renew its oath of allegiance to Henry VI.

In spite of all the official demonstrations of Anglo-Burgundian friendship, Bedford reaped no practical advantages from the Duke of Burgundy's visit except the purely symbolic one of a few companies of soldiers from Picardy for whom in any case he had to pay 20,000 livres to the Duke of Burgundy. Moreover, he had to give him back the city of Meaux.

On July 16 Philippe le Bon left Paris, and from Laon, where he stopped before continuing to Dijon, he sent an embassy to

Charles VII, for his policy of the balance of power between France and England was his only means of retaining his independence.

In Reims de La Trémouille and Régnault de Chartres, acting on the Duke of Burgundy's advice, tried hard to postpone the advance on Paris. It took Jeanne three days to obtain the King's agreement to her plan. On July 21, followed by his entire army, the King set out for Soissons. On the way, in obedience to tradition, at the Priory of Saint-Marcou he touched those suffering from scrofula. Everywhere during his progress he received deputations presenting him with the keys of Laon, Château-Thierry, Provins, Coulommiers and towns of lesser importance. On the 23rd he entered Soissons, where de La Trémouille persuaded him to visit all the towns that had opened their city gates to him. So leaving the road to Paris, the King, much to Jeanne's resentment, took himself to Château-Thierry (July 29), then to Montmirail (August 1), and finally to Provins (August 2), thus wasting precious time with receptions and festivities.

Bedford did not fail to take advantage of the breathing-space the King gave him. While he sent emissaries to the Duke of Burgundy, offering him the lieutenancy-general of all regions of France occupied by the English except Normandy, he urged his uncle the Cardinal Bishop of Winchester, who held the reins in London, to send him reinforcements as quickly as possible. The old cardinal, who at long last began to appreciate the blunder of not crowning young Henry VI as king of France, decided to send six thousand men to the Continent. That army did not cost him anything since it was destined to become the core of a crusade directed against the Hussites in Bohemia, and the Pope gave the money for it. Crossing Normandy at great speed those six thousand men reached Paris and considerably strengthened the garrison. The Cardinal Bishop of Winchester arrived on July 25. Without losing an instant the Duke of Bedford took the field with a large army against Charles VII.

On August 5 the King of France was in Laon, where he intended to cross the Seine and fall back on the Loire. Notwithstanding Jeanne's remonstrances—she did not cease urging him to march on Paris—the King, listening to the advice of the Royal Council, signed a fortnight's armistice with the Duke of

Burgundy. In the end de La Trémouille and Régnault de Chartres had won the day, and things were made even easier for them by Philippe le Bon who promised to withdraw from the English camp when the truce expired.

Happy at the thought of conquering his capital without resorting to arms the King was only too eager to accept the Duke of Burgundy's suggestions and was practically willing to entrust him with the government of his kingdom. He did not realise that the astute tactician only wanted to provoke a decisive battle between the English and the French armies, after which all he would have to do was to crush the weakened victor with the help of his intact army.

The retreat to the Loire caused great apprehension in all the towns that had gone over to the King, and from everywhere letters were sent him, begging him not to abandon them.

To persuade the King to go back on his unfortunate decision Jeanne wrote to the inhabitants of Reims.

✠ Jhésus   ✠ Maria

"My dear and good friends, the good and faithful Frenchmen of the city of Reims, Jehanne the Maid gives you her news, and asks and requests you to have no misgivings about the good fight she is engaged in on behalf of the blood royal. And I promise and swear that I shall not abandon you as long as I live. And it is true that the King made a fortnight's truce with the Duke of Burgundy, at the end of which he has to surrender the city of Paris peacefully. Nonetheless do not be astonished if I do not enter there shortly; for truces made like that do not fill me with content, and I do not know whether to keep them. But if I keep them it will be only for the sake of the King's honour. Believe me too that they will not shame the blood royal because I will keep and maintain the King's army together to be ready at the end of the fortnight if no peace is made. For this, my dear and perfect friends, I ask you not to cause yourselves worry as long as I am alive, but request you to keep a good look-out and guard the King's good city. And let me know if anybody importunate harasses you, and I will free you from him as quickly as I can. And let me have your news. I commend you to God to keep you.

106

"Written on this Friday August the fifth near a dwelling in the field on the road to Paris."

In no sense did Jeanne's letter modify the King's decision. He ordered the army to continue falling back on the Loire, though at the same time he made it execute a series of manoeuvres which took it from Bray to Crépy-en-Valois, where it arrived on August 11 after having gone through Château-Thierry on the 8th and La Ferté-Milon on the 10th. In each place the population assembled as the royal procession passed, shouting, "Noël! Noël!" and acclaimed the King and Jeanne while the church bells rang loudly.

After staying the night of August 12 in Lagny-le-Duc the army arrived before Dammartin and camped in the open fields. In that locality the King of France received an insulting letter from the Duke of Bedford in which he reproached him for rising against young Henry VI, the lawful king of France and England; also for using witchcraft in order to win over the townsfolk and the villagers. After some disagreeable words about the Maid he ended his letter calling on Charles VII to make peace "but not to violate it as at Montereau," or to let his fate be decided by arms, himself fixing the day and place of the battle.

The King's sole answer was to entrench his army in Dammartin and send out scouts to find out where the English were. On August 13 La Hire ran into Bedford's troops near Thiers, but as they occupied Mitry in strength he wisely withdrew towards Senlis, which Bedford immediately reinforced with roughly six thousand men who had just come over from Dover. The following day was spent in skirmishes without appreciable results. The English retrenched themselves behind the River Nonette while the French pitched their camp at Montèspilloy.

On August 15 the French army, deployed in four divisions, tried to make contact with the English, but could not give battle, as in the course of the night Bedford's soldiers built a trenched camp with waggons and timber, and stakes with sharp points round it, and refused to come out in spite of the loud and constant challenges of the French.

At dawn on August 16 the English raised camp and fell back on Senlis. The Duke of Bedford was, in truth, in a state of alarm caused by the negotiations between the French and the Burgundian. Moreover, he was haunted by the fear of a popular rising in Paris. On top of that he received news that the Constable de Richemont, who waged war in Normandy on his own account, had taken Evreux, whence he could advance either on Rouen or Paris. In those difficult circumstances Bedford did not want to take the risk of being beaten by the French in pitched battle. His only thought was to regroup his forces in order to fend off the worst danger: the loss of Normandy.

Jeanne wished to take advantage of the unexpected opportunity to repeat her victory of Patay, but the King, who in any case had a few days before sent to Arras Régnault de Chartres, Christophe d'Harcourt, Raoul de Gaucourt and Jacques de Chastillon to negotiate with the Duke of Burgundy's counsellors, opposed her plan, and ordered the army to withdraw on Crespy while he waited for the return of his emissaries.

At Arras, the King's delegates who were joined by Jean Tudert, Dean of Paris, were on the verge of success when envoys arrived from Bedford and were received by the Duke of Burgundy whom they reminded of his oath. Faithful to his usual tactics Philippe le Bon, who in truth was the arbiter of the situation, gave the English envoys all the pledges they could wish for, while he sent a mission to Charles VII, consisting of Jean de Luxembourg, David de Brimeu and Hughes de Cayeux, Bishop of Arras, asking him to extend the truce.

Meanwhile the burghers of Compiègne sent their city keys to the King, and Senlis, abandoned by its English garrison, swiftly imitated their example. Pierre Cauchon, Bishop of Beauvais, appreciating that the majority of the people stood by the King of France, moved discreetly into the background lest trouble befell him.

To Jeanne's great anger the King accepted the idea of new negotiations with the Duke of Burgundy. In Compiègne, where the King had installed himself on August 18, he was waiting in an irritated state of mind for the outcome of the negotiations.

On August 23 Jeanne said to the Duc d'Alençon, "My handsome duke, get your people and those of the other captains moving. Upon my staff I want to have a closer view of Paris!"

What the King really wanted was to have his hand forced, for he realised that once again the Duke of Burgundy had tricked him. And it did not displease him to show the Duke's envoys that he was perfectly capable of taking his capital without their master's help. The same day Jeanne, the Duc d'Alençon and part of the army began their march on Paris.

The Burgundian envoys quickly sent a messenger to Arras with the news, and asked for instructions. Frightened by the French move and fearing that Paris could be taken by assault in the absence of Bedford, who had left the capital to organise the defence of Rouen against the advance of the Constable, the Duke of Burgundy instructed his envoys to sign a treaty with the King. The King wanted the envoys to dance to his tune, but then he heard on the 28th that Bedford had retaken Evreux the night before and was preparing to go back into Paris. So he felt constrained to accept the prolongation of the truce till Christmas, and, furthermore, he had to promise not to undertake any military operations north of the Seine and to acknowledge the Duke of Burgundy as the protector of Picardy. Then he left Compiègne and accompanied by the main army he took up temporary residence in Senlis, waiting to see how things turned out. During that time Jeanne and the Duc d'Alençon occupied Saint-Denis.

In Paris, after a moment of panic, the authorities once again had the situation well in hand. Louis de Luxembourg, Chancellor of France in the name of Henry VI, Jean Rattley, an intimate of the Duke of Bedford, Villiers de l'Isle-Adam, Military Governor, and Simon Morhier, Provost of Paris, took the necessary decisions for the town to withstand a siege pending the arrival of English reinforcements. They had under their orders two thousand men whom Bedford left with them, a strong Burgundian garrison to which were attached a large number of mercenaries paid by the Duke of Burgundy and who came into the city in vast numbers. The breaches in the walls were repaired, the outside moat cleaned and deepened, cannons were raised on to the roofs of houses near the enceinte, and in all the streets barricades were raised. As an answer to the clandestine propaganda of the preaching brothers and the partisans of the Armagnacs they spread the rumour that the King's soldiers were resolved to sack the town and exterminate the entire population.

Every day that passed was to the advantage of the defenders who continually strengthened the fortifications. Jeanne was well aware that precious time was being wasted, and urged that the attack should take place as soon as possible. On her insistence the Duc d'Alençon went to Senlis on September 1 to ask the King to move the main body of the army to the walls of Paris. As the King would not budge he repeated his request on September 5, but only on the 7th did the King decide to leave for Saint-Denis with his troops. Those days of waiting were not lost in so far as a wooden bridge was thrown across the Seine to facilitate the advance.

On September 8 the military operations began. It was high time too, because inside the town the King's partisans were becoming impatient and could not understand the reason for the delay. In the morning the main body left the village of La Chapelle, where it spent the night, and under the command of the Duc d'Alençon took up its position near the Porte Saint-Denis, while Jeanne, followed by about a thousand troops, sought contact with the garrison on the side of the Porte Saint-Honoré..

After having drawn up her men on a vast earth platform known as the Marché aux Pourceaux, Jeanne lined up her cannons and ordered fire to be opened on the fortifications. The cannonade lasted over two hours and caused serious damage to the ramparts. Towards one in the afternoon the Seigneur de Saint-Vallier dashed forward and took possession of the Boulevard Saint-Honoré outside the walls, pushing the Anglo-Burgundians back behind the ramparts. Jeanne thought that it was time for her to intervene and brandishing her standard she led the men to the assault. To cross the first ditch she had wattle and faggots brought, and working courageously they soon surmounted the first obstacle. It was not the same when they reached the second which was a large canal full of water as the Provost of Paris had ordered the sluice gates that kept back the water of the Seine to be opened.

The defenders of Paris did not remain inactive. From the top of the walls the garrison sent a rain of arrows on the assailants, also tried to crush them with a hail of stones.

Jeanne exhorted her men and summoned the defenders to lay down arms.

"Give back the town to the King of France," she cried, "or you will all be put to death without mercy!"

The Anglo-Burgundians answered by calling her "the whore of the Armagnacs."

Towards two o'clock in the afternoon the assailants found a spot where the water of the canal rose only shoulder high and started to fill it up, which caused great alarm among the defenders. And the partisans of the King who watched it all from their rooftops, rushed into the streets, shouting that the defences were crumbling. Straightaway panic took hold of the inhabitants and the ordinary clergy did not miss the chance to add to the confusion by ringing all the church bells. The battle seemed to be won.

Impervious to the arrows and cannon balls whose target she was, Jeanne measured the depth of the water with the staff of her standard, searching for new likely spots for her men to cross over. As she was thus engaged an arrow from a crossbow hit her right thigh. It was a serious wound. She had herself carried by La Hire to an elevation distant enough from enemy fire and ordered the onslaught to continue.

But her absence immediately dampened French morale. The attack lost strength, and the garrison, fired by the energy of despair, sent another rain of arrows and stones down on the attackers who, when night approached, tired and discouraged, obeyed de La Trémouille who urged them to withdraw.

In the morning of September 9 Jeanne, having spent the night in the camp of René of Anjou, went out of her way in trying to convince her host and all who were with him of the necessity of renewing the battle. Then something quite unexpected came to her aid.

About a hundred Armagnacs, led by the Baron de Montmorency, came out of Paris without encountering any obstacles and appeared before her, bringing her their assurance that a new attack would certainly be crowned with success because the defences of the town were much weaker than the royal army believed, the garrison was demoralised and the King's followers would rise like one man once the ramparts were taken.

"Upon my staff," cried Jeanne, "I will not leave here before taking the town!"

Ignoring her painful wound she mounted her horse and gave the signal for departure. However, as the troops got ready for the decisive assault the Comte de Clermont brought them an order straight from the King to withdraw to Saint-Denis; for the Duke of Burgundy, who had no illusions of Paris resisting the royal army, had asked the King to stop hostilities and promised that the town would surrender on its own. On the advice of his Council once again the King of France put his trust in the Duke of Burgundy's word. With fury in their hearts the Duc d'Alençon and Jeanne obeyed the royal command: the army fell back on Saint-Denis.

Jeanne had every intention of persuading the King to annul the fatal order, and if she failed, to assault Paris with the whole army without his consent, but in the night of September 9–10 de La Trémouille, acting on the Duke of Burgundy's instructions, had the wooden bridge across the Seine destroyed. That put an irrevocable end to the operation.

The King thought only of his enthronment in the Abbey of Saint-Denis. That ceremony, which was traditionally the complement of the coronation, took place with great pomp. When it was over, accompanied by a few friends who included Pierre d'Arc, Jeanne went silently to the basilica, and laid on the altar her sword, lance, armour and standard. According to the customs of her time that meant that she renounced further pursuit of the campaign.

On September 13 the King left Saint-Denis. On the 21st the army reached Gien, where it dispersed. The noblemen returned to their estates, and because of lack of money the King dismissed his mercenaries. Jeanne, though she would have preferred to share the dangers the small garrison left behind at Saint-Denis was bound to encounter, eventually joined the Court.

For her task was still incomplete. She had succeeded in raising the siege of Orléans, also in taking the Dauphin to Reims to be anointed King of France, but to fulfil her mission she had firstly to obtain the liberty of Charles d'Orléans, head of the House of Orléans, whom was still prisoner in England, and secondly and above all to lead a crusade into the Holy Land to recapture the Tomb of Christ from the Infidel.

Ten

When Philippe le Bon heard that the King had disbanded his army he hurried to Paris, where the authorities gave him a triumphal reception. Already on September 29 he had a long interview with the Duke of Bedford from whom he obtained not only the Champagne as a personal possession but also the lieutenancy-general of all the provinces occupied by the English. Compared to young Henry VI, whose star continued to decline since the defeats of his troops on the Loire, and to Charles VII, who had to raise the siege of Paris and was at the moment without an army, the Duke of Burgundy appeared to be the true king of France. Following his policy of duplicity, which brought him so many advantages, the Duke of Burgundy took no action against the few remaining troops of the King, but kept strictly secret his agreement with Bedford. It was only made public when Henry VI's Council ratified it on March 10, 1430.

At the beginning of October the Duc d'Alençon asked the King to give his permission for him, seconded by Jeanne, to take action in liaison with de Richemont to chase the English out of Normandy. De La Trémouille and Régnault de Chartres intervened to stop the King agreeing to the proposition. The first feared a victory by de Richemont who was an ally of Yolande of Anjou, and the second dreaded that Jeanne's presence was sufficient to lead d'Alençon's men to victory, in which case the Duke of Burgundy's entire policy would crumble, in fact he would be forced to hand over Paris. The King was weak enough to listen to them, and Jeanne had to resign herself to staying on at Court.

In high good spirits the Duke of Burgundy, who was kept informed in detail of all that took place in the King's Council, left Paris and went to Flanders to celebrate, with unheard of lavishness, his marriage with Philippa of Lancaster, daughter of the bastard John I who recently founded a new dynasty in Portugal.

Abandoned by the King, the Duc d'Alençon was forced to give up his plan to reconquer his duchy, and left de Richemont without help, who had to limit himself to keeping in check the English, who pillaged mercilessly all the districts they occupied. During that time the King, falling back into his natural indolence and still believing in the promises the Duke of Burgundy made him, spent his days travelling from one royal residence to the other, taking with him most of his counsellors. Jeanne remained almost constantly in his company and was officially heaped with honours and kind attentions. Her half-brother, the King, presented her with beautiful dresses and expensive furs and himself paid for the upkeep of her household which he wanted to be worthy of her royal origin and of the essentially important part she had played in recent events.

Her rank at Court and the affection the King held her in did not stop his councillors from pursuing a secret campaign of calumnies and disparagement against her. De La Trémouille did his best to minimise her military rôle, assuring his listeners that due to her impestuous initiatives fifteen hundred casualties had occurred. Régnault de Chartres let it be known in an unctuous episcopal voice that if the King's troops failed before Paris it was because the Maid, who made a display of profound piety and pretended to be inspired by God, did not hesitate to attack the capital on September 8, which was the feast of the Nativity of the Virgin Mary.

It must be said that those insinuations found little credit with those who heard them since they knew that the raising of the siege of Paris did not devolve on Jeanne but firstly on the men who worked against her incessantly; and secondly and definitively on the King himself who gave the order to retreat to the Loire.

Far more serious for her was the charge that she considered it her duty to perpetuate the revolutionary programme of the Templars whose banner she used in public as her own. With the exception of the noblemen who were on the side of Yolande of Anjou, all the great lords had a deep hatred for her which they hardly concealed even for convention's sake. Thus a great void was created round her.

Showing indifference to all those attacks in which jealousy and hatred vied with stupidity and treason, in her soul Jeanne was hurt, nonetheless, by being kept at arm's length from the decisions of the Royal Council.

Gone from her presence were her "handsome duke" who had returned to his wife in his castle of Beaumont; Gilles de Rais, whom de La Trémouille managed to detach from her by sending him on a tour of inspection to Western France; and her page, Louis de Coutes, who left her on the day after the coronation. On the other hand, she had the satisfaction of staying in Bourges with Régnier de Bouligny, financial councillor of the King, whose wife was a close friend of Queen Marie. As a token of the esteem the Queen had for her half-sister-in-law she decided to call Jeanne the daughter she was soon expecting to give birth to.

Jeanne remained simple in the world of luxury that surrounded her; pious too, hearing Mass every morning. She preferred to the courtiers the ordinary clergy and the decent, ordinary people who never ceased to flock to her home, asking to see and speak to her. When the manifestations of respectful sympathy of which she was the object risked degenerating into a sort of feverish adulation she went out of her way to stop the excesses of admiration she caused by forbidding her feet to be kissed or the hem of her skirt touched, and exhorted them to give all that fervour to the cult of the holy saints of France. To the women who brought medals, rosaries and other objects of piety for her to touch, she said laughingly, "Touch them yourselves. It will do just as much good."

At the beginning of November she heard that a small army under the command of the Sire d'Albret had assembled with the aim of taking back some of the places the English still held in the region. Immediately she asked for the King's permission to take part in the expedition. Gilles de Rais made the same request. The King began with saying no, but eventually gave in. For once de La Trémouille made no opposition since the command of the troops was vested in his brother-in-law, and as the hostilities were strictly limited to local action they could not interfere with the Duke of Burgundy's plans. Taking it all in all, he preferred to see Jeanne exposed to the dangers of the battlefield than having her at Court, where her influence over the King was still strong.

About October 25 the small column that consisted of only a few companies of mercenaries besieged Saint-Pierre-le-Moustier. Fortunately, Jeanne brought along all the artillery she could muster which balanced the inferior number of the assailants to that of the defenders. After two days of uninterrupted bombardment part of the ramparts of the fort crumbled, and Jeanne ordered the assault, which was repulsed. Practically alone before the wall, not in the slightest discouraged by the lack of success, and totally impervious to the dangers that surrounded her she refused to listen to d'Aulon who asked her to move back.

"I am not alone," she said. "I still have fifty thousand men, and I shall not leave before the town is taken! "

Her courage brought back all who had decamped. On her order they carried faggots to the ditches and filled them up. When that was done she ordered a second assault. That decided the issue. With an irresistible dash the soldiers broke open the gates of the citadel, and spreading out in the town they butchered everybody they caught and set fire to the houses. Only with an immense effort and using all her authority did Jeanne succeed in saving the church from being burnt down; and the lives of women and children who sought refuge there.

After this resounding success the Royal Council decided on besieging another town, Charité-sur-Loire, much stronger than the previous one. Jeanne did not share the Council's opinion: she would have preferred to push towards the Ile-de-France and Picardy, but de La Trémouille and Régnault de Chartres obtained the King's consent to their plan: first the banks of the Loire were to be cleaned up.

At that time first at Jargeau, then at Montfaucon-en-Berry, Jeanne met an adventuress, Catherine de la Rochelle, who pretended to be inspired by God, and whom several members of the Royal Council—those who pulled the strings for the Duke of Burgundy—thought they could use in opposition to Jeanne. To that woman, who was in the hands of Régnault de Chartres, it seemed essential to make immediate peace with the Duke of Burgundy. Brother Richard, who ever since Troyes followed the Court wherever it went, sang her praises. That Franciscan, as a matter of fact, was very upset that in spite of all his hopes Jeanne had not taken him as her confessor. First Jeanne took Catherine for a poor, unbalanced woman, and with deep irony advised her to look after her hearth and her children. But soon she realised that her adversaries in the Royal Council were truly trying to set the woman up as her rival. Catherine was wont to declare that every night she received the visit of a "white lady wearing golden garments" requesting her to find the King and tell him to send heralds to every town, commanding all those who hid silver or gold to hand them over to him, thus enabling him to pay the troops he needed.

In order to show the Royal Council the foolishness of such a proposition Jeanne felt compelled to put her to the test, especially as, pushed by those who made use of her, the adventuress declared that the fort of La Charité should not be attacked. As she maintained that every night she received the visit of the famous white lady Jeanne invited her to spend the night in her room. Catherine could not refuse. Though neither of them closed her eyes till the morning the white lady did not appear. There was no other way out for the adventuress than to disappear, and those who imagined that they could thwart Jeanne's plans with that poor tool were compelled to think again.

Jeanne decided at once to lay siege to Charité-sur-Loire, the town of which Catherine de La Rochelle said that the rigour of its climate made it impossible for her to be present. The destroying of the Anglo-Burgundian forts was in Jeanne's eyes the surest means of coming to terms with the Duke of Burgundy, with whom, so she said, "one will not be able to make peace except at the swords' point."

On November 24, accompanied by the Sire d'Albret and the Marshal de Boussac Jeanne set out for La Charité. Since it could not stop the expedition from leaving, the Royal Council made certain that it should become a complete failure. Not only were Jeanne's arms ridiculously insufficient for the task she set out to accomplish but the Council saw to her leaving without any siege material. Jeanne tried to solve her difficulties by writing to several towns in the region, asking them for money and reinforcements. To the inhabitants of Riom she wrote the following letter:

"Dear and good friends, you are aware of how the town of Saint-Pierre le Moutiers was taken by assault. And with God's help I have the intention of cleansing the other places of the King's enemies. But for that great expense in gunpowder, missiles and other war material which it cost us to take that town, and which the lords who are in that town and also myself now lack, to be able to lay siege to La Charité, where we are going presently, I beg you, if you care for the welfare and honour of the King, to send forthwith to help the said siege, powder, saltpetre, sulphur, missiles, crossbows, sword-blades and other materials of war. And do not take long about it; so that none shall say you were negligent or refused. Dear and good friends, the Lord keep you all.

"Written in Moulins on the 9th day of November."

Only the town of Orléans made a serious effort in sending mortars and cannons with the personnel they needed. The other towns either did not reply or made insignificant contributions. Probably de La Trémouille gave them secret instructions not to give Jeanne any appreciable aid.

In spite of the shortage of men and arms Jeanne persisted in laying siege to the fortified town, counting on her artillery balancing the inferior number of the troops. For over three weeks she tried in vain to reduce the town. It was a particularly rigorous winter, and the lack of food, and soon of ammunition also, forced her to raise the siege. On top of it all her artillery fell into enemy hands. With hatred in her heart she was forced to return with the remnant of her army to Mehun-sur-Yèvre. That defeat became even more smarting when on January 11, 1430, the commandant of the town, Perrin Grasset, bought in secret by de La Trémouille for 1300 gold ecus, surrendered to the King the city he was in charge of. Thus the rascally councillors of the King could sustain the claim that they had obtained, at least in recent days, greater success with their diplomatic negotiations than Jeanne with her military actions.

The King was cognisant of the true reasons of Jeanne's defeats of late, and, therefore, showed her no sign of disfavour. He had many long conversations with her, thanked her warmly and sincerely for the magnificent work she had done and assured her of his lasting gratitude. However, he thought the moment was propitious to tell her that he had no desire to change the line of action he had chosen for himself, which consisted of waiting for the Duke of Burgundy to bring back Paris to him. He also let her know that he disapproved of the position she took when she assumed with the Templars' banner, a programme of reforms which frightened the whole aristocracy as well as the lords temporal and spiritual of the kingdom. In brief, he considered that Jeanne's mission was over.

There remained Jeanne's private position to be settled. It was not an easy problem. There could be no question of Jeanne being officially recognised as the King's illegitimate sister. In those days bastards were not yet rejected systematically by the family as happened later. However, only those were openly accepted in society who were the fruit of a husband's sin against conjugal fidelity, whereas children born from a married woman were, except in rare cases, taken as the offspring of the man "*quem nuptiae demonstrant.*" The fundamental principle that a married woman could give birth only to legitimate children was so deeply embedded in people's minds that even when at Troyes in 1420 Isabeau of Bavaria treated her son in public as "the so-called Dauphin" the population south of the Loire saw in that humiliating declaration which shocked them to the core no more than an ugly manoeuvre of the English, forcing the captured Queen to confess a fault she never committed.

The Comte de Dunois, son of Louis d'Orléans and Mariette d'Enghien, his mistress, bore the title of Bastard of Orléans to remind everybody of his princely origin. But, on the other hand, Jeanne, issue of the criminal love affair of the same Duc d'Orléans and his sister-in-law, Isabeau of Bavaria, could officially never be treated as the bastard daughter of the Queen of France. Unofficially, things were vastly different. Several members of the Court were acquainted with her royal origin. First the King to whom at Chinon Jeanne entrusted the secret of her birth, which filled him with joy; then Queen Marie and the whole House of Anjou; the bastard Dunois and the Duc d'Alençon, who were all her relations or allies under different titles, as well as de La Trémouille and Régnault de Chartres, who in spite of their enmity in matters of policy, retained some fundamental respect for her, and among others Gérard Machet, confessor to the King and Raphaël, almoner to the Queen of Sicily, and the Belliers and the Bouchers, laymen and faithful partisans of the Houses of Anjou and Lorraine.

Moreover, to those who understood heraldry the coat of arms the King gave Jeanne following the deliverance of Orléans was a highly significant proof of her royal descent. It reminded them neither of the arms of the heroic town she liberated nor of the religious signs painted on her banner at the time. It was the true coat of arms of the House of France, with one of the fleurs-de-lys omitted and cunningly replaced not by the bar sinister, the usual symbol of the bastard, but by a sword surmounted by the royal crown.

Her royal brother having decided that her mission was at an end, Jeanne, as much for the sake of their relationship and mutual affection as for the great services she rendered him, had to content herself with the important position he gave her at Court. To play the part that was designed for her it was necessary to define her position officially, especially as suitors were not lacking, the more ardent among them the brilliant knight, scion of the high Breton nobility, Marshal of France Gilles de Rais. That was the reason why Charles decided on giving letters patent of noble rank to establish her precedence at Court.

The d'Arc family belonged to the small though true nobility, and as Jeanne's position was well out of the ordinary it was not easy to find the correct text for those documents. The clerk who wrote them out found no other way out of his embarrassment than the use of obscure sentences and sybillic twists which, nevertheless, were clearly understood by everyone who knew the secret of Jeanne's origin.

Even in the first sentence after "Charles, by the grace of God King of France, in perpetual memory of an event . . ." a blank was left with the idea of it being filled in according to the evolution of the situation, since the truth could not immediately be revealed. It stipulated that Jeanne and her foster-parents were raised to the nobility in consideration of "laudable services rendered Us and Our Kingdom," adding the words only the initiated could comprehend: "and also for certain other reasons that induce us to do so . . ." Further in the text was indicated that the newly ennobled should participate "in the privileges of the other members of the nobility," but added this curious sentence: "notwithstanding, as it is said, that they are not of noble extraction and are perhaps not even free men," a thought more significant if one considers that even if Molière, who drew up the document, and the witnesses who signed it—the Bishop of Séez and de La Trémouille in person—did not know Jacques d'Arc's social position in Domrémy, they could not avoid knowing that some members of that family belonged to the clergy, while others had for a long time filled important positions with the d'Orléans family and in Isabeau of Bavaria's household.

However, Jeanne did not resign herself to play the part of a simple supernumary at the Court of Charles VII because that was his will. At Mehun-sur-Yèvres, laden with honours and presents, dressed in magnificent robes, while one feast in her honour followed another without end, she sadly thought of her mission, two conditions of which she had not yet fulfilled: to obtain the freedom of Charles d'Orléans, the head of her family, who was prisoner in England, and to lead the crusade to the Holy Land to liberate the Tomb of Christ. Chafing, she waited for her hour.

The winter was passed in complete inaction. On February 15 the King, followed by his household, went to Sully-sur-Loire at the invitation of de La Trémouille, and in spite of her repugnance Jeanne was compelled to rejoin the King there three weeks later.

In the middle of March the people of Reims wrote to Jeanne, asking her for her help against the English who announced their intention of attacking the town if it did not surrender to them, since it was their will to anoint Henry VI as king of France in Reims. On March 16, 1430 Jeanne replied to them,

"Very dear and much beloved, and wishing to see Jehanne the Maid, I received your letters, making mention of the siege you fear. Please know that it will not take place if I meet them. And if it happens that I meet them not when they go against you, lock your city gates for I will soon hasten to you. And if I find them there I will make them put on their spurs so quickly that they will not know where to find them, and their ruin will quickly follow. I ask you only to remain good and loyal. I pray God to keep you safe."

A few days after this letter was despatched bad news reached the Royal Council. The Duke of Burgundy had obtained the counties of Champagne and Brie from the English (which in any case the King had ceded him) as well as the sum of 1,200 *livres* on the condition that he made peace with them. And showing his true colours Philippe le Bon was preparing to attack the French forts in Picardy. Furthermore, his agents were stirring up strife in all the towns which had recently surrendered to the King; and all this at the very moment when a rising was expected in Paris at the instigation of the begging brothers working for the Armagnacs. In addition to that Henry VI and a strong English contingent had disembarked at Calais.

Caught napping the Royal Council did not know which way to turn. On the advice of Queen Yolande the first move was to nominate Arnaud de Barbazon, a valiant soldier, as governor and lieutenant-general of the Champagne, with the order to cooperate with René of Anjou. Then negotiations were entered into with the Duke of Brittany who was asked to supply men-at-arms, and in order to take the Duke of Burgundy in the rear the Royal Council endeavoured to conclude an alliance with the Emperor Sigismund and the Duke Frédéric of Austria.

On March 28 Jeanne sent a letter to the people of Reims to recomfort them:

"Very dear and good friends, please you to know that I received your letters wherein you mention how it was reported to the King that in the good town of Reims there were many bad people. Also please know that what was reported was very true. Verily there were many who were in alliance with the Burgundians and wanted to betray the town, bringing them inside. And since then the King learnt the contrary because you assured him, sending him proof of it. Therefore, he is very pleased with you. And, believe, you are in his grace and if you have need of him he will help you if there is a siege. And you know well that you will have a lot to suffer by the wickedness of the Burgundian traitors. But also you will be delivered shortly by the pleasure of God, which will happen as soon as it can. Also, I ask and request you, very dear friends, to guard the good town for the King and keep a good lookout. You shall soon have more ample news from me. One more news I give you at the present moment, namely that the whole of Brittany is French and the Duke has to send the King 3,000 combatants paid two months in advance. I commend you to God. May He look after you."

The measures the Royal Council took could have no immediate effect; the agreement with the Emperor and the Duke of Austria could be of advantage only at a later date; and the Bretons had not yet put in an appearance. To calm the fearful, whose number was rising and who were to be found everywhere, it was decided to send Xaintrailles with four hundred men to reinforce the garrison of Compiègne where was expected the Burgundian advance guard commanded by Jean de Luxembourg.

Eleven

The Royal Council's decision to take up arms again raised the morale of the supporters of the Armagnacs who were but waiting for this occasion to recommence guerilla warfare against the English. At Melun and Saint-Denis the resistance had already begun. In Paris the partisans of the French cause were plotting to raise the population on Palm Sunday, April 9.

Jeanne was acquainted with all that was happening. Trembling with impatience as she thought of her mission being resumed, she went to see the King, asking him to give her the command of an army. Not only did the King refuse to agree but went as far as to forbid her to leave the Court. His decision was the result of the constant underhand dealings of de La Trémouille and Régnault de Chartres, the first insinuating that the military leaders refused to serve under her, the second overwhelmed by the reproaches the Duke of Burgundy heaped on him, and fearing that new victories by Jeanne would turn the Duke definitely against him.

At first aghast at the unexpected refusal Jeanne nevertheless returned to the charge and obtained from the King, as changeable as ever and also in his heart regretting the pain he was causing her, his permission to join the army on her own without command or his approval. She had to accept that half-measure.

In the morning of March 29, without taking leave of the Court, she mounted her horse and left Sully, followed by Jean d'Aulon, Brother Pasquerel, Pierre d'Arc and a small escort consisting of some servants. In a few short stages the small group reached Lagny-sur-Marne, where she received the precious reinforcement of a hundred archers and crossbow men of the local militia. The town's garrison, which had gone over to the King at the time of his coronation, had in any case to fight hard against the Burgundian bands which ravaged the countryside, the most dangerous of them being under the command of a hardened old soldier, Franquet d'Arras, renowned for his ferocity.

Hardly had Jeanne arrived at Lagny than she attempted to rid the district of all the looters who infested it. Her intention was warmly approved of by Jean Foucault, commandant of the town, and soon after by the Lombard captain Baretta and the Scotsman Hugh Kennedy, not to mention the many mercenaries who came to fight under her banner. The two adversaries, each about five hundred men strong, met in the open country. The battle was long and bloody. Twice the French tried to push back the Burgundians who were entrenched on high ground; thrown back with heavy casualties the French were on the verge of withdrawing when Jeanne ordered a third attack which was successful. The Duke of Burgundy's men either perished or were taken prisoner, Franquet himself among the latter.

Jeanne hoped to exchange the old soldier against the proprietor of the Hôtel de L'Ours in Paris who was imprisoned for having conspired against the English, but when she heard that that supporter of the Armagnacs had been put to death as well as other Parisians detained for the same reason, she handed Franquet over to the local magistrate who, after trying him for the crimes he was guilty of, ordered his execution.

While she was in Lagny they brought to Jeanne a three days' old baby which could not be baptised because it gave no sign of life. Jeanne had the child taken to the church, and asked the young girls of the town to accompany her to pray before the statue of the Blessed Virgin. Then taking the babe in her arms she held it over the baptismal fount. All of a sudden the pale babe's cheeks turned rosy, it struggled to get out of its swaddling clothes and yawned three times. In great haste it was baptised. The good people called that a miracle, and coming so quickly on top of the pitiless execution of Franquet it spread all over the countryside and Jeanne's reputation rose again by leaps and bounds. A few days later she had an army of over four thousand men under her command.

On April 22 Jeanne went to Melun, which place the Burgundian garrison swiftly evacuated. In the afternoon while she was praying beside the moat of the town she heard her Voices which had not spoken to her since the siege of Paris was raised. SS Catherine and Marguerite told her in a clear voice that she would be captured "before the feast of St John"—that is to say before June 24—"and so it must be." That awful revelation was tempered by the advice that "she should accept it" and she was assured that "God would help her." Not to discourage those around her Jeanne refrained from revealing what her Voices had told her.

On April 23 Jeanne went to Senlis, where she met Régnault de Chartres. The Chancellor had heard that she was on her way to Compiègne. Now the possession of that town on the Oise controlling the north road leading to Paris was of capital importance to the outcome of the hostilities which had just started. Therefore, Régnault de Chartres did all he could to let it fall into Burgundian hands. To make sure that no new success by Jeanne interfered with his agreement with the Duke of Burgundy he found no other solution than to go there in person to see his plan carried out unhindered.

A few days later Jeanne left Senlis so as to escape the Chancellor's vigilance, and went to stay in the castle of Borenglise. Close to it, being no more than four leagues' away from Compiègne, was a chapel dedicated to St Marguerite, and convinced that she would, as her Voices told her, be taken prisoner before the feast of St John, Jeanne had decided to go into retreat for a week there before starting on new military operations.

In the evening of May 3 Jeanne entered Compiègne, accompanied by her usual escort, and was the guest there of Marie Le Boucher, the wife of the King's Attorney. On the following morning the Maid, whose arrival the Chancellor could not pretend to ignore, assisted at the council of war held in the house of Guillaume de Flavy, commandant of the town, at which were also present the Comte de Vendôme, commander-in-chief of the royal army, Régnault de Chartres, Xaintrailles and several captains. The news was bad. The Duke of Burgundy's troops had taken the offensive, seized Gournay-sur-Aronde, and were besieging Choisy-sur-Aisne, which was of strategic value as it controlled the road to Compiègne. The council of war decided to go to the help of the besieged. A *coup de main* was tried in the direction of Pont-l'Evêque to force the passage across the Oise, but after violent fighting the French were forced to withdraw. The Comte de Vendôme then decided to make a new attempt at some other point, and made his way to Soissons. Régnault de Chartres insisted on taking part in the expedition, for Guichard Bournel, Governor of that town, was his secret ally.

Following the instruction he received from Régnault de Chartres, the Governor let the Comte de Vendôme know that tradition forbade the entry of armed men into the town, adding that the burghers, even if admitting that times were not normal, had not the slightest intention of agreeing to the upkeep of an extra garrison While Régnault de Chartres's heart glowed with pleasure the King's troops were compelled to withdraw. Next day Guichard Bournel opened the city gates to Jean de Luxembourg, the Duke of Burgundy's captain. For his treason the disloyal governor was paid the sum of 4000 *saluts d'or*. Almost at the same moment the fortress of Choisy capitulated, whose governor, the very brother of Guillaume de Flavy, was bought for 3000 *saluts* by the emissaries of the Duke of Burgundy. Régnault de Chartres was winning all along the line.

The capitulation of Soissons and the occupation by the Burgundians of the fortresses of Gournay and Choisy crowned the expedition with final failure. The King, as short of money as ever before, ordered the troops to be disbanded. The Comte de Vendôme fell back on the Loire; Régnault de Chartres took himself to Senlis, where he could continue putting into effect his plan, the first part of which had already gone according to his instructions.

Jeanne withdrew to Crépy-en-Valois, followed only by Xaintrailles, de Baretta and about four hundred mercenaries.

Meanwhile the Burgundians were closing in on Compiègne. The Duke drew up the main body of his army near Condun-sur-Aronde, and sent the advance guard under Jean de Luxembourg to occupy Clairoix, while Noyelle, another of his lieutenants, took possession of Margny. The English under Montgomery held Venette in strength; in brief the Duke was master of the whole of the right bank of the Oise.

In the evening of May 22 messengers of Guillaume de Flavy came to Jeanne, bringing the news that Compiègne was being invested from every side.

"Upon my staff," she exclaimed, "I am going to see my good friends of Compiègne! "

In vain they tried to make her see reason by pointing out that she had but a handful of men to put against ten thousand Anglo-Burgundian soldiers. She dismissed all the objections of her friends, and though the night was well advanced she gave the troops the order to get ready to leave. At dawn Jeanne entered Compiègne.

During the forenoon of May 23 the local authorities met in Guillaume de Flavy's house. The Governor put his plan to them namely to free Compiègne from the Burgundians by chasing them first out of Margny, then of Clairoix, and then, depending on the results of the two operations, to turn at once against Montgomery, or wait for reinforcements to attack the Duke of Burgundy himself in his general headquarters at Condun. It was a mediocre plan inasmuch as the objectives were but of secondary importance. Even if Margny and Clairoix were taken the victors could not have maintained themselves there for long since the Anglo-Burgundians possessed a crushing numerical superiority which Jeanne in this instance could not counter-balance—as she had done in the past—by putting powerful artil-lery into action. The most the plan could have achieved was a prestige success which Armagnac propaganda would not have failed to exploit.

Jeanne appreciated the dangers involved in such an action and hesitated to give her consent. Guillaume de Flavy insisted on his plan being adopted, adding that he would put a hundred men of the garrison at the expedition's disposal. He also promised to use his artillery and crossbowmen on the ramparts which defended the high road and, he even had thought of using covered boats to bring back the fighting men from the other bank if they had to fall back before the enemy. The burghers, who wanted to see the Burgundians go as soon as possible, gave their approval to the plan. Lest they doubt her courage Jeanne felt compelled to give her approval too.

In the afternoon while the soldiers were getting ready for the sortie she went to the church of Saint-Jacques, where she prayed for a long time before taking communion. On her way out she leaned against a pillar and said to the good people and the children who followed her in large numbers, "My good friends, a man has betrayed me. I am betrayed. Pray for me!"

Towards five o'clock Jeanne left the town with her entire contingent. Soon they reached Margny, where, surprised by such a late attack, Baudon's and Noyelle's Burgundians were quickly overthrown and forced back to Clairoix. In haste Jean de Luxembourg assembled his men and went to meet Jeanne's soldiers. The battle raged for quite a while. Jeanne and her troops might have won in the end if the rumour had not spread among them that the English, having left Venette, were marching along the Oise to cut off their retreat. The French soldiers all panicked, ran away, many of them shouting, "*Sauve qui peut!*" The Maid tried to save the situation by shouting, "Be quiet! It depends only on you to beat them! Think only of hitting them hard!"

And as an example to them she threw herself into the mêlée, hitting the Burgundians hard with the flat of her sword. D'Aulon, seizing her horse's bridle, managed to drag it in the direction of Compiègne, but obstinately she insisted on remaining with the rear-guard as she wanted to see all her men reach safety behind the ramparts of the city. She was expecting the artillery, in accordance with the decisions taken at the war council in the Governor's house, to sweep the high road, thus stopping the English from advancing. Not a single cannon shot was fired.

Without meeting any resistance the English occupied the approaches to the bridge, and on Guillaume de Flavy's orders the drawbridge was raised when Jeanne and some of her followers reached the river empty of boats. They were still battling ferociously. Within a few minutes her small escort was reduced to impotence. Burgundian, English and Picards surrounded her, shouting, "Surrender and give up your oath!"

"I swore my oath and gave it to somebody else!" she answered, refusing to surrender.

Eventually an archer, "a lean and thin man" in the service of Captain Lionel de Wandomme, who was one of Jean de Luxembourg's lieutenants, managed to catch hold of her by her velvet doublet and threw her "quite flat on the ground."

The Governor made no attempt to save her; the garrison, which had the means of making a sortie in strength remained behind the walls; and the artillery stayed silent.

In the evening of May 23, 1430, the Maid was taken prisoner, betrayed as she predicted during the day, and as her Voices had told her.

Twelve

Night had fallen by the time Jeanne and her companions in captivity, d'Aulon, Pierre d'Arc and Poton de Xaintrailles, reached Margny surrounded by a strong escort of Burgundian soldiers led by the bastard son of de Vendôme who was "happier than if he had a king in his power." The Comte de Luxembourg, to whom the Maid belonged since her capture, came at once to see her in the inn, where she was held for the time being. Courteously he invited her to share his supper, and treated her with the highest regard, not only because of the high standing of his prisoner but also because several members of his family had contracted marriage alliances with the House of Orléans.

Next day the Duke of Burgundy came to call on Jeanne. They had a long conversation. As a matter of fact Philippe le Bon harboured no resentment against Jeanne, for, taking it all in all, the deliverance of the town of Orléans and the coronation of Charles VII in Rheims had given him the opportunity of obtaining immense personal advantages from the English, and at the present moment he was engaged in secret negotiations with the Court of France, with which he was seeking a rapprochement in letting men like Régnault de Chartres and the Papal Legate take the initiative. Also, he could not forget that Marguerite, his elder sister, before being married to the Comte de Richemont, was the wife of the Dauphin Louis, half-brother of Jeanne, and that his first wife had been Michelle of France, Jeanne's half-sister. All those family ties, united with his policy of the moment, made him careful to treat with the greatest circumspection a prisoner who by her birth was not only the half-sister of Charles VII, King of France, but as well of the mother of Henry VI, who styled himself King of England and of France. For the aforesaid political and family reasons Jeanne's capture placed the Duke of Burgundy in a dilemma. Yet a solution had to be found.

Jeanne should be put to ransom according to custom; but the

Duke could not help asking himself whether it was in his interest to hand her over to his official allies who would lock her up in a fortress, or to the French with whom he was negotiating in secret. He wavered between the two alternatives, wondering which could bring him the biggest personal advantage. At the moment Jeanne, according to the rules of war, belonged to his vassal Jean de Ligny, Seigneur of Beaurevoir, a scion of the House of Luxembourg, who could not, however, give up his prisoner without the approval of his overlord.

The first move was to let it quickly be known that the Maid was taken prisoner. The Duke of Burgundy hastened to spread in all quarters the astounding news that, "the Creator did us the immense favour of making the one, who is known as the Maid, our prisoner. We write in the hope that it will give you joy, comfort and consolation, and that you will thank the Creator who sees and knows everything." Within a few days her capture was known all over the country.

On his side Régnault de Chartres, Chancellor of France, showed his joy almost indecently when he wrote to Reims of which town he was archbishop, "God allowed the Maid to be taken because she was filled with pride and because of the rich robes she wore and because she did not do what God commanded, but acted according to her own will." And to console his flock the prelate added, "there came to the King a young shepherd, a keeper of lambs, from the mountains of the Gévaudan who said neither more nor less than Jeanne," and who had, "orders from God to discomfit the English and the Burgundians."

In the provinces faithful to the King of France the news caused deep stupor, and in many towns they followed the example of Tours where the authorities ordered public mourning and days of prayers for the liberation of the prisoner.

At the Court, while Jeanne's enemies rejoiced more or less overtly the friends of the House of Orléans got busy in looking for ways and means to have her freed as quickly as possible. The venerable Archbishop of Embrun did not hesitate to tell the King in public, "that he was showered with blessings thanks to the arms and consolation of a girl," and recommended the King,

132

"not to save means or money or whatever the price is so as not to be ineffaceably blamed for very unworthy ingratitude."

All the supporters of the French cause had no doubt whatever that after negotiations which might take a fairly long time the King would ultimately pay the ransom the Duke of Burgundy demanded and after that the freed Maid would continue fighting the English till final victory.

In Paris the occupiers lit large bonfires at the cross-roads and celebrated a solemn Te Deum in the church of Notre-Dame. And to avoid the possibility of the Maid being bought back by the French they hastened to claim her from the Duke of Burgundy through the intermediacy of the University of Paris. On May 26 Brother Martin Bélorme, Vicar of the Inquisition in France wrote a long letter to the Duke, summoning him to hand over the prisoner. The inquisitor first reminded him that "all loyal Christian princes and all other true Catholics are in duty bound to extirpate all errors against the Faith," then he named "a certain woman called Jeanne whom the adversaries of this kingdom call 'The Maid'," who had committed "diverse errors, great injury and scandals against Divine honour and our holy Faith, which things cannot be committed without good and suitable reparation," and he requested the Duke to send him, "the said prisoner Jehanne, suspected vehemently of several crimes smelling of heresy, to appear before us the Procurator of the Holy Office." The document bore the signature of Le Fourbeur, notary to the Inquisition and Hébert, notary of the University.

Immediately after receiving the letter the Duke of Burgundy ordered Jean de Ligny at once to transfer his prisoner to a safe place for the added reason that the battle continued raging round Compiègne—Margny was only a league away—and the Duke feared that an untimely action by some English captain or an intrepid move by some French mercenary chief might take his precious hostage away. Jean de Ligny swiftly led his prisoner to his own castle of Beaulieu in the Vermandois, which was eight leagues to the north, a strongly fortified castle that could withstand a long siege.

Once Jeanne had gone the Duke of Burgundy wrote to the Vicar of the Inquisition, and, in order to save time, explained that she could be considered only as a prisoner-of-war and as such entitled to ransom.

In Beaulieu, where she was reunited with her military household, Jeanne thought only of escaping to rejoin the besieged of Compiègne who continued resisting the Anglo-Burgundian attacks. In vain her squire d'Aulon, who was returned to her, Pierre d'Arc and the others who were made prisoners at the same time as she, tried to make her appreciate that the town was in a desperate situation as the fort that controlled the access to the bridge across the Oise was already in enemy hands.

"No," she said, "no. The fortresses, which the King of Heaven handed to gentle King Charles, will not be taken as long as an effort is made to hold on to them."

One morning while everybody was still sleeping in the castle she hauled herself up to the ceiling of the tower in which she was locked up, pushed aside the two wooden beams that held the roof, and slipping between them, succeeded in leaving her prison. To make sure of reaching the open fields unhampered she wanted to lock her jailers in, but as she turned the key the creaking lock awoke the porter who gave the alert which put an end to her escape. In despair she had to return to her prison.

On Whit Monday Jean de Ligny, who wanted her even farther away from the theatre of war, sent her to his castle of Beaurevoir, thirteen miles north of Beaulieu. Her new enforced residence was more pleasant than the one she left behind, for several members of his family spent most of the year there, particularly his wife Jeanne de Béthune, Vicomtesse de Meaux, her daughter-in-law Jeanne de Bar and her old aunt Jeanne de Luxembourg, whose vast fortune he expected soon to inherit. The three women hated the English as much as the Burgundians, the first two because they were the widow and daughter of Robert de Bar killed in the battle of Agincourt in 1415, the third because she was the King's godmother. They showed Jeanne sincere and deep affection, doing all they could to alleviate her lot.

The only thing about Jeanne that upset the three women was her refusal to stop wearing man's clothes. The Maid justified her attitude by assuring them that "she not yet had the permission to discard them," and explained that dressed like that it was easier to keep at arm's length importunate suitors, one of whom, a certain Raymond de Macy one day treated her with such familiarity that he had to be put in his place.

While, in spite of the tender concern of the three ladies, Jeanne fretted and worried because of her helpless position and no chance of action, Yolande of Anjou worked desperately hard to come to her help. It was not an easy problem to solve. The easiest way out was to buy out the prisoner, however not only would the Duke of Burgundy refuse to lose the opportunity to ask for an enormous ransom—at the moment the Royal Treasury was completely depleted and Yolande of Anjou was in the throes of terrible financial difficulties—but Jeanne's return to freedom would cause fresh trouble in the Royal Council, since one could not expect her to renounce carrying arms. The Royal Council had always maintained that the war would be won by diplomatic means; and more than ever it was convinced that it was in the right: for months now the Duke of Burgundy had been making overtures to Charles VII.

Régnault de Chartres supported the Duke's policy in every sense, and the tribe of de La Trémouille was certain of his intentions being sincere. Everybody knew that the Duke was busily preparing himself to take over the splendid inheritance his uncle, the Duke of Brabant, was any minute expected to leave him. Besides, most of the Maid's supporters in the Royal Council believed that Jeanne had conspicuously gone beyond her assignment when she took over the Templars' programme of reforms, and her friendship for the common people and the minor clergy—her two strongest allies—whose very symbol she was, considerably worried the high nobility and the dignitaries, who, not without reason, were of the opinion that if Jeanne achieved total victory over the enemies of the kingdom the paradox would result of France finding itself under the same sort of rule as England, where the monarch's powers were limited by an assembly composed of chosen representatives of the people.

As to Yolande of Anjou, it was exceptionally difficult for her openly to take the part of one she had always supported and protected, because she knew only too well that her intervention would immediately be reported to the Duke of Burgundy against whom she fought with pitiless hatred. Furthermore, as a riposte to the Duke of Burgundy who, in spite of his friendly overtures to the Court of France, was cynically making ready to despoil Réne of Anjou of the Lorraine inheritance which was soon to come to him, she was negotiating in secret a marriage between one of her daughters with the Duke of Brabant. That would have put an end to the Duke of Burgundy's hopes of gaining the vast inheritance from his uncle.

For the moment it was most important for Jeanne's defenders to find out what the exact intentions of the Duke of Burgundy were. On their intervention the King sent an emissary to the Duke, asking him to name the price of the ransom. The Duke, who had become cognisant of Yolande of Anjou's secret dealings with the Duke of Brabant, refused to give a precise answer, and the French King's envoy had to depart empty handed. From then on it became evident that the Duke of Burgundy would not deliver Jeanne to the French however high a figure they offered him, but would sooner or later hand her over to the English as it was more than likely that the members of the University of Paris, who claimed her on May 26, could find sufficient money to pay the ransom.

In the English camp Jeanne's fiercest enemy was Henry de Beaufort, Cardinal Bishop of Winchester, great-uncle of Henry VI, the real ruler in London, who had been in a continuous rage ever since Jeanne's victories had interfered with his plans. As an answer to Charles VII's coronation the terrible prelate decided in person to anoint his nephew as king of France in Notre-Dame-de-Paris. But since August 26 the little king and his retinue were held in Calais because the French based on Compiègne barred the roads of Picardy and Louviers and the way through Normandy.

Terrified by the idea of fighting against Jeanne's troops the English mercenaries deserted en masse on the pretext that their pay was in arrears. Without any effect on them the angry Cardinal published an ordnance, scolding those "who feared the witchcraft of the Maid."

The Queen of Anjou realised that since according to all evidence the Duke of Burgundy would hand Jeanne to the English, it was essential not to let her be given to the Cardinal, who would without a doubt have her executed as much to satisfy his rancour as to give his troops confidence again. For not all the English leaders were as ferociously intransigent as the Cardinal, who recently had had a poor woman burnt at the stake because she sang the Maid's praise in public. Among the less intransigent was John, Duke of Bedford. Though of a forceful personality he had a supple mind and a strong political sense. He hid as well as he could his hatred of his uncle the Cardinal. He looked at everything and everybody through the eyes of his wife Anne of Burgundy, sister of Philippe le Bon and cousin of Jeanne.

Jeanne was taken prisoner in the diocese of Pierre Cauchon, Bishop of Beauvais who, though ostensibly on the English side, was entirely devoted to his protector, the Duke of Burgundy, thanks to whom he had reached episcopal rank. Nor did the Bishop neglect remaining in close contact with the Court of France, especially with Chancellor Régnault de Chartres, who as Archbishop of Reims was his ecclesiastical superior, since the bishopric of Beauvais depended on the archbishopric of Reims.

Now that it was certain that the Duke of Burgundy would deliver her up to the English it was considered sufficient to save her from death for the Duke not to hand her over to the Cardinal, who would have given her short shrift; but to the Duke of Bedford's agents, particularly to Bishop Cauchon whose knowledge of law and legal procedure was universally respected. Charles VII, whom Yolande of Anjou acquainted with the plan, found nothing to say against it. Pleased at being rid of the immense worry the Maid's fate caused him, and following his mother-in-law's wishes he ordered Régnault de Chartres to enter as soon as possible into communication with the Duke of Burgundy, Bishop Cauchon and the Duke of Bedford. This solution of the problem did not displease the Archbishop of Reims. He did not want Jeanne to die. After all, she was the sister of the King of France, aunt of the King of England, cousin of the Duke of Burgundy and related to other powerful families. However, he did want to eliminate from the political scene the girl who, after her arrival in Chinon, had changed the scheme of things within a few months. So nobody was more willing to execute his master's orders than the Archbishop. The Archbishop of Reims hastened to do as his royal master bade.

Already at the beginning of June Cauchon had written a letter to Henry VI, King of England and France, asking for the Maid's trial to be handed to him, as she had been taken in his diocese. The Cardinal Bishop of Winchester could not refuse the Bishop of Beauvais a privilege he was entitled to by canon law, but as he had only very limited confidence in Pierre Cauchon, and because he had no desire to have trouble with the University of Paris which had been the first to claim the prisoner, he replied in an official letter dated June 2, saying that the Bishop and the Inquisitor would judge her together and concurrently.

As it had received no answer from the Duke of Burgundy to its request of May 26 the University of Paris addressed him a new one dated July 14 in the following terms:

"Very high and puissant Prince and our most honoured Lord,

"Once before in duty to Your Highness we have written very humbly begging that the woman, known as the Maid, who, God be praised, is in your power, should be put into the hands of justice so that her trial for idolatry and other matters touching our Holy Faith and the scandals caused by her in the kingdom can take place.

"Nonetheless we received no answer to that, and we did not hear what provision was made for appropriate discussion about that woman; but fear that through the falsity and seduction of the enemy from Hell and the malice and subtlety of wicked persons, your enemies and adversaries who with all their care want to save that woman by dubious means, she might be taken out of your realm in some fashion God does not permit; for in truth, in the judgment of all good Catholics who are aware of this great injury of the Holy Faith, this enormous peril, inconvenient and damaging to the good of this kingdom, nothing comparable to which having happened in the memory of mankind, if she went away without appropriate punishment, it would greatly be to the prejudice of your honour and to the most Christian name of the House of France of which your very noble progenitors were, as now you are, constantly faithful protectors and very noble principals.

"For these reasons, our dreaded and honoured Lord, we very humbly beseech you again that for the sake of the faith of our Saviour, the conservation of the Holy Church and the protection of Divine honour and also for the purpose of the most Christian kingdom, it may please Your Highness to hand this woman to the Inquisitor of the Faith and send her safely to Paris as we begged the last time, and give her or have her given to the Reverend Father in God, Monsignor the Bishop of Beauvais, in whose spiritual jurisdiction she has been apprehended, so that the trial in Faith of this woman should take place to the glory of God and the exaltation of our Holy Faith and to the edification of good and faithful Catholics and the public interest of this realm, and also to the honour and praise of Your Highness whom may Our Lord keep in prosperity and give His glory at the end."

To give more strength to its request the University the same day sent a letter to Jean de Luxembourg in which one finds again the fear of the Parisian clergy that Jeanne should escape or be freed either by an action of the French troops or as a result of negotiations between the Court of France and the Duke of Burgundy.

After underlining that "the first oath of the order of knighthood is to defend the honour of God, the Catholic faith and the Holy Church" the University pointed out that "this woman who calls herself the Maid" did "offend the faith and dishonour the Church, for because of her idolatry, errors, false doctrines and other evils, inestimable troubles followed in this kingdom"; then after thanking Jean de Luxembourg for "having done a great service to our Holy Faith and the whole kingdom" by capturing Jeanne, the letter went on to say that it would be an "intolerable offence against the Divine Majesty if that woman were freed or lost" as one hears that "all the adversaries are striving by every roundabout means to do so, and, what is worse, by money or ransom." And the letter ended in the same manner as the one written to the Duke of Burgundy to hand over "this woman to the Inquisitor of the Faith" or to "deliver her up to our very honoured Lord Bishop of Beauvais, who also asked for her."

To make sure that the letters the University wrote reached their destinations Pierre Cauchon offered to take them in person. After he made the English provide expenses of hundred *sols* a day for his journey—he never forgot his material interests—the Bishop of Beauvais appeared before Compiègne at the headquarters of the Duke of Burgundy and addressed the following summons to Jeanne's keepers:

"That this woman who is commonly called Jehanne the Maid, prisoner, be sent to the King to be delivered to the Church to be tried because she is suspected and slandered for having committed several crimes such as witchcraft, idolatry, invocations to demons and other several acts touching our Faith and against it. And therefore she cannot be considered as a prize of war according to what is said; nonetheless for the remuneration of those who took and detained her the King wants generously to give up to the sum of six thousand francs, and to the bastard who took her to give and assign a revenue of two or three hundred *livres* for the upkeep of position.

"The aforesaid bishop requests from him and from all of them, as the aforesaid woman was taken in his diocese and is under his spiritual jurisdiction, that she be given to him so that he can try her as it behoves him. He is ready to hear her with the assistance of the Inquisitor of the Faith, and if need be with the assistance of the Doctors in Divinity and Law and other eminent persons who are experts in legal procedure as the seriousness of the affair requires, so that it should be done with mature consideration, holiness and in due form to the exaltation of the Faith and the instruction of several persons who in this matter were deceived and abused in the circumstances by the aforesaid woman.

"Lastly, if in the above-mentioned manner they do not want to or not one of them is satisfied or obeys the summons as said above, despite that the capture of this woman is not similar to the capture of a king, a prince or other people of high estate (who, however, if they were taken or found themselves in a like situation, whether king, dauphin or other prince, the king could have what he wanted by giving to the captor the sum of ten thousand francs according to the law, usage and custom of France) the aforesaid bishop summons and requests the above-mentioned that the so-called Maid be delivered to him against the surety of the sum of ten thousand francs. And the said bishop, according to the form and penalties of the law, requests that she be given and delivered to him as stated above."

To justify the ample travelling expenses he received, and to give the English proof that he truly performed the task entrusted him, Pierre Cauchon took care to have the following certificate drawn up:

"In the year 1430 of the Lord on the 14th day of the month of July, 8th indiction, 13th year of the pontificate of our very Holy Father the Pope Martin V, in the fortified castle of the very illustrious prince, His Highness the Duke of Burgundy, established in his camp before Compiègne, present the noblemen, Messeigneurs Nicolas de Mailly, magistrate of Vermandois, and Jean de Pressy, knight, and other witnesses in large number were presented by the Reverend Father in God Monsignor Pierre, by the grace of God bishop and Count of Beauvais, to the said very illustrious prince His Highness the Duke of Burgundy a summons on paper containing word by word the above transcribed five articles, which summons my Lord the Duke truly transmitted to the noble Nicolas Raulin, his Chancellor, who assisted him in transmitting it to Messire Jean de Luxembourg, Lord of Beaurevoir; and the said Seigneur Jean de Luxembourg having arrived unexpectedly the said Chancellor gave him the summons which, as it seemed to me, the said Lord read. That took place in my presence.

"Signed, Triquellot, Apostolic Notary."

The summons by the Bishop of Beauvais did not impress the Duke of Burgundy at all. He was resolved to act only in his own interest. But it was not easy to decide whose side to take to the best advantage as the case had become rather involved since the first letter from the University.

On one hand, an emissary of Charles VII let the Burgundians know that if Jeanne were delivered to the English to perish by their hands "he would inflict like treatment on those who were in his hands." This threat, which ignored the laws of war as conceived in all contemporary minds, was a matter one had to reflect on seriously before taking a decision. On the other hand, the Duke of Burgundy could no longer labour under the illusion that if given to the English Jeanne would be sent to some prison in London to join there her half-brother Charles d'Orléans, because the royal ransom they offered for Jeanne clearly showed that they wanted to put the young girl to death. Now, Philippe le Bon wanted under no circumstances to be held responsible for the death of the Maid.

As to the plan Cauchon unveiled to him and which consisted of sending Jeanne before a tribunal presided over by him, and which he could manipulate as he pleased, the Duke of Burgundy had no faith in it. Not that he doubted the word and ability of the Bishop of Beauvais, whom he had known for a long time and whose skill he had had occasion to appreciate, but because he found it almost impossible to execute it without the risk of a false move even if the fanatics of the University were kept out of it; for in any case the trial would take place in Paris; not forgetting that the deputy of the Inquisition, of whose intentions one could not yet form a judgment, had a considerable part to play. For all these reasons the Duke of Burgundy thought it preferable to give the bishop no answer whatever, but wait to see how events were shaping.

Jean de Ligny strongly approved of Cauchon's plan, but was unwilling to act against the wish of the Duke of Burgundy, the more so as he needed the unreserved support of his overlord to be able to get hold of his old aunt's inheritance all for himself.

Anyhow, for the plan produced by the Bishop of Beauvais to have any serious chance of success it first was necessary to begin the trial, and obtain the agreement of the interested party without whom nothing could be done. For that reason Jean de Ligny and Pierre Cauchon went to the castle of Beaurevoir. A great disappointment awaited the two men: the moment Jeanne de Luxembourg was informed of the presence of the unexpected guests she formally refused to receive the bishop whom she considered an instrument of the English. Moreover, she threatened her nephew with disinheriting him if he did not pledge his word never to surrender Jeanne to the English. Jean de Ligny immediately gave his word. And Jeanne de Bar threw herself at her husband's feet, begging him not to commit an infamous act which would soil his name for ever. Before the attitude of the two women on whom he had counted to reason with the prisoner, Pierre Cauchon could do nothing else but take his leave.

Cauchon's visit to Beaurevoir gave Jeanne one further reason for trying to escape. Jeanne de Luxembourg and Jeanne de Bar could not keep the bishop's unusual mission from her. She knew too that the besieged of Compiègne were still fighting desperately to remain faithful to the King of France, and she suffered because she could not go to their help. Rumour had it that once the town was taken the whole population would be put to the sword. She realised that sooner or later she would be handed to the English. After a long interior struggle she decided to break out.

The Voices continued to counsel her to accept her fate, assuring her that "God would come to her aid, also to those in Compiègne." One day St Catherine told her that "she would not be delivered before she saw the King of the English."

"I do not want to see him," Jeanne replied. "I prefer death to being in the hands of the English!"

As the weeks went by, so her decision to escape strengthened, and one night the temptation to regain liberty, escape the English and join "those of Compiègne" overruled the advice of her Voices. She tore up all the material she could find: hangings, bed sheets, blankets, shawls and garments which she tied together to make a rope. Then she tied one end to a heavy chest, and from the second floor window of the tower in which she was kept prisoner she slid down the rope. But the rope was either six or seven yards too short or broke during her descent—in any case after a heavy fall she landed in the dungeon's ditch.

Though she suffered horribly from concussion caused by the fall she still dragged herself as far as the tower of La Follemprise, from where, she hoped, she might reach the open after providing herself with a horse from the stables. But then she collapsed and at dawn the watch found her lying unconscious in the grass. Taken back to her room she was admirably looked after by the de Luxembourg ladies. For three days she could not eat anything. However, her robust constitution helped her quickly to get well again.

Her Voices reproached her for not trusting them and commanded her to "ask God's forgiveness for having jumped." In order to comfort her St Catherine assured her that "Compiègne would receive help before St Martin's Day in winter."

Feeling death approaching Jeanne de Luxembourg made her

will on September 10, leaving all her possessions to Jean de Ligny, then went home to her castle of Crotoy five miles from Abbeville. With no more worries on that score Jean de Ligny, whom Jeanne's second attempt to escape had truly frightened, and fearing that his prisoner might bolt in the end, asked the Duke of Burgundy to have her transferred to one of his own fortresses. The Duke agreed since it was as much in his as his vassal's interest to keep the precious hostage. His position was no longer as buoyant as it had been when he left unanswered the summons the University had sent him. The town of Compiègne continued heroically to resist all the assaults of his troops, sustained by the hope of seeing at last the arrival of the reinforcements the King promised them. And since July 9 the Cardinal of Winchester forbade English merchants to go to Antwerp to buy linen and sell wool, which was an awful blow to the Flemish industry.

On September 20 Jeanne left Beaurevoir, accompanied by a strong escort commanded by Jean de Ligny, and two days later reached Arras, where the Duke of Burgundy assigned his castle of Bellemotte as her residence.

A few days after her arrival she received twenty-two gold crowns sent by the magistrates of Tournai to whom she had written, explaining that she needed money. Tournai was the nearest town loyal to Charles VII.

Though she was separated from her household and was strictly watched for fear of another attempt to escape, Jeanne, nonetheless, was given far more freedom inside the castle and even in the town. She was allowed to go under heavy guard every morning to hear Mass in the cathedral of Arras. To see her ride past dressed as a man and mounted on the best horse the castle's stable could provide, the townsfolk crowded the streets. They did not want to miss the opportunity of seeing the woman of whom all France was speaking, her supporters encouraging her with a discreet gesture or look, all seduced by the gracefulness and simplicity of her carriage.

Back in the castle Jeanne received everybody who asked for an audience. Among the many visitors there was one who became of capital importance to her: Jehan de Pressy, the Duke of Burgundy's personal secretary, brought her a letter from his master and in the course of a long conversation he acquainted her with the plan conceived by Yolande of Anjou, accepted by Charles VII, approved of by the Duke of Burgundy and which the Bishop of Beauvais was to put into execution.

Since her failure during her last attempt at escaping in Beaurevoir Jeanne had promised herself never again to leave the road her Voices advised her to follow. She had a new proof of the accuracy of her visions, namely the raising of the siege of Compiègne which was now announced to her. The French army had entered the town on October 26, before St Martin's Day as St Catherine told her; and it was the same saint who constantly exhorted her to take her sufferings patiently, assuring her that she would not be set free "before she saw the King of the English."

She meditated on all that while Jehan de Pressy talked to her. First she was distressed by the precise details she received on the attitude the Court of France took towards her, then though saddened by the thought of being kept from the battlefields for a long time she resigned herself to her fate.

At the beginning of the month of November Jeanne de Luxembourg let her nephew know that she wanted to see Jeanne again. Jean de Ligny could not but comply with his aunt's wishes, so he arrived at the castle of Beleemotte on the 6th and left with the Maid on the 7th. After a stop a Lucheux and another at Drugy, where they stayed the night, the two of them reached the castle of Crotoy, where the old lady, whose agony began several days before, eventually died on the 13th.

Since the month of June the Bishop of Beauvais had not ceased bestiring himself on behalf of the secret task he was entrusted with, yet officially giving the impression that he was doing his duty by the English. That was not easy. To begin with he had to avoid the trial taking place in Paris, where it was impossible to manipulate the clerks of the University who were enraged against Jeanne and who were masters of legal procedure. On that score he quickly obtained results from the Cardinal Bishop of Winchester whom he persuaded first that the Parisians were under the influence of Armagnac propaganda and, there-fore, that one might legitimately fear a popular uprising, which could be hurtful to the proper conduct of the trial; secondly, the possibility of some foolhardy attack by partisans, ready to remove the accused before the eyes of her judges.

To avoid such possibilities he suggested Rouen as the seat of the tribunal. The bishop of that town had recently died. The Cardinal thought that Cauchon used that as an excuse to remind him that he had declared himself candidate to that See. Rouen, fully garrisoned by the English, was also the normal residence of the Duke of Bedford, Regent of France in the name of Henry VI. The Cardinal fell into Cauchon's cleverly prepared trap. He agreed to the Maid's trial being held in Rouen as soon as the Duke of Burgundy handed her over.

Having won the first round there remained for Cauchon the task of keeping the Inquisition out of the trial, as it was most competent in dealing with matters touching the faith, and had already on May 26 summoned the Duke of Burgundy to deliver up "the said Jeanne, vehemently suspected of several crimes smelling of heresy." As a matter of fact Brother Bellorme allowed himself to be carried away by his zeal when he asked for the "appearance of the prisoner before the procurator of the Holy Office," for at the moment the Pope was far from inclined to be agreeable to the English. In fact Martin V was very dissatisfied with the Cardinal Bishop of Winchester who, on the pretext of organising a crusade against the Hussites, had succeeded in taking large sums of money from him which were used without scruple to pay the English soldiers fighting in France. The Pope, who put all his efforts into the war against heresy in Europe, felt extremely humiliated for having let himself be cheated out of the moneys he had patiently collected especially as he was of a miserly disposition.

The Bishop of Beauvais did not fail to use the Holy Father's present mood to his advantage. He alerted Régnault de Chartres and Gérard Machet who, using their influence with the Papal Legate, persuaded the Grand Inquisitor of France, the Dominican Jean Graverand, not to persue the Maid in the name of the Inquisition. Jean Lemaître, who also belonged to the Dominican Order, hastened indirectly to disavow Brother Martin Bellorme by letting it be known that he was ignorant of whether he was authorised or not to continue with the action.

The Bishop of Beauvais won all along the line, but was careful not to show his satisfaction, as that might easily have aroused suspicion. On the contrary, he got very busy preparing for the trial, sending out commissions to collect evidence in different localities, and setting up boards of inquiry in the Barrois, particularly in Domrémy, Moutiers-sur-Saulx, Neufchâteau and Vaucouleurs. He continually urged the Chapter of Rouen to give him Letters Patent of the Territory, that is jurisdiction in the town. However, the canons feared that such authority could be interpreted as a sort of anticipated taking possession of the diocese so they let him coax them in vain. In any case they had a different candidate for the See.

When the Duke of Bedford heard of Jeanne de Luxembourg being on the verge of death he ordered the English treasurer to let him have 10,000 gold *livres* for Jean de Ligny. On the morning of November 10 the convoy carrying the ransom for Jeanne left Rouen protected by a strong cavalry escort. It was followed by the Bishop of Beauvais who had already arranged with Jean de Ligny all the details concerning the handing over of the prisoner. On October 20 the Duke of Burgundy had agreed to Jeanne being handed over on the conditions Cauchon had outlined and the Duke accepted, but it was reciprocally understood that it would not take place before the death of the old Demoiselle de Luxembourg.

On November 15 the convoy entered the courtyard of the castle of Crotoy. It was early in the morning; and early in the afternoon it left with Jeanne, who put up no show of resistance. Calm and decided to listen only to the advice her Voices gave her she made no attempt to escape from the twenty archers who guarded her, though she had several opportunities to do so. They crossed one of the arms of the Somme in boats and crossed Saint-Valéry before arriving in Eu, where the night was spent. The following day the convoy reached the castle of Arques, which it left next dawn, entering Rouen on Friday the 17th towards four in the afternoon.

Thirteen

The castle of Bouvreuil to which Jeanne was taken on her arrival in Rouen was as solidly constructed as most castles of the period. It consisted of a vast central building and a number of outbuildings surrounded by a thick wall strengthened by high towers, one of which is still in existence. The Duke and Duchess of Bedford had been residing there for a long time, and since the month of July young Henry VI and his mother Catherine stayed there.

Jeanne was given a suite of three rooms, at one end of it, in a tower named Devant les Champs, at the other end of the private apartments of the Duke of Bedford. The room in the middle was assigned to Jeanne as her own room, the other two were used as office and waiting room. Thus the prisoner could easily be watched.

Immediately after her arrival in the castle Jeanne received a visit from the Bedfords. The Duke confirmed to her all Cauchon had explained during the journey about the trial and the fate that was in store for her. The Duchess, who was her cousin, showed her true tenderness. The same day she made the acquaintance of Queen Catherine, her eldest half-sister, who was accompanied by her son little Henry VI, King of England and France. Once again Jeanne perceived that her Voices spoke but the truth, for did they not say that "she would see the King of the English before she was saved"? The evidence of all the friendliness she was treated with, and the reassurance given by her Voices lifted her a little out of her gloom.

The Earl of Warwick, Governor of the castle, was brutally rude both in language and behaviour on the first day; but suddenly his attitude underwent a change. The Bishop of Beauvais, obliged to take him into his confidence, had explained to him the real aim of his mission. First he was astounded by the disclosure, but when the Duke of Bedford confirmed all the Bishop had said he hastened to offer his services for the happy outcome of the affair. Opportunist and unscrupulous Warwick considered it better to attach himself to the Regent whom he saw as the future ruler, than to continue serving the old Cardinal of Winchester who had always helped him.

There were still difficulties ahead for Cauchon. Hardly had he set foot in Rouen than a letter from the University reached him.

"To our Reverend Father in God,

"Monseigneur,

"We behold with extreme astonishment that the sending of the woman vulgarly called the Maid has been so long deferred to the prejudice of the Faith and ecclesiastic jurisdiction, especially as one hears that she has in fact been handed over to our king and master Henry VI.

"The Christian Princes in their zeal for the interests of the Church and the Faith are accustomed to expect that when an outrageous attack is made against Catholic dogma, the culprit should be delivered over to ecclesiastical judges called to lay hands upon him and punish him. And if you, Reverend Father, had shown more severe exactitude the case of the aforesaid woman would already be in front of the Tribunal of the Church. Clothed as you are by your high episcopal dignity you cannot be indifferent to repressing the scandals in the bosom of religion above all when chance willed that that case take place in your diocese.

"In order that the Church's authority does not suffer much longer condescend in your zeal, Reverend Father, to provide with extreme diligence that the aforesaid woman be promptly handed into your keeping and into the keeping of Monseigneur the Inquisitor of heretic perversities.

"That done, be so good as to take care that the said woman is conducted to Paris, where are to be found many doctors and learned men, so that the case be better examined and more surely judged to the holy edification of the Christian people and the honour of God who should direct you, Reverend Father, in all matters with special grace.

"Written in Paris in our general assembly solemnly collected at Saint-Mathurin on November 2, 1430.

"Signed: Hébert."

149

The University did not deem it sufficient to write only to the Bishop of Beauvais: it intervened as well with the English in these terms:

"To the very excellent Prince, the King of France and England, our very dreaded and sovereign Master;

"We heard it said again that at present into your power the woman known as the Maid has been handed, which fills us with joy, trusting that by your order the said woman be put on trial to repair the great witcheries and scandals which notoriously happened in this kingdom because of her, to the great prejudice of Divine honour, our holy Faith and all your good subjects.

"And as it belongs to us because of our profession to extirpate such disturbing manifestations when our Catholic Faith is thereby touched, we cannot conceal the long delay of justice which must displease every good Christian, and your royal Majesty more than anybody else because of your great indebtness to God in recognition of the high gifts, honours and dignities he gave your Excellency.

"Although we wrote several times, we do it this time again, offering our always humble and loyal recommendation, in order that we should not be accused of any negligence in this so necessary matter; we very humbly beg and in the honour of our Saviour Jesus-Christ we very strongly pray your high Excellency that this woman, if it please you, be shortly put by your order into the hands of the Justice of the Church, that is to say into the hands of the Reverend Father in God, our very honoured Lord Bishop and Count of Beauvais, and into the hands of the Inquisitor of France too, to whom belong the knowledge of the misdeeds of the said woman, especially where they touch our Faith, so that either by reason, or decent discussion of the charges against her and such amends as belong, guarding the holy truth of our Faith and putting all errors, false and scandalous opinion out of the minds of your good Christian subjects.

"And it seems to us very fitting, if that is the pleasure of your Highness, that the said woman be brought to this city to be tried in public, and surely, for themselves, doctors and other notabilities being there in large number, her trial will have greater repute than in any other place. Moreover, it is fitting that amends for the said scandals be made in this place, where her actions were divulged and spread excessively.

"Doing so your royal Majesty will keep his great loyalty, to the Sovereign and Divine Majesty who may give your Excellency continuous prosperity and endless good fortune.

"Written in Paris at our general congregation celebrated at Saint-Mathurin, November 21, 1430.

"Your very humble and devoted daughter, the University of Paris."

All this intervention could not but worry the Bishop of Beauvais who urged the Chapter of Rouen to give him the letters patent he had asked for, but the canons remained obstinate, always finding some good reason to hold back their agreement. Meanwhile Cauchon continued his feverish activities, writing to all the commissioners whom he had sent to different spots in the Barrois, in short he showed meritorious zeal. So that all and sundry should know that Jeanne was truly in his power he authorised visits to the castle of Bouvreuil. For several days, long queues of all kinds of people pushed their way into the castle, enemies of Jeanne who came to mock her; the simply curious who wanted a close look at the woman who had had so many adventures; and friends and sympathisers, particularly preaching brothers, who wanted to speak words of comfort.

Far from being dejected Jeanne received her visitors with great assurance, expressed herself as always with that same mixture of simplicity, sweetness, irony and firmness that impressed everyone who heard her. She answered all questions put to her with precision, ignoring no question and often leaving her interlocutors confused, especially as she repudiated not one of her beliefs, bravely taking the responsibility for all her actions, and averred that the moment she registered her freedom she would continue with her mission.

On December 5 Warwick entered her chamber followed by the Bishop of Luxembourg, Chancellor of King Henry VI, the Earl of Stafford, member of the English Royal (Privy) Council, and two unexpected visitors, namely Jean de Ligny, her erstwhile keeper, and the Comte de Macy whom at Beaurevoir she had put in his place because of his importunate gallantry. His aunt's legacy having given him possession of a considerable fortune, and full of remorse for having surrendered Jeanne (he had added to his arms the sad device, "Nobody can do the impossible"), and harried by his wife who wanted him to undo what he had done, he asked his master's permission to buy back the prisoner. The Duke of Burgundy was not opposed to his request since the English were causing him a thousand difficulties in Flanders, but he did make it a condition that Jeanne should promise never again to take up arms, for he was convinced that if she reappeared on the battlefield her presence would galvanise the French forces to such an extent that the English would at once be forced to evacuate the whole kingdom of France, in which case he would cease to play off Charles VII and Henry VI against each other, which would put an end to his game of balance of power that had been so profitable to date.

Relieved by his answer, Jean de Ligny sounded Charles VII on the subject, to find out what his feelings were, also to ask him whether he agreed to the Comte de Macy marrying Jeanne. The King gave a favourable reply, even adding that if Jeanne wished to marry de Macy he would repay the ransom to de Ligny. On that Jean de Ligny handed back to the English chancellor the 10,000 gold *livres* which he had been paid, and he came to the castle of Bouvreuil to retrieve the prisoner to whom he was entitled in accordance with the laws of war.

After greeting Jeanne, Jean de Ligny came straight to the point.

"I am here to ransom you if you promise that you will never again bear arms against us."

Jeanne answered at once. "In the name of God, you laugh at me!" And she added, "I perfectly well know that you have neither the wish nor the power to achieve what you say."

"I promise that I am ready to save you by paying ransom, and if you promise to live far from the battlefields."

The Earl of Warwick confirmed what Jean de Ligny said and in his own name asked her to make an undertaking not to fight against the English again. But Jeanne, who was assured by her Voices that she would be freed, and who wanted to continue with the mission her capture had interrupted, and moreover who feared falling into a trap since neither Cauchon nor Bedford was present among the visitors, although they were the two who had promised to save her, refused to accept de Ligny's offer.

"I very well know," she exclaimed in an angry voice, "that the English want to kill me in the belief that after my death they could win the kingdom of France. But even if they had a hundred thousand soldiers more than they have now, they could never conquer the kingdom!"

The Earl of Stafford, who was present at the meeting only to voice his government's agreement with the proposal, could not listen to more. "Female of the devil," he shouted, and drawing his sword he threw himself on Jeanne. Luckily Warwick pulled him back in time.

"You see for yourself," exclaimed Jeanne, "what the English want to do with me."

"You will die by fire and not by steel," Warwick retorted, who was forced by his official position to use such expressions.

"If I do not leave you before!" Jeanne retorted.

It was Louis de Luxembourg's turn to speak.

"Jeanne," he said, "I have deep pity for you and beg you to stop wearing man's clothes. You will not be taken to an ecclesiastical prison except on that condition."

Jeanne who refused to give up wearing male attire and who on top of it had no desire to exchange the suite in the castle of Bouvreuil for a dark dungeon, where nobody could come to her rescue if need arose, answered in simple tones,

"In that case I shall stay here as long as it pleases Our Lord."

"You can see that she is mad and full of the devil," Stafford said.

Warwick put an end to the futile meeting by pushing the visitors towards the exit. In the yard the Comte de Macy complained, repeating that he loved Jeanne and Charles VII had promised to give her as wife to him; Jean de Ligny bowed his head, infinitely upset by the failure of his mission.

The canons of the Chapter of Rouen persisted in their dilatory manoeuvres, so the Bishop of Beauvais persuaded the Duke of Bedford to order them to deliver the requested letters patent. They were forced to give in "with regard to the circumstances" but did not forget to maintain the "archiepiscopal dignity" in the following document:

"To all those who see the present, the Chapter of Rouen which, during the vacancy of the see is charged with the administration of all the spiritual jurisdiction, greeting.

"On behalf of the Reverend Father in God, Monsignor de Beauvais, it was set forth to us that according to ordinary jurisdiction it belongs to him to make investigations in the case of a woman commonly known as the Maid, suspected and accused of divers crimes against the Faith, which the aforesaid bishop began at the moment when the said woman was taken in his diocese and while she remained there before she was taken to another place.

"That fact having come to the notice of the aforesaid bishop he in his own name addressed himself to the Duke of Burgundy and M. de Luxembourg, asking and requesting them to deliver the woman to him. Thus summoned, and also requested in the same vein by King Henry, our sovereign lord, and the University, those lords delivered the woman who was taken to Rouen and entrusted to the Reverend Father.

"A number of considerations based on the present and foreseen circumstances induce the Reverend Father to take proceedings in this town of Rouen against the aforesaid woman, such as investigate, question and detain her in prison, and to exercise, in brief, all the rights necessary in pursuit of justice.

"The aforesaid Reverend Father however does not intend to reap another's field without our permission, and in order to provide himself with the necessary rights he requested us kindly to give him judicial territory to enable him to exercise those rights within our jurisdiction.

"As we consider that request just and according to law we gave him the letters patent of territory to be used everywhere and whenever he considers it necessary in this town of Rouen as well as in the whole diocese. Consequently we notify the faithful of each sex, whatever their condition, and enjoin them in virtue of holy obedience to comply with all the demands of the Reverend Father whether to appear as witness or to give opinion or in any other capacity.

154

"We concede and consent to all acts of justice being thus done in our territory by the said bishop, whether separately or in unison with the Inquisition, to be carried out freely and with the same legal procedure as if the Reverend Father had performed them in his own diocese.

"We give him by these presents in case of need the authority and the faculty except the archiepiscopal dignity of the diocese of Rouen.

"Given in Rouen on December 28, 1430.

Signed: R. Guérould."

The moment Pierre Cauchon took possession of the letters patent he hurried to inform the Duke of Bedford. As early as January 3, 1431 the Cardinal Bishop of Winchester issued an ordnance which set out that Henry VI "requested by the Bishop of Beauvais, exhorted by his dear daughter the University of Paris, ordered the warders to take the accused to the bishop because she was known to be suspected, noted and libelled for superstition, false doctrines and other crimes of lése-majesté against God."

The text contained a sentence which left no doubt about the Cardinal's sentiments: "It is our intention to recover this woman if it happens that she is not convicted and sentenced to death on the accusations touching our Faith . . ."

Furnished with the necessary authority the Bishop of Beauvais could now start proceedings. First of all he had to set up the tribunal over which he was to preside. According to canon law, even if the judge was the only person to pronounce the sentence he considered just, the rule enjoined him to sit with learned assessors whom he chose himself, and whose opinions, though purely advisory, had to be recorded during the whole trial. Their number was not limited, and Cauchon decided to summon all whose opinions might be of some interest. With that he gave the trial so wide a publicity that the Cardinal ceased to mistrust him. And to disarm the University he asked for the help of some of the most famous doctors of divinity in Paris, among them Nicolas Midi, Gérard Feuillet, Jacques de Touraine and Thomas de Courcelles. The last named was later put in charge of collecting and translating into Latin the minutes of the clerks of the court.

In all thirty-three theologians and other doctors expressed their opinion in the course of the trial, among whom were six bishops, ten abbots, twenty canons, and monks belonging to the Benedictine, Carmelite, Franciscan, Augustinian and Dominican Orders.

On January 9, 1431 Pierre Cauchon summoned into the king's council room eight assessors to whom he read out a declaration written by himself and which constituted the opening of the trial:

"To all those who will see the present. We, Pierre, by Divine mercy Bishop of Beauvais, and Brother Jean le Maistre of the Order of the Preaching Brothers, deputising for Jean Graverent, Inquisitor of the Faith and of heretic perversity for the Kingdom of France, greetings in Our Lord Jesus Christ."

In fact, Brother Graverent, the Inquisition's delegate in Rouen, had not yet revealed the attitude he intended to take, but as his consent was indispensable for the opening of the trial Cauchon did not hesitate to use his authority.

The document went on to say that "a woman, commonly called the Maid," was taken on the bishop's territory and "it was rumoured that the woman, forgetful of the dignity becoming her sex, without shame and feminine modesty, wore through a singularly monstrous distortion unusual clothes suitable only for men, and her presumption went as far as to dare to hold up assertions contrary to several articles of the Catholic Faith, heinous crimes which she committed not only in our diocese but also in the entire kingdom."

Then after mentioning that the University and the Inquisition had urged "Our lords the Duke of Burgundy and Jean de Luxembourg who held her," to deliver her as "suspected of heresy," which took place through the intervention of "the Most Serene and Most Christian Prince, our Sovereign the King Henry of France and England," Cauchon declared that "anxious at all costs to strengthen the Christian Faith" he considered it meet and proper "to investigate these facts thoroughly." And the "Venerable and famous Chapter of Rouen having given him the right of residence in that town in order to conduct the trial," he considered it "opportune even before bringing action against this

156

woman to deliberate with learned men and experts in Divine and human law."

To that meeting, Cauchon invited Gilles de Duremont, priest of Fécamp, Nicolas Le Roux, priest of Jumièges, Pierre Mignet, prior of Longueville, Raoul Roussel, treasurer of the cathedral of Rouen, Nicolas de Vendères, archdeacon of Eu, and three priests of the diocese of Rouen, Robert Barbier, Nicolas Coppequêne and Nicolas Loiseleur, all of them experts in theology and canon law.

The Council was of the opinion that "certain special officers" were needed, and on the advice of Cauchon Jean d'Estivet was named as promoter (prosecutor), Jean de La Fontaine as examining commissioner, Guillaume Collès, known as Boisguillaume, and Guillaume Manchon as notaries, and finally Jean Massieu as court usher.

Then the Council decided that all information collected about the Maid would be read out at their next meeting. Cauchon ruled against the objection that some of the information dealing strictly with the Catholic faith belonged exclusively to the Inquisition.

Thus overriding the Inquisition which, in spite of his inclination, he had to associate with the trial, Cauchon justified the procedure he had adopted. The absence of Jean Lemaître, the Norman delegate, whom he himself had provoked with his interventions, helped him infinitely, not only because he was now free to conduct the trial in his own fashion, but also because the presence in the tribunal of the delegate of the Inquisition would automatically have been followed by the transfer of Jeanne to an ecclesiastical prison, in this case the prison of the archbishopric. Now Cauchon wanted to look after the prisoner personally, and in Bouvreuil he could talk with her every day.

As a matter of fact Jeanne did not understand the bishop's attitude in certain instances, and often his decisions irritated or disconcerted her. In spite of her Voices who told her to have faith and assured her that she would be saved, with her purity of outlook and truthful disposition she did not succeed in having real confidence in a man whose legal subtleties seemed to her but a lot of falsehoods.

At the very beginning of the trial Cauchon thought it

indispensable for Jeanne to submit to an examination of her virginity. He had the delicacy to entrust that to the Duchess of Bedford and not to some vulgar midwife. Jeanne saw it as an outrageous insult. But in fact the proof of her chastity allowed the bishop to set aside, even before it could be formulated, the serious accusation of her having had carnal intercourse with demons which certainly one or the other assessor would have brought against her. Carnal intercourse with demons was punished by torture followed by execution.

Jeanne was exasperated too, by the continuous presence of five English soldiers in the two rooms next to her chamber. Often they allowed themselves the liberty of flouting her in coarse English. However, Cauchon had to keep up appearances, so was forced to leave the guard to please the Cardinal's men. To avoid the risk of the soldiers doing violence to her he permitted Jeanne to wear male attire which protected her better than a woman's dress, and besides he attached three professional warders, Berwoit, Gris and Talbot, charged specially to protect her, to the five soldiers.

For the same reason he was forced to accept her being daily tied at certain hours to a heavy piece of wood by a long chain. She swore continually that she was waiting for the first chance to escape and rejoin the soldiers of the King of France as soon as possible. Nonetheless they took off the chain at night and even in day time if there was no visit announced. Anyway, after the first day of the trial she obtained from Cauchon an order to have the chain removed. At last she began to understand that it was to her advantage to behave docilely and listen to his advice.

Even so Jeanne could not grasp that the whole show had been put up with the sole object of saving her. In her opinion Cauchon, who knew the truth about her birth and claimed that he was saving her from the fate the English had in store for her, should set her free at once. But things were not as simple as she thought, and Cauchon did his utmost to make her understand that he could not rescue her without first confounding her enemies. And he certainly could not tell her that the Court of France, the King and Yolande of Anjou also desired to see her kept as far as possible from all political action and the battlefield. Hence the clashes between the two of them. Jeanne, who was proud and impatient by nature, had become very touchy since her capture. The bishop's attitude irritated her and she often refused to listen to the advice he gave her. Resolved to save her, and if necessary in spite of her wishes, he now and then spoke to her severely, and to force her to give in did not hesitate to inflict on her the hardest punishment for so pious a person, namely forbidding her to go to Mass. For Cauchon's task was singularly difficult, and he acutely needed help from Jeanne; she could help only by remaining docile. Difficulties rose in every quarter and it was essential to nip them in the bud.

On January 13 Cauchon assembled at his residence six of the assessors whom he acquainted with the information already collected on Jeanne. He decided to appoint a commission presided over by Jean de La Fontaine to examine the question whether the prisoner ought to be arraigned in matters of faith. Ten days later the commission handed in its report, stating that there were valid reasons to proceed against her.

There arrived in Rouen an envoy of Nicolas Bailli, notary royal at Andelot, whom Cauchon the previous winter had charged with the investigations in the Barrois and Lorraine. The man brought very favourable reports on Jeanne, summarised in one sentence. "One found out nothing about her that would not but give pleasure if told of one's own sister." Such a report asked for an immediate adjournment pending further inquiries by the tribunal; but as the Cardinal was complaining of the slowness of the proceedings there was a risk, if the tribunal adjourned, of the trial being transferred from ecclesiastical judges to the sectarians of the University. Cauchon trembled with fear, confiscated the dangerous report, and in a panicky voice ordered the unfortunate messenger to leave Rouen.

On February 14, 15 and 16 Cauchon and the assessors heard some of the witnesses, and divers reports sent in by the investigators were read out. On the 19th someone reminded them of the representative of the Inquisition not being present, an inconceivable situation at a trial dealing with a matter concerning the faith. Cauchon had no alternative other than to adjourn the proceedings at once. Then he hurried to see the deputy of Brother Graverent and between them they drew up the plan of the future line to be taken.

At the next sitting, which was on the following day, Brother Lemaître appeared, but declared that he could not stay because he had not the authority from his superior to do so. He withdrew. Cauchon sent the Grand Inquisitor "a summons to transport himself to this town" as "it devolved on his office" if "his work or other reasonable excuse" kept him away "to accredit Brother Jean Lemaître." But the Inquisitor restricted himself to authorising Brother Lemaître to assist at the trial without taking part in it; and Brother Lemaître did not turn up before March 13. Thus Cauchon won again. Though the Inquisition was present at the trial he alone conducted it and he alone would pronounce sentence.

On February 20 Massieu, the usher, was ordered to let the prisoner know that she would have to appear next day, February 21 at eight in the morning, before the tribunal, sitting in the royal chapel of the castle. When Jeanne received the summons she replied that "she would appear willingly and would tell the truth in her answers," and asked for two favours to be granted, firstly, that "priests from her part of France" be added to the tribunal, and secondly, to be authorised "to hear Mass before appearing." The first request greatly infuriated Cauchon because it showed that Jeanne was still far from trusting him. Even if he had been weak enough to grant the favour the Cardinal of Winchester would certainly not have allowed the presence in Rouen of judges who were favourably inclined to the prisoner; as in that case it was practically sure that she would be sent before the University of Paris, where she would infallibly have become the victim of her enemies' hatred. So Cauchon refused, and to show her how much he disapproved of her answer, on the pretext that she still wore male attire he did not grant the second request either.

The refusal of the second request deeply pained the Maid. Cauchon took his decision only with great regret. However, that was the most efficacious means at his disposal of forcing her to fall in with his views. In spite of their several meetings Jeanne was not yet ready to put her trust in him. Neither the assurance the Duke of Bedford gave, nor the encouragement of her Voices could make her entirely change her mind. She could not admit to herself that a lot of legal subtleties were needed to save her from the fate her enemies reserved for her.

Cauchon, who well knew on which points the more wicked among the assessors would question her, tried in vain to explain the deft answers she should give in reply to certain accusations—not to stick to the truth if it became necessary—and he went out of his way to convince her that it was very much in her interest to give proof of her flexibility and docility before her judges and speak in a moderate voice. Such an attitude filled with good will and the semblance of repentance would have drawn at least the indulgence if not the sympathy of some of the assessors on whose moderation Cauchon had to rely so as not to risk the possibility of finding himself unsupported when passing sentence.

Indignant because of her sense of rectitude and rigid in her feelings, Jeanne refused to hold back her convictions in public without comprehending that such declarations would but further prejudice a tribunal the majority of whose members were decided on condemning her even before she was heard. No compromise was possible between the noble and proud attitude of the Maid whom her detention and her impatience to take up arms again had even more inflamed, and the subtle game based on a profound knowledge of legal procedure that the bishop had to play in order to hoax the tribunal and the Cardinal. Hence the constant tussle which offended Jeanne and irritated Cauchon.

On one point however they did not differ: Jeanne promised not to reveal the secret of her origins. Thus for Henry VI's English subjects and those Frenchmen who were on his side Charles VII would continue to be the "so-called Dauphin," disowned by his mother and disinherited by the Treaty of Troyes. For the same reason Catherine of France, daughter of Isabeau of Bavaria and mother of Henry VI, did not have to fear the awful scandal that would follow if Jeanne revealed who were her real parents, a scandal that would particularly have been dangerous to the future of the double monarchy because it would easily have made the people suspect Catherine's legitimacy, and consequently her son's right to wear the crown of France.

Though out of necessity she agreed to declare herself her

foster-parents' daughter, Jeanne insisted on Cauchon not dwelling on the matter, and she let him understand that she would only vaguely answer the questions put to her on that subject, especially as she refused to deny her attachment to the House of Orléans. And as regards the very basis of the trial she refused in advance to give any precise replies to questions put to her about what her Voices revealed, or in any case not tell the whole truth.

If from the theological point of view the 'bishop could not object against the principle of mental reservations which she intended to use in some of her answers, on the purely legal side he could not help warning her repeatedly of the disastrous consequences if she refused to enlighten the tribunal on the subjects he would bring up. As much as Cauchon wanted to keep the trial, wherever possible, within its essential religious scope Jeanne strove to have it put on the political level which fundamentally was its true essence.

Her intransigent attitude singularly complicated Cauchon's task. Nonetheless he was determined to defend Jeanne—against herself if necessary—and so to save her.

On the morning of February 21, 1431 the tribunal, consisting of Pierre Cauchon, Jean d'Estivet, Jean de La Fontaine, prosecutor, Boisguillaume and Guillaume Manchon, notaries, Jean Massieu, usher, and thirty-six priests, canons, priors, doctors of theology or of canon law, and other clerks secular and laymen, met in the chancel of the royal chapel of the castle of Rouen. In the nave and side-aisle were seated a number of distinguished people who had received permission to be present at the solemn session.

Cauchon who presided read out several documents in detail relative to Jeanne's capture, her transfer to Rouen. Then the charges against her and the decision that had been taken to bring her before the tribunal to answer the charges laid against her were read out. When those long-winded formalities were over—they lasted for about three hours—Cauchon ordered the accused to be brought before him.

Surrounded by several warders Jeanne entered the chapel and went to her seat, to which Jean Massieu led her, in front of the tribunal. Pale and emaciated by her detention, her long hair falling on her shoulders, still dressed as a man, but her suit beginning to wear threadbare and its black colour strongly contrasting with the white chancel lit by many torches, Jeanne sat down on the stool reserved for her. Everybody regarded her carefully. Some pretended to be shocked by her attire, others thought that her attitude was insolent and defiant, but there were those too who could hardly master the sudden admiration she inspired in them.

Calm and serene, supported by the encouragement of her Voices, not at all weakened by the fast she had imposed on herself from the night before till noon—it was Lent—Jeanne waited to be questioned, firmly resolved to defend herself and not to lie about her mission.

Cauchon began with presenting her to the tribunal in these words:

"This girl whom you see, Jeanne, was taken prisoner in a district of our diocese of Beauvais. She is accused of several crimes against orthodoxy which she committed inside our diocese and other places. The Most Serene and Most Christian Prince and Lord our King Henry handed her over to us to be tried in matters of Faith. Also we summoned her to appear today before our tribunal." Then turning to the accused he added, "Jeanne, swear on the Gospel to tell the truth in answer to all the questions we will put to you."

She answered at once. "I do not know on what you want to question me. You might ask me things I do not want to tell you about."

Thus did she let the tribunal clearly know that she would not tell the whole truth.

Cauchon, who wanted to keep the debate strictly in the domain of religion and leave it there, declared, "They will concern matters of Faith."

Jeanne wanted to put her position precisely. "On my father and mother, on my actions since I came to France, I willingly take the oath, but as to my revelations which came from God I spoke of them and confided only in Charles, my king. I would say nothing of my visions to you even if you cut my head off. My secret counsellors forbid me to do so." She stopped for an instant, then added, "In any case I will know in less than a week whether I am authorised to reveal them."

Cauchon abstained from making any comment on the strange declaration, and fearing that Jeanne might take back her promise not to disclose in public the secret of her birth, before anybody had time to ask her what she meant in the last sentence he quickly said in a conciliatory voice, "I repeat: will you swear to speak the truth in answer to the questions concerning the Faith?"

Jeanne hesitated before replying. Then she stated, "on the Faith and only on that," and falling on her knees she put her hands on the Gospel which a clerk brought to her and took the oath. Satisfied and relieved Cauchon hurried through the procedure of questioning her on her identity. "Your name and surname?"

It was a delicate question but Jeanne replied skilfully. "At home they called me Jeannette. Since I came to France, Jeanne." Then she quietly added, "I do not know my nickname!"

Before any of the assessors had time to be astounded by such a flagrant lie by the accused who signed all her letters "Jehanne the Maid," Cauchon hastened to ask, "Place of birth?"

Taking advantage of the right of mental reserve Jeanne replied, "Domrémy."

"Name of father and mother?" continued Cauchon.

On that score Jeanne gave him a truly subtle answer. Separating one word from the other she said, "My ... father ... was called ... Jacques d'Arc." Putting her answer into the past though her foster-father was still alive she intended to recall that her real begetter, the Duc d'Orléans was assassinated twenty-four years ago.

"Name of your mother?" asked Cauchon imperturbably.

"Isabelle," replied Jeanne without hesitation but not adding Romée, and in this her mental reserve was confined to the truth since the surnames of Isabelle and Isabeau are the same, one often used instead of the other.

After asking for a few details concerning her christening Cauchon inquired, "Your age?"

"More or less nineteen years old," Jeanne answered, choosing her words carefully, for this statement which gave her four years less than her actual age was necessary for the cause.

Cauchon said, "Recite Our Father."

"Hear me in the confessional and I will willingly recite it," Jeanne replied.

The bishop refused to. He knew very well that Jeanne would take advantage of the circumstance to ask him for absolution which theologically speaking he would have to give her for the mental reservations she made. Moreover, he could not help thinking that if she were absolved of her sins it would be impossible to refuse her going to Mass which she wanted so much, but in that case he would lose the best means he had of bearing pressure on her. To save himself embarrassment he limited himself to saying, "If I gave you one or two trustworthy persons belonging to the French party then would you recite Our Father to them?"

Cauchon obstinately clung to her reciting the Pater Noster because in those days one firmly believed that those who were possessed by the devil were incapable of reciting the Lord's Prayer, and he wanted to avoid at any price her being suspected of having intercourse with demons.

But Jeanne was obstinate too: shocked in her deep piety because she was forced to play with the truth she badly wanted to receive absolution from a confessor. Stubbornly she replied, "No! Except if they hear me in the confessional."

Cauchon decided to give up the subject, for he saw that she would not give in. He looked at her severely, then said, "Now, Jeanne, I forbid you to leave," he put emphasis on the next three words, "without our consent the prison which was assigned to you in the castle of Rouen."

Trusting her Voices which assured her of her salvation Jeanne loudly replied, "I accept no interdiction! If I escape nobody can accuse me of betraying my Faith: because I give it to nobody! And I protest against the bonds I am tied with."

"*Eh!*" exclaimed Cauchon. "You tried several times to escape from other prisons. Jeanne! That is why we put you in irons," and he added a sentence the real meaning of which she alone could appreciate, "so that you should be guarded more safely."

"True enough," Jeanne conceded, "that elsewhere I wanted to

escape and even now I still should like to." Letting her voice drop she went on, "Every prisoner has the right to escape."

Jeanne's anger frightened Cauchon in so far as he feared that she might make unwise declarations on that very delicate subject, so he quickly closed the session.

Using the intense cold in the chapel as his excuse, Cauchon decided to hold the further sessions in the "parliament chamber" at the end of the great hall of the castle. That room had the welcome advantage in winter of possessing a fine fireplace; moreover, it was much smaller than the royal chapel which allowed him considerably to reduce the number of those who were present at the trial. For he realised that the session of the day before was plainly to the Maid's advantage, and the commentaries in the town and among the assessors of the tribunal made him fear of being accused of softness or inefficiency and the conduct of the trial taken from him.

On Thursday February 22 a few minutes before eight o'clock Massieu, the usher, went to fetch Jeanne to take her before the tribunal. On their way through the courtyard they went by the chapel, and Jeanne asked his permission to enter for a moment. Massieu thought it was right to give it. Jeanne was praying before the altar when d'Estivet appeared on his way to the tribunal. Through the open door he saw the accused praying fervently, and started insulting the usher, shouting, "Criminal, who makes you so bold as to allow this excommunicated harlot approach a church without permission? I will have you flung into a dungeon, where you will see neither moon nor sun if you do that again."

With tears in her eyes Jeanne followed Massieu whom these low insults had also shocked. From that day onward the chapel was carefully guarded to stop Jeanne from praying there on her way to the tribunal.

Already, at the beginning of the second session Cauchon, wishing to recover his reputation, wanted to make a show of his authority, and said in a firm voice to the accused, "Jeanne, we request you under the penalty of canonical sanction to take the oath as you took it yesterday to tell the whole truth, nothing but the truth, in all that concerns the trial."

166

Jeanne, whom the attitude of the tribunal on the day before only strengthened in her determination to make it dance to her tune, and who was still trembling at the thought of the insult of the prosecutor, answered drily, "I took the oath yesterday. That should suffice."

In a softer voice Cauchon said, "You must take the oath, Jeanne. Nobody, whoever he is," he put emphasis on the following words, "prince or commoner, if he is required in a matter of Faith can refuse to take the oath."

"I did so yesterday. That should suffice," said Jeanne, then could not resist blurting out, "You weary me too much!"

A scene similar to the one of the day before repeated itself. Cauchon insisted on the oath and the Maid continued stubbornly to refuse it. In the same fashion as on the day before he had to be content with the oath "solely concerning matters of Faith." After that the bishop asked Jean Beaupère, theologian of the University of Paris, to do the questioning. He began clumsily, telling Jeanne to "answer the truth."

"Some questions I will answer truthfully," she said, "but there might be others which I shall not answer at all."

Beaupère realised that it was useless insisting, and at once he put the question, "How old were you when you left your father's house?"

Jeanne, who could not remember precisely what she said the day before concerning her age, replied rather insolently, "I do not know!"

Beaupère did not insist but went on with the cross-questioning. Jeanne explained that she had learnt to sew and to spin, and in her youth she looked after the house but did not go "into the meadows with the sheep and other animals."

The assessor asked her whether she went "each year to confess her sins." She answered that she went to confession regularly, either to the vicar or some other priest, adding that on several occasions "she confessed to mendicant priests," which again was unnecessary and clumsy, for the begging orders had already for a long time indulged in untiring propaganda for the French party in the provinces occupied by the English. Jeanne perceived the blunder she made, and when Beaupère asked how frequently she took communion she answered violently, "Leave me in peace!" And in order to get rid of the subject she made a declaration concerning her Voices in which with great precision she explained the circumstances wherein the visitations took place.

Expecting to confuse her Beaupère interrupted, "How could you see the light that accompanied the voices if the light came from the side?"

"Leave me in peace!" Jeanne replied, and took up the thread again.

The theologian stopped her and asked a question which, though sounding innocent enough, was of remarkable black subtlety. "What advice did the voice give you on the salvation of your soul?"

Her answer was swift, to the point and perfect. "To behave myself well and go frequently to church." Then she went on with her declaration, stating that the Voice said to her that "it was necessary for her to come to France." She spoke of her reticence in the beginning, then of her submission to the order God gave her. When she related that going through Auxerre she heard Mass in the cathedral of that town Beaupère asked,

"On whose advice did you don male attire?"

Jeanne refused to answer; when pressed she became annoyed. "I leave to nobody such a heavy charge!" and continued her story.

Several of the assessors managed to interrupt her when she stopped to take breath. One of them said, "What do you think of the Duc d'Orléans?" Deeply shaken since it touched her on the raw Jeanne replied in words that made Cauchon tremble, "I know that God loves the Duc d'Orléans. I had more revelations concerning him than of any other living man the King excepted!"

Fortunately for Cauchon another assessor began to question her on the male attire she wore. Though annoyed to hear the same question again she nevertheless understood that she owed the tribunal some explanation on that score. "It was necessary for me to wear men's clothes. I think that my Counsellor was right in recommending their wear." After that she continued her tale, relating how she reached Chinon, where she told the King that she wanted to "go to fight against the English."

Beaupère asked for details about the meeting, adding, "Was there any light?"

"Leave me in peace!" answered Jeanne.

"Did you see an angel above your king's head?"

"Spare me! Leave me in peace!" cried Jeanne, and in her irritation could not refrain from saying, "the King saw many apparitions and had beautiful revelations," and carried away she added the unnecessary words, "he also."

On that subject Beaupère wanted to hear more details. "What revelations? What sort of apparitions?"

"I will not tell you," Jeanne replied insolently. "Go and ask the King and he will answer you."

Regaining control of herself she went on with her story. When she mentioned her Voices again one of the assessors asked her, "Do you often hear those voices?"

"No day goes by without hearing them," she answered. "In fact, I very much need them."

Beaupère wanting to confuse her: "What reward did you ask from your voices?"

Her answer touched straight the hearts of several assessors. "Never any other final reward than the salvation of my soul."

Then she want back to her story, and when she was speaking of the siege of Paris Beaupère put the insidious question, "Did you not order the attack on a feast day?"

Completely exasperated Jeanne said again, "Leave me in peace!"

In fear lest in her anger the Maid went beyond the limits of impudence or uttered serious indiscretions in the course of her declarations Cauchon decided to intervene, that is he closed the session.

The third public session took place on the following Saturday. Cauchon summoned sixty assessors, and as there was not enough room he had to reduce the number of the English guests. It was a clever stroke because not only did he bring in new councillors but also managed to eliminate most of the spectators who spent their time telling all and sundry that he was unfit to preside over the tribunal.

The sitting began with the taking of the oath.

"Take the oath, Jeanne, unconditionally."

Jeanne made no answer.

"Come, take the oath," Cauchon repeated.

The accused remained silent.

Losing his patience a little the bishop said, "Will you take the oath?"

Irritated by the repetition of the formality even though it was obligatory Jeanne still refused to take it without her conditions. "On my faith, you may ask me questions I refuse to answer, especially about my revelations. Peradventure you might force me to reveal what I promised not to, and then I would perjure myself. Is that what you want? I say to you: take care!" And referring to their daily meetings in her room she added these words the real meaning of which Cauchon alone could understand, "You who call yourself my judge you have a heavy task. You heap too much on me."

Cauchon tried to appease her. "Come, Jeanne, purely and simply take the oath."

"Leave me in peace," Jeanne replied. "I took the oath twice. All the clergy of Rouen and of Paris could not condemn me even if they had leave to. On my behalf I will willingly speak the truth, but I cannot tell everything." She added in a low voice which, however, everybody heard, "In any case a week would not be long enough for it."

Once again Cauchon tried to reason with her by telling her that she should take the advice of the councillors present, some of whom felt strongly for her. "Ask your assessors whether you should or not take the oath?"

But obstinately Jeanne refused to understand that her trial could be of very short duration, and that would automatically be followed by a death sentence. She remained adamant. "On my part I am willing to tell the truth, and that is all. Do not speak of it again!"

Cauchon warned her again. "You arouse suspicion if you refuse to take the oath," he said, and as she still refused he said in an angry voice, "I advise you, Jeanne, I order you to swear, otherwise you greatly risk being condemned for the crimes you are accused of."

"Leave me in peace!" was all she answered.

"For the last time I request you to take the oath," Cauchon said. Then he delivered a long sermon explaining why it was necessary to take the oath, and for the sixth time he told her to take it.

Inflexibly Jeanne replied that she was ready to swear to the truth of the facts "concerning the trial." Tired out, Cauchon gave in, and she took the oath on her conditions.

Beaupère began to cross-question her, putting many questions to her about her Voices and the circumstances in which they appeared. Without hesitation Jeanne explained that she had asked "advice on what to answer at the trial," and added that the night before the Voice said to her, "Answer bravely and God will help you!"

The theologian wanted to know whether the voice "forbade her to reply to certain questions."

"I shall not answer you," Jeanne said, explaining that "And I had revelations about the King too but will not tell them to you." Then she went on, "Last night the Voice said many things for the good of the King. Ah! I should like the King to know of them even if I do not drink wine till Easter—because he will be much happier with it at his dinner."

In a wicked fashion Beaupère tried to trip her up by making her agree to her having supernatural means of corresponding with Charles VII which would be proof of her having relations with the powers of Hell, and then she could be charged with being possessed by the Devil.

Jeanne gave a skilful answer. "I do not know whether the Voice would obey me unless it were God's wish."

The theologian was defeated, the politician made one more effort. "Did your counsellor reveal that you will escape from prison?"

When he heard the question Cauchon trembled with fear, but there was no cause for it because with sharp insolence Jeanne said, "Is that any business of yours? Am I to tell you?"

Beaupère harped again on the voices, putting one insidious question after the other about the light that accompanied the visitations. With admirable prudence Jeanne said, "You will not yet get this one. Children say that people are often hanged for speaking the truth."

With that answer Jeanne finally conquered part of the tribunal, not only the secret partisans whom Cauchon had specially brought in as assessors, but also some of the others who were impressed by her dignity and her excellent replies. Murmurs of sympathy began to be heard in court.

To make good his losses Beaupère put a frightening and unsolvable question to her. "Are you in a state of Grace?" First there was complete silence, then protests rose from every side. Unable to hold himself back Jean Lefèvre, one of the assessors, called out, "That is an awful question, the accused need not answer it!"

An answer in the negative would have condemned her as a sinner, and if she said yes it would have been sheer heresy full of false pride, for nobody has the right to be certain of being in a state of Grace.

Jeanne's sublime answer frustrated the theologian's wicked plot. "If I am not," she said, "may God put me in it. If I am may God keep me in it!"

Intense emotion followed her words and many of the assessors, even among those who were hostile to Jeanne, could not hold back their admiration for an answer on a point that specialists would have feared to tackle. Beaupère swiftly changed the subject: he asked Jeanne about her childhoon in Domrémy, seeking unsuccessfully to find proof of witchcraft while she was near the fountain of Groseilliers under the Arche-aux-Dames. He did not succeed in getting the better of her: every answer was clear and to the point. Towards the end of the session the representative of the University tried to lay another trap. "Would you accept a woman's dress?" he asked.

"Give me one," Jeanne replied, "and let me go. Otherwise no. I am satisfied with this one since it pleases God that I wear it."

Once more Beaupère was defeated.

Cauchon adjourned the court. In his heart he was well satisfied with the way the session had gone.

In the afternoon he went to see Jeanne to compliment her on the excellent answers she gave to Jean Beaupère. The Duchess of Bedford was present, and added her congratulations to those of the bishop, and the two of them, taking advantage of the Maid's good mood, obtained her agreement to have female attire made for her and to prove her good will appear in it before the tribunal. Soon after her visitors left her a tailor, Jeannotin Simon, came to see Jeanne, sent by the duchess. On the pretext of having to take exact measurements he began to behave indecently; but the prisoner only strengthened her decision to continue wearing male attire.

For her dinner Cauchon sent her a splendid carp to show his satisfaction with her becoming sensible at last. In the night she became sick, vomited and ran a high temperature. The watch called Warwick who came at once and sent for physicians. Two of the best doctors of Rouen, Guillaume de la Chambre and Guillaume Desjardins, after consulting with Jean Tiphaine, the Duchess of Bedford's physician, bled Jeanne which greatly relieved the sick girl. The news of the bad state of her health soon spread through the castle. On Sunday morning, February 25, d'Estivet was one of the first to hear that she was ill. He hurried to her and asked her what the cause of her ailment was. Jeanne explained that she ate the carp Cauchon sent her and she suspected she had been poisoned. The prosecutor became furious, and pretending to believe that she accused the bishop with wanting to kill her, he showered coarse insults on her, treating her as a whore and a lewd woman till Warwick appeared, and reminding him that he was the governor of the castle, threw the odious prosecutor out, then gave the strictest orders to have all food given her first tasted.

The Maid remained in bed for two days during which the Duchess of Bedford never ceased watching over and comforting her.

In the morning of Tuesday, February 27, the tribunal sat again as Jeanne seemed well enough to answer the questions the assessors would put her. Surrounded by twenty-three assessors Cauchon asked her again to take the same oath. Jeanne declared that she would swear only as regards "the objects of the trial" and assured them once more that she "would not tell all she knew." Cauchon did not insist too much and called on Jean Beaupère to question her.

"And how do you feel Jeanne since Saturday?" he asked.

"You can see for yourself. I am as well as I can be," she replied. She was still far from well.

After having asked her "whether she fasted every day during this Lent," which was answered by the sharp reply, "Has that anything to do with the trial? Yes? Good. In that case I fasted throughout Lent," Beaupère again questioned her on her Voices.

Jeanne upheld her previous declarations, affirming that the Voice told her to "answer bravely," and repeated that she would not answer certain questions because "there are revelations that are for the King of France but not for you!"

The theologian tried to confuse her by speaking of her apparitions, their frequency and the physical shapes they had. To all that Jeanne gave clear answers, though not without obvious irritation. Then he spoke to her of her man's clothes, and Jeanne, who was still smarting from the insolence of the tailor the Duchess of Bedford had sent to her, made this reply: "All I do is by the command of God. If He ordered me to dress differently I would do so because it was ordered by Him."

Beaupère did not insist, but moved on to another subject. "When you saw your king for the first time was there an angel above his head?"

Jeanne perfectly understood the intention behind the question: namely to accuse her and Charles VII of witchcraft. "By Our Lady," she replied, "I do not know whether there was. I did not see him."

Disappointed by her answer which he could not use to incriminate her he still harped on the same subject though from a different angle. "Was there light in that place?"

Jeanne extricated herself with a joke that made everybody laugh: "I bet there was! More than three hundred knights and fifty torches! Not to mention the spiritual light."

Beaupère continued questioning her: "How did your king come to believe you?"

Keeping her promise not to reveal the secret of her birth Jeanne simply said, "He had excellent proof." Aiming at him she added, "And the advice of the clerics!"

The University's representative tried to take advantage of her. "What kind of revelations did he have?"

"You shall not get that out of me this year," said Jeanne who nonetheless did point out "that the King had a sign concerning her," but she refrained from explaining it, and maintained that "other doctors, other theologians and other investigators" had approved of her mission. "The clerics were of the opinion that there was only good in me."

Beaupère had to retreat. But he put to her a number of questions about the sword which she had brought from Sainte-Catherine-de-Fierbois, yet he did not succeed in convincing her of having bewitched it. She explained that when she was taken prisoner she no longer had that sword, and refused to tell him in what circumstances she abandoned it. As a matter of fact, Jeanne broke it on the back of one of the many prostitutes who followed the army during the siege of Paris. She told him that later she used a sword taken from a Burgundian, "a good sword for fighting and giving good hits and good cuts." She mentioned in passing that the sword, her horses (she had an excellent stable), and "other objects worth more that 12,000 ecus" were looked after by the brothers d'Arc.

Beaupère spoke of the standard she carried at the siege of Orléans. She willingly gave him a description of it and said there was "written on top the names Jhésus—Maria." With that she admitted in public that she belonged to the Third Order of St Francis. The rest of the interrogation was taken up with secondary matters, mostly the military operations round Orléans and Jargeau. Then the court rose.

The fifth public session took place on March 1. In accordance with canon law Cauchon requested her "to take an oath to tell purely and simply all the truth."

This time again Jeanne agreed to swear to say the truth but only on "what concerned this trial." Cauchon did not force the issue and Jeanne took the oath, saying she would speak the truth on "what concerns this trial" and tell as much as she would before the Pope in Rome. That gave Beaupère the chance to ask her, "You speak of Monseigneur our Pope? Which one you consider the real one?"

"Are there two?" Jeanne asked ironically.

"Did you not receive," he insisted, "a letter from the Comte d'Armagnac to ask you which one of the three pontiffs to obey?"

Jeanne did not deny that she received in July 1429 a letter from the Comte d'Armagnac asking her to let him know to which one of the three candidates to the Holy See—Martin V, Clement VIII, and Benedict XIV—one owed obedience. But she firmly stated that the correspondence read out to her contained "only part of the answer" she gave at the time, and added, "As far as I am concerned I believe that we have to obey Monseigneur the Pope who is in Rome."

Beaupère asked "whether it was her habit to put the names of Jesus and Mary with a cross in her letters."

"That depends," she answered. "Now and then I put a cross to tell the person I wrote to not to do what I said in my letter."

They read out some of the letters she sent to the King of England, the Duke of Bedford and other English captains. Jauntily she accepted the responsibility for all she had written, though she queried some details such as "Give back to the Maid" when it should have been "Give back to the King." She realised that her letters made a bad impression on most of the members of the tribunal. To get back the initiative she made a prophecy which was sure to make the fifty-eight assessors who sat with Cauchon think twice. "I tell you that within seven years the English will lose a bigger battle than the one before Orléans, and they will lose the whole of France! "

The interrogator tried to overcome the effect her words made on the opportunists. "How do you know that?" he asked.

"Through the revelation I had, and I am as sure of it as I am of seeing you all in front of me."

Beaupère quickly changed the subject and spoke of the apparitions. "Who told you that that would happen?"

"St Catherine and St Marguerite; and not a day goes by without my hearing them."

The theologian questioned her on the physical aspects of the apparitions, endeavouring to get her to contradict herself, which would have given him his chance of catching her out on the details, and then to argue that she lied all along the line. But she gave her answer without the slightest embarrassment and with a remarkable subtlety of mind.

"How do you recognise whether that . . . that thing that appears before you is man or woman."

"By their voices! "

"The saints who appear before you have they hair?"

Jeanne could not resist making an ironical remark. "What a funny question," she said.

Tenaciously Beaupère continued to insist, "Is there something between the crown and the hair?"

"No."

"Was the hair long and did it reach down to the shoulder?"

Infuriated by that kind of question Jeanne replied, "I know nothing."

Nonetheless Beaupère went on and when Jeanne said "the voice was lovely, sweet and humble," and spoke "the language of France" he interrupted her: "So St Marguerite does not speak English?"

Jeanne gave this smart reply: "Why should she speak English when she does not belong to the English party?"

"On their heads did they have gold ringlets or not?"

"I know nothing about that."

"And you, Jeanne, did you wear rings?"

She did not reply but addressed Cauchon. "You took one. Give it back." Then turning to Beaupère, "The Burgundians took another. If you have it let me see it." She explained that on that ring was the Franciscan devise "Jhésus-Maria" engraved, and she asked him to give to a church another ring, a present from Jean d'Arc. For at the moment of her capture Jeanne possessed many gold rings she had been given, and due to her remarkable memory she remembered every piece of jewellery she had ever worn. She did not forget to add, in order to save herself from a supplementary accusation, "I never cured anybody with my rings."

Beaupère returned to the voices. "What were the promises your voices made?"

"This is not the way to conduct a trial," she said. But she added, "Among other things they tell me that the King will get his kingdom back."

"Were you promised anything else?" Beaupère insisted.

"Yes, but I will not tell you. It has nothing to do with the trial. Before the three months are up I will reveal another secret."

But Beaupère wanted to know more. "Did your voices tell you that you will be freed within three months?"

"It has nothing to do with the trial," Jeanne said. "I do not know when I will be set free. Those who want to take me away from this life might have to leave before me."

Determined to force her to betray her secret thoughts Beaupère continued to insist. "Did your counsel tell you that you would leave your present prison within three months?"

"Speak of it again in three months' time and I will reply," said Jeanne, then turning to Cauchon she said, "Ask the assessors whether that has anything to do with the trial?"

Thus appealed to, Cauchon, who feared she might say something rash, was compelled to consult the assessors. The majority were of the opinion that it concerned the trial. Cauchon dared not contradict them.

"Well then," said Jeanne when he gave her the results of their deliberations, "I always told you that I shall not tell everything. Some day I will have to be set free, but if I tell you I want to be given notice. Also I ask for a respite."

After that skilful answer Cauchon breathed more freely, whereas Beaupère looked like one who achieved victory. "Ah! Ah! Your voices forbade you to tell the truth!"

"Do you want me to tell you what will happen to the kingdom of France?" she retorted and stated again, "I do know that the King will gain the kingdom of France."

Beaupère insisted no more. He moved quickly on to another subject, and spoke again of her apparitions. About St Michael he put a question which, coming from a priest, sounded rather curious. "Was he naked when he appeared?"

Jeanne replied with ironical contempt. "Do you think that Our Lord has not the money to clothe him?"

Beaupère stopped putting those sort of questions to her, for they made him look ridiculous, and he asked her once more on a matter she hitherto refused to speak of. "What proof did you give your king of your Divine mission?"

"I never stop telling you that you will not get it out of me," Jeanne answered. "Go and ask him," she added, losing her temper a little.

But Beaupère went on insisting. Under Cauchon's watchful eyes he queried, "Do you know what the proof was you handed your king?"

"I shall not tell you! I made a promise in a certain place and it would perjure me if I revealed it."

"Whom did you promise?"

"To St Catherine and St Marguerite. And I showed it to the King. I promised without them asking me to. It was on my own initiative because far too many people would have asked for it if I had not made the promise to the saints."

"When you revealed the proof to your king was there anybody with him?"

"I don't think so," Jeanne answered cautiously, conjuring up the scene in Chinon, in the course of which she brought Charles VII formal proof that Isabeau's bastard was she and not he. "But there were many people nearby," she added.

Having been unable to make her speak on a subject he wanted to know so much about, Beaupère ceased questioning her, and Cauchon, strongly displeased by all questions asked on that subject, quickly put at end to the session.

The sixth and last public sitting took place on the following day, March 3. The little comedy of taking the oath did not occur this time. Cauchon simply asked her to take the oath, and Jeanne replied, "I have already done so, but I am ready to take it again."

Cauchon did not insist and let Beaupère start questioning her. He put several questions again on the physical shapes of St Michael, and SS Catherine and Marguerite. Skilfully Jeanne avoided the traps he set her, and when he attacked her on very subtle theological points she replied, "You will have nothing more than what I already said in my answers."

Beaupère returned to a subject to which he attached immense importance. "Did you find out through revelation that you would escape?"

"That does not concern the trial. Would you want me to speak against myself?"

Beaupère did not let her rebuff him with her answer. "Did not your voices tell you anything on that score?"

"That is not for the trial! I call God as my witness!" said Jeanne and in a loud voice she added as if it were an afterthought, "On my faith, I know not the day and the hour of my escape."

"Did your voices say a few words about that ... in a general sense?" Beaupère inquired.

"Really!" replied Jeanne, then explained, "They told me that I would be freed but I do not know the day and the hour."

As satisfied with the answer as Cauchon was embarrassed by it, Beaupère spoke again of her male attire "which she could not leave off wearing without God's approval," adding that if she had to do so "it would have been on the request of Mlle de Luxembourg and Mme de Beaurevoir." Then he sought to convince her that it was superstitious to turn her banner round and round before altars or churches and have it sprinkled with holy water. To all those allegations she formally answered by denying them and declaring, "To my companions-at-arms I said, 'Go in bravely among the English!' and I went in myself."

Then Beaupère tried to convince her that she was idolatrous, reproaching her with having allowed "her hands, feet and robe be kissed."

"I could not help it if they kissed my hands, feet and clothes." Then she said touchingly, "Poor people came to me unbidden."

She was then questioned on details of very secondary importance—a palfrey she was supposed to have taken from the Bishop of Senlis and maintained that she had "bought it for two hundred gold *saluts*," but sent back "because it had no stamina"—her relations with Catherine de la Rochelle and Brother Richard. Beaupère hoped that her answers would compromise her with that mad woman and the visionary, but did not succeed in spite of the insidious questions he put. As regards her incarceration in Beaurevoir she denied that she attempted to kill herself "when she jumped," and as Beaupère treacherously tried to connect her attempted escape with one of her previous declarations, she allowed herself the pleasure of repeating what she had said at the time.

"I prefer to give my soul back to God to being in the hands of the English."

Beaupère asked her whether she had ever "blasphemed the name of God."

"Never. I curse not the saints. I have not the habit of swearing," Jeanne said.

Considering that the session had lasted long enough Cauchon ordered Jeanne to be taken out. Then he told his assessors that the public sessions were over and the answers of the accused would minutely be examined so as to decide on whether it were necessary to question her again on certain points. Finally he forbade all who had assisted in court to leave the town before the end of the trial.

From March 4 to 9 Cauchon assembled many of the assessors in his residence to examine Jeanne's replies. After discussing the text for a considerable while the assessors reached the conclusion that it was necessary to put a number of supplementary questions to her. Cauchon did not object, and on the pretext of it being more practical he decided on the new sessions taking place in Jeanne's own room, which allowed him to reduce the number of his aides.

The complementary sessions took place from March 10 to 17. They were endless. Cauchon went out of his way to drag it out as long as possible since the Grand Inquisitor had not yet given his deputy permission to take part at the meetings. At last the permit arrived on March 11, but Brother Lemaître asked first to examine carefully all the relative documents and was not present at the trial before March 12. Besides, he reduced the Inquisition's rôle to one person—himself. He did not nominate law officers as was his duty; was content with the assistance of his chief collaborator Brother Isambart de la Pierre, and two theologians, Thomas Fieftot and Pasquier de Vaux, though he did not forget to nominate Jean Taquel, general notary to the Inquisition, as investigator and registrar, which allowed the last-named to take copies of all the papers concerning the trial.

For an entire week Jean de La Fontaine, chosen by Cauchon as examiner, questioned Jeanne in the presence of Nicolas Midi, Gérard Feuillet, Massieu and Jean Sécard. The questions brought no new light on the case. At the most they gave Jeanne the opportunity to explain some points about her childhood in Domrémy, her arrival in Chinon and her battles with the English.

At the session of March 10 she gave details of her capture at Compiègne, and reminded them, as she already had told them at the trial, that her Voices had warned her that "she would be taken before the feast of St John, that it had to happen like that, and she would have to accept it all" because God would help her.

On March 12, in answer to a question put by Jean de La Fontaine concerning the young man who had her summoned to appear in court in Toul for breach of promise, Jeanne explained that she "had taken the vow to remain virgin as long as it pleased God," and pointed out that the Voices often called her "Jeanne the Maid."

When de La Fontaine asked, "When you left father and mother did you not think of sinning?" Jeanne answered, "As God commanded it it had to be done." And she added these words which calmed her conscience a little because of the lies she said when the names of her parents was asked, "Had I a hundred fathers and a hundred mothers, were I a king's daughter, even so I should have left! "

In the afternoon without him being aware of it Jean de La Fontaine gave her a further opportunity to speak of her real family. "How would you have freed the Duc d'Orléans?" he asked.

"I would have taken enough prisoners to get him back," said Jeanne. "And if I had not enough I would have crossed the sea to take him out of England by force."

In the course of those two days the questions dealt chiefly on the proof Jeanne gave Charles VII and which she refused to divulge. That subject was still to the fore during the next sessions. Interrogated without respite on that point Jeanne feared that she might blurt out by mistake something that could betray her, and she replied, speaking in a sort of parable, her aim to deceive the assessors who tried hard to make her admit that at Chinon an angel put a crown on the King's head. She pretended to give in as they wanted her to, yet was careful to mix true details with sheer fiction, confusing all to such an extent that the assessors could make neither head nor tail of most of her answers.

On March 14 Jean de La Fontaine, while preparing the questions he was going to put to Jeanne, informed Cauchon that he intended to ask her why she had implicated and threatened him at the public session of February 24. The cunning prelate, who had no desire to enter into a discussion with Jeanne in front of witnesses, especially as he knew what was behind her words, quickly told de La Fontaine that he could not assist at the afternoon session because he had to watch over the procedure to be adopted when dealing with the answers the accused had given.

In the morning de La Fontaine interrogated Jeanne. After he had questioned her as was his habit, on her saints he suddenly said, "You said that Monsignor de Beauvais incurred danger when he charged you. What does that mean? What sort of danger did Monsignor de Beauvais incur, and what about the others?"

To that leading question Jeanne answered with remarkable subtlety. "What is was," she explained, for she knew that Cauchon would be told of it and she wanted to remind him of their secret agreement, "and what I said to Monsignor de Beauvais: 'You say you are my judge. I do not know whether you are. But you will do well not to pass judgment on me because you would put yourself in great peril. I warn you because if Our Lord punishes you I did my duty by telling you in advance?'

De La Fontaine wanted to know more on the matter. "What kind of danger is that?"

"St Catherine told me that I would receive succour. I do not know whether I will be freed or whether during the trial some perturbation will bring about my freedom. I think it will be either one or the other." Then she added these words, "My Voices tell me that I will be freed, and they say: 'Accept everything, do not worry about your martyrdom, you will eventually come to the Kingdom of Paradise.'" So that there should be no misunderstanding she explained, "I call martyrdom the pain and adversity from which I suffer in my prison."

The assessor tried to confuse her by asking whether "she was sure to be saved" and certain that she would not be "damned in Hell."

"I firmly believe in what my Voices told me: I will be saved!"

"This is a weighty answer," de La Fontaine could not help saying.

"I also consider it a great treasure," Jeanne said.

During the afternoon session de La Fontaine brought up the declarations she made in the morning. Jeanne confirmed them. Then he asked her if she had ever denied God. She loudly defended herself against such an accusation, though admitted having occasionally said, "Oh my God!" or "St John!" or "Our Lady!" without them being anything else but a familiar exclamation.

Questioned again on Thursday March 15 Jeanne answered not only the inevitable questions put to her about her saints, but also several others, asking for details on her attempted escape from Beaulieu and her constant refusal to wear female attire. It was the same at the two sessions of Saturday the 17th, which, as the three previous ones, were held without Cauchon being present, without any new light being shed on the trial, except for Jeanne refusing at the morning session to rely on the Church Militant—the Pope, the prelates, the clergy and the mass of the people—but completely on the Church Triumphant—God, the saints and the angels.

"I rely on Our Lord," she said, "who sent me to Our Lady, and all the blessed saints in Paradise. To me Our Lord and the Church are one. That is not difficult to believe, so why do you make difficulties?"

Before the afternoon session Jean de La Fontaine came to see Jeanne in her room. The assessor, who had assisted at all the public sessions and at all the supplementary ones, had come in the end to feel deep sympathy for her. It had struck him that it was his solemn duty to warn her of the grave dangers she incurred if she refused to submit to the Church Militant. He had decided on the visit in order to calm his conscience; and to give it greater weight he brought with him two preaching brothers, Isambart de la Pierre and Martin Ladvenu, assistants of the vice-inquisitor who shared his views.

Using their great persuasive powers they succeeded in convincing her to take a less intransigent attitude in matters of religion. Towards the end of the afternoon session Jean de La Fontaine put to her the question she was expecting. "Does it seem to you that you are in duty bound to tell the Pope, the vicar of God, the whole truth on all matters affecting your faith and conscience?"

"I request you to take me before him," Jeanne replied, "and before him I will answer all I have to answer."

De La Fontaine had that answer added to the records, and after questioning her on different matters, especially on the inscription of Jhésus-Maria engraved on one of her favourite rings he put an end to the proceedings for the day.

In the evening Cauchon was informed of Jeanne's replies. When he read that Jeanne made an appeal to the Pope he became furious, for the entire plan he had so carefully prepared would collapse, as the English would never agree to her being sent to Rome, but would take the prisoner from him and try her for political reasons. He made inquiries on who saw Jeanne between the sessions, and when he found out he immediately summoned Martin Ladvenu and Brother Isambart de la Pierre, and made a terrible scene. Fearing for his life Martin Ladvenu hastened to leave Rouen with the intention of never coming back; Brother Isambart at once went to complain to Jean Lemaître, who protested to Cauchon, warning him that if even the slightest misfortune befell any of his assistants he would definitely withdraw from the trial. All Cauchon could do was to ask the preaching brothers to hold their tongues, but could not resist letting Isambart de la Pierre know that "if he interfered once more by trying to help Jeanne he would be thrown into the Seine."

That was not the first occasion that Cauchon thought himself forced to intervene in so violent a manner to avoid the impetuousness of others to thwart the clever plan he had carefully prepared in all its minute detail. Already he had unhesitatingly on a trivial pretext sent to prison Nicolas de Houppeville, who at the beginning of the trial opined that "Jeanne having already been examined" by the clergy of Poitiers and the Archbishop of Rheims, superior of the Bishop of Beauvais, Cauchon had no right to judge her. Later another cleric, Jean Lohier, whom Cauchon had requested to give his opinion, declared that legally the trial was void in law because several fundamental principles were not observed. This so infuriated Cauchon that Lohier judged it prudent at once to leave the town. And Jean de Chatillon, Archdeacon of Evreux, who during the first sessions voiced similar opinions without the same firmness, was forbidden by Massieu, on Cauchon's order, to set foot in court again.

As regards Jeanne's request for an appeal to the Pope Cauchon decided to consider it as null and void. Since the beginning of the trial Cauchon had taken similar liberties. Several times he ordered the clerks of the court to ignore certain replies of the accused which he believed were against her interests in so far as they might cause the case to be taken away from him. Jeanne had not failed to notice that not all her replies were put exactly and completely into the records. She complained, saying, "Ah, you write down everything that is against me, but you do not want to write down what is for me . . ." Cauchon pretended not to have heard her observation, but when one of the assessors, believing that it was his duty to draw his attention to what the Maid had said, spoke up, in an irritated voice he shouted to the tiresome man, "Hold your tongue, the devil take you!"

The person who in public could thus treat one of his collaborators had even less scruple when the tribunal was not sitting to give orders to suppress such and such a passage if he considered that it went against Jeanne's interests. Every means was acceptable to him as long as it helped him to achieve success in the enormously ticklish work he had set out to accomplish.

As Jeanne continued, in spite of their daily conversations, to withhold her entire confidence from him, Cauchon thought of indirectly strengthening his influence over her by authorising her to confess to one of his assessors, Nicolas Loyseleur, Canon of Rouen, who was all for him and who, like so many others, was secretly for the French party. Going to her some time in the evening, at other times during the day, depending on the occasion, the priest brought her great comfort by his very presence. He used their meetings cleverly to suggest to her some of the answers to the leading questions that would be put to her. Then he went to relate everything to Cauchon who due to him was informed in detail of the state of mind of the accused, which, however, did not stop Cauchon, since he believed that one could never be careful enough, from having Loyseleur watched by his clerks who, hidden behind the hangings, recorded all their conversations.

On Sunday March 18 Cauchon called a dozen of the assessors to his residence to deliberate on what course to adopt next in the trial. The study of the records of the public sessions and supplementary sessions took over two days. Finally, it was decided to extract from Jeanne's recorded answers a certain number on which Cauchon would ask the opinions of the doctors of Rouen and Paris before passing sentence.

On Saturday March 24 Jean de La Fontaine, accompanied by six assessors went to Jeanne's room. Guillaume Mauchon read out the long records that contained the questions put to the accused and the answers she gave. In the morning of Palm Sunday March 25, Cauchon, bringing with him four assessors, went to see Jeanne and made this offer: he would give her permission to go to Mass since she did not cease asking to on condition that she agreed to dress as a woman.

Jeanne refused, saying, "I ask to be allowed to hear Mass in male attire. This attire does not interfere with my conscience and to wear it is not against the Church!"

Cauchon did not fail to take notice of this further refusal to wear clothes of her own sex which in any case he had expected and for which he was grateful, for in the plan he had conceived to save the Maid, the matter of her attire played an essential part. As for Jeanne, she never was more adamant in refusing to discard her male clothes, as several English soldiers had quite recently tried to rape her while she slept. She defended herself vigorously; her shouts brought the professional warders to her side, and Warwick when told of it meted out severe punishment to the authors of the aggression. Since then instead of sleeping naked as was the custom of the time she slept fully dressed, realising that her doublet and breeches were the most efficacious protection.

On March 26 Cauchon declared the preparatory trial closed, and announced to the twelve assessors he summoned to his residence that the trial proper was now opened. He invited d'Estivet, the prosecuting advocate of the case, to present his conclusions in the shape of articles on each of which Jeanne would be requested to give an explanation, it being understood that if she refused to do so she would automatically be considered convicted of the charges brought against her.

On March 27 the trial proper opened in a hall near the great gallery of the castle. Cauchon presided, surrounded by the Vice-Inquisitor, Brother Lemaître, and thiry-seven assessors. Cauchon ordered Massieu to have Jeanne brought before him. When she had sat down on a stool Jean d'Estivet developed the argument on the conclusions he had reached, inviting Jeanne to swear to speak the truth in answer to each article of the indictment, pointing out that if she refused to do so she would *ipso facto* be declared guilty and excommunicated.

Several assessors addressed the tribunal to make their own observations, which generally were favourable to the accused, for example Ducrotoy who, basing himself on canon law, declared that Jeanne was entitled to three delays before she could be excommunicated; Pierre Miget, Prior of Longueville, who opined that she should not be forced to answer either with a simple yes or no, but had the right to qualify her answers; and Gatinée who explained that if Jeanne refused to take the oath he would examine the procedure in canon law, for he was not altogether certain that she had not the right to refuse.

The prosecutor in his reply declared that all the articles he had drawn up were "inspired only by his zeal to uphold the Faith."

Then Cauchon addressed Jeanne. "All the persons you see here are very learned clerics, well versed in human and Divine law, their intention now as always to act with kindness and piety towards you. We seek no vengeance." Then he added words the real meaning of which Jeanne alone could understand, "We desire no chastisement" before continuing, "We seek only to instruct you and to lead you back to the road of truth and salvation." In conclusion he proposed that she should "choose among the assessors one or several doctors to assist her in her answers, and requested her to "swear to speak the truth on all points dealing with the trial."

Jeanne could have shown among those present one or more defenders—for instance Loyseleur in whom she had complete faith—but following the advice she had received she declined the offer, saying, "I have no intention of acting differently from the advice of Our Lord. As far as the oath you ask from me I am ready to swear that I will speak the truth about everything that concerns the trial."

Cauchon did not ask for more. He hastened to make her take the oath on the Gospel. After that, he asked Thomas de Courcelles to read out one by one the articles of the indictment, written down in Latin but immediately translated into French, so that the accused should understand all she was charged with. The reading out of the seventy articles of the indictment, which were based on the essential passages of her interrogation, took two days, March 27 and 28.

The act of accusation was preceded by a preamble which explained that the accused was brought before the tribunal in order that "the woman Jeanne, commonly called the Maid, be judged by you, declared sorceress, soothsayer, false prophet, invoking evil spirits, superstitious, devoted to magic, evil thinker in matters of the Catholic faith, schismatic, misled, sacrilegious, idolater, apostate, blasphemer of God and His saints, seditious, trouble maker, bellicose, thirsting for human blood, without shame and mocking the decency of her sex by wearing irreverently an unusual suit and behaving like a man-at-arms, abominable by so many crimes to God and men, prevaricating on Divine and natural law as well as on ecclesiastical discipline, seductress of princes and of the people, accepting the scorn of God to be venerated and adored herself, exhibiting her hands and garments to be kissed, usurper of the honours and worship due to God alone, heretic, or at least strongly suspected of heresy, be canonically and legally chastised for her crimes."

To every article of the indictment read out to her Jeanne made a brief reply, restricting herself most of the time to denying the accusations, or simply to saying "I answered that elsewhere," or "I refer you to what I said at the trial." But to a number of them she answered in detail though she had already answered them before. She felt it was necessary.

To the first article which was about the jurisdiction of the bishop and the ecclesiastical tribunal she gave this reply: "I well believe that our Holy Father the Pope in Rome, the bishops and other churchmen are here to safeguard the Christian Faith and those who are weak. But I will submit only to the Church in

Heaven, that is to say God, the Virgin Mary and the saints in Paradise. I do firmly believe that I did not fail our Christian Faith, nor I do not wish to."

When the sixty-first article was reached—it spoke of her rebellion against the Church Militant—she repeated what she had said the first instance. "To the Church Militant I bring my respect and reverence with all my strength. However, to submit my actions to the Church Militant I have first to consult Our Lord who made me do them."

"Do you submit to the Church Militant?" insisted the promoter who wanted to obtain a straight answer.

"Send me your clerk on Saturday and I will answer him," said Jeanne who wanted to gain time.

On the "unusual garments" with which the thirteenth article dealt d'Estivet tried to confuse her, saying, "The Holy Canons and Holy Writ say that the women who wear men's clothes or *vice versa* are spurned by God."

Tired by her long detention and the interminable trial, where she had to be continuously on the alert to avoid the traps some of the investigators laid for her, Jeanne could not be bothered any more to point out that the canons of the Church could not be definite on that score since St Catherine, in front of whose statue in Domrémy and Maxey-sur-Meuse she used to pray with all the fervour of her soul, also dressed as a man after having cut her hair short, yet was later canonised. She answered in simple words, though she retained her right to return to the subject, "I said enough about that. If you want me to answer give me time and I will answer you."

When the fifteenth article, which dealt with the admonition in Arras and in Beauvais not to wear male attire, was read out to her she again stated, "I refused and I still refuse."

The twenty-second article contained her "letter to the English." She clearly told the tribunal that "before seven years are up they will perceive the truth of what I wrote to them," and unhesitatingly she added, "The peace the English need is to go back to England their country! "

On her previous declaration that "God loved some men more," she upheld what she had said before, namely that, "I do know that God loves my King and the Duc d'Orléans."

The fiftieth article concerned her Voices. Her answer was that she begged "Our Lord and Our Lady" for her Voices to give her "aid and support." She raised her voice. "And they do."

One of the assessors inquired how she called to her Voices.

"Like this: 'Very sweet God, in honour of your holy Passion I request you if you love me to reveal what I should answer these men of the Church. As to the clothes, I know by which commandment I took to wearing them, but I do not know how to give them up. May it please You to instruct me.'" Then she added these unexpected words, "My Voices often give me news of Monsignor of Beauvais."

Cauchon jumped, then, because of the general astonishment her words produced, could not avoid asking her, "And what do they say?"

"I will tell you in private."

The fifty-fourth article was about her "companions and servants." On that score she explained, "My subordinates consisted of men, but in billets and resting-places at night I most often had a woman with me. And when I was fighting I slept dressed and armed in places where I could not find a woman."

To the last question: "If you have committed any sins against the Christian Faith are you willing to submit them to the Church and to those who are entitled to correct them?"

"I will tell you Saturday after dinner," said Jeanne who wanted to gain time to be able to consult her Voices.

On Saturday March 31, which was the eve of Easter, Cauchon went to Jeanne's room to hear the answer she promised to give on her submission to the Church Militant. He was accompanied by Jean Lemaître, the deputy of the Inquisition, and by the following assessors: Jean Beaupère, Nicolas Midi, Pierre Maurice, Jacques de Touraine, Gérard Feuillet, Guillaume Haiton, Thomas de Courcelles and Guillaume Mouton.

Jean Beaupère asked her whether she would accept "the judgment of the Church which was on earth to judge all she did and said."

Jeanne began her answer with, "I agree with the Church Militant . . ." but immediately added the proviso which annulled her affirmation, "as long as she does not command me to do something that is impossible to do. What I call impossible is to deny the facts and the words I said at the trial, the visions and revelations to which I confessed, and which I accomplished and received from God." And so that there should be no misunderstanding concerning her belief she explained, "If the Church wanted me to do something contrary to the orders I received from God, then I will not obey!"

Beaupère continued to insist. "Do you think," he asked, "that it is your duty to submit to the Church here on earth, that is to our Holy Father the Pope, the cardinals, archbishops, bishops and other prelates of the Church?"

"Yes," answered Jeanne, but then added, "Our Lord is first served."

After those clear declarations the tribunal rose. Within himself Cauchon was very pleased with the answers Jeanne gave.

The days of April 2, 3 and 4 were spent by Cauchon and some of the assessors in extracting from the seventy articles of the prosecutor's indictment twelve propositions, that is, a concise summary concerning "the many statements and assertions of the said Jeanne" on which Cauchon had to ask for the opinion of a number of doctors famous for their knowledge of theology and canon law. The first three propositions dealt with Jeanne's visions, the fourth with the revelations she claimed to have received from God, the fifth with her male attire which she refused to give up and in which she took the Eucharist several times, the sixth with the inscription of *Jhésus-Maria* which accompanied all her letters, the seventh with her leaving Domrémy and coming to Chinon, the eighth with her attempted escape from Beaurevoir, the following articles with the talks she claimed frequently to have had with St Michael and SS Catherine and Marguerite, and the last with her refusal to submit to the Church Militant.

On April 5 Cauchon sent copies of the twelve propositions to the churchmen whose opinions he needed, asking them to reply not later than the 10th.

"We beg and request you," said the accompanying letter, "for the good of the Faith to give us in writing under your own seal a salutary counsel on the subject concerning the assertions here transcribed, for us to know whether after having seen, considered and pondered those assertions or some of them, they are contrary to the tenets of the orthodox Faith or could be suspected of being against Holy Writ, or scandalous, brazen, obnoxious in any sense."

Cauchon took care to associate the deputy of the Inquisition with this new move, and was specially careful to put on the list of the learned persons the names of certain doctors whose secret sympathy for Jeanne was known to him. Thus he avoided a unanimous reaction which would have made things embarrassing for him since he had very little room in which to manoeuvre.

Two bishops, seven canons, eleven lawyers and four specialists in theology, not one of them belonging to the tribunal, were asked to give their opinions in writing. They assembled in the episcopal palace of Rouen on Thursday April 12, and pondered over the propositions submitted to them. The majority of them "having diligently considered, compared and weighed her words, apparitions and revelations" found in the "aforesaid articles only fabricated lies, scandalous and irreligious acts, blasphemy, lack of piety, and idolatry."

Master Denis Gatinée declared that in his opinion, "if the accused did not mend her ways she should be handed to the secular arm to expiate her crime; if she abjured, absolution should be given her, and according to custom she should be locked up in a prison, fed on bread of pain and water of anguish, to bewail her sins and never again to commit them," a valuable piece of advice which Cauchon took note of. Guillaume, Abbot of Cormeilles, and Nicolas, Abbot of Jumièges, first refused to give their opinion on the pretext that they had not been present at the trial. They were twice requested to give their opinion. Eventually they did give it, declaring that they would accept the theologians' views though with the important reservation that "if the accused was in a state of mortal sin God alone could know that . . ."

Raoul le Sauvage believed that the case should be submitted to the Pope "for the honour of the King and yours, and the peace of your conscience," while Jean Pigache, Richard de Grouchet and Pierre Minier unhesitatingly maintained that "if her revelations came from God or a good spirit they should not be wrongly construed." Jean de Saint-Avit, the old Bishop of Avranches, whose opinion was taken down by Brother Isambart de la Pierre in his diocese, did not fear to declare, basing himself on St Thomas, that "when there is doubt in matters concerning the Faith one should always apply to the Pope or the Council in Rome." The chapter of Rouen did not want to give an opinion, and gave in only after being threatened with disciplinary sanctions. The opinion said that Jeanne was guilty, but asked for the University of Paris to be first consulted.

Two essential points emerged from all those answers: firstly, that the accused should be warned to mend her ways before the rigour of the law was applied; secondly, that the case be submitted to the doctors of the University of Paris for their opinion. Cauchon did not oppose the opinions expressed by the majority of those he had consulted since not one of them could upset the plans he had so carefully worked out in order to save the Maid.

The first "charitable exortation" took place on April 18 in the prison because Jeanne had fallen ill again, and Jean Tiphaine, personal physician to the Duchess of Bedford, had to treat her for several days for a violent bout of fever. Surrounded by several assessors Cauchon spoke to Jeanne in these words, "All these doctors and masters, Jeanne, have come here with a wholly charitable intention to help and comfort you in your illness." Then he turned to those who accompanied him. "Masters, we exhort you by the loyalty that binds you to the true doctrine of the Faith to give Jeanne fruitful advice for the salvation of her soul and body." Then he warned Jeanne that if she refused to submit to the Church "that never closes her bosom to those who return to her" he would feel compelled to leave her to her fate.

"It seems to me," Jeanne answered, "that because of my illness I am in great peril of death. If that is so and God wants it so then I request you to confess me, give me Our Saviour and Christian burial."

"If you want the sacraments of the Church," Cauchon replied, "you must behave like a good Catholic and submit to the Holy Church."

"I cannot say more at this time," she said.

194

Cauchon insisted, Jeanne maintained her position.

"Whatever happens to me," she said, "I shall neither act nor speak differently than I did at the trial."

Cauchon and each of the assessors exhorted her to submit to the Church, and Nicolas Midi pointed out that if she refused she would be "abandoned like a Saracen."

Jeanne protested, saying that she was a "good Christian, properly baptised." Nonetheless she continued refusing to submit.

The second charitable exhortation took place on Wednesday May 2 in the hall of the castle of Rouen, where the trial had been conducted. Sixty-three assessors, almost the entire tribunal, assisted at the session.

To begin with Cauchon recalled the entire case, then concluded, observing that after having tried in vain to persuade the accused to submit to the Church he "judged it was right that in the presence of all of you here solemnly assembled, this woman be exhorted to submit, hoping that your presence will make it easier for her to return to humility and obedience." Then the accused was brought in, and Master Jean de Chatillon, whom Cauchon had appointed to do so, delivered a general admonition, embroidering on the absolute necessity in which all faithful Christians found themselves of making their peace with the Church. At the end of his admonition Jean de Chatillon asked her, "Do you accept to mend your ways according to the deliberations of these men of integrity?"

Jeanne was by now completely restored to health and had found her assurance again. In a voice full of contemptuous condescension she demolished whatever effect the Archdeacon of Evreux's words could have had on the assembly. "Read out all you wrote down," she said. She was referring to the pages he held in his hand, "and then I will answer you!" Then she added, "I rely on God, my Creator, my Judge, the King of Heaven and earth."

Jean de Chatillon then enumerated in six articles the principal charges drawn up by the tribunal against her: revelations, male attire, divination, rash beliefs, predictions and refusal to submit to the Church Militant. In conclusion he requested her to submit on all these points.

All Jeanne answered was that if she "truly believed in the Church down here she still referred her speech and action to God in person."

"Do you want to say," he insisted, "that you have no judge on earth, not even the Holy Father?"

"I will not tell you more," said Jeanne who with her health had recovered her early intransigence and retracted unhesitatingly some of her earlier declarations. "I have a good master, who is Our Lord to whom I submit, but to nobody else!"

Jean de Chatillon warned her that if she did not recognise the Church and the article *Unam Sanctam* she would be declared a heretic "and sentenced to the flames by other judges."

The threat did not frighten her. "If I saw the flames," she simply said, "I could only say the same, and nothing else."

Jean de Chatillon realised that out of sheer stubbornness she had put herself in a very difficult position. So he said. "And if the General Council with our Holy Father, the Cardinals et cetera were here would you submit to them?"

"You will get nothing more out of me," Jeanne replied.

Jean de Chatillon tried hard to save her from the terrible consequences that would follow her refusal. "Will you submit to our Holy Father the Pope?"

This time she understood that it was wiser to qualify her answers. She said with great skill, "Take me to him and I will answer him." And she could not resist adding, "That is all."

Jean de Chatillon moved on to the next subject. "Have you anything to add on the subject of your clothes?"

"I would willingly put on a long dress and a woman's bonnet to go to church and receive my Saviour. I said so before. On the condition that afterwards I can wear the same as I wear now." Though it would condemn her even more she added these words in order to set her conscience at rest, "When I have finished doing what God sent me to accomplish, I will wear woman's clothes again."

Then Jean de Chatillon spoke of her apparitions and the proof she gave Charles VII. He hoped to confuse her when he said, "The sign you gave your king? would you give it also to the Archbishop of Reims, the Lords de Boussac, Charles de Bourbon, de La Trémouille and La Hire?"

Jeanne did not doubt La Hire's attachment to her cause, but knew well the sentiments of sullen hostility which the Great Chancellor and the Constable of France had for her. Moreover, she knew that nothing would happen on that score. She answered in a bantering tone, "Give me a messenger and I will write to them about the whole trial. Otherwise no!"

Chatillon did not insist. He admonished her again, repeating that she should submit to the Church and concluded with these words, "If the Church abandons you you will be in great peril of your body and soul. Eternal flames for the soul, temporal flames for the body, by the sentence of other judges."

Stubborn in her refusal to submit Jeanne answered him with a direct threat. "If you do against me what you say here, it will burn your body and soul!"

Chatillon tried for a last time to make her submit to the Church. "Tell us only one reason why you do not return to the Church?"

Jeanne did not bother to answer. Now other assessors endeavoured to convince her. Deaf to their exhortations she persisted in remaining silent.

Then Cauchon spoke, asking her again to reflect.

"How long a delay will you grant me to reply?" asked Jeanne.

"You must answer at once," said Cauchon who very well knew that she would refuse.

She did refuse, and Cauchon, pleased with her attitude, had her taken back to her room, and then the court rose.

The torture that aimed to persuade a recalcitrant accused to admit to the faults with which he was reproached was, according to the canon law of the time, automatically applied to all who refused to submit to the Church. Horribly tortured, the unfortunate person nearly always ended up by confessing to all the crimes he was accused of, in order to put an end to the abominable treatment. Frequently it was but a mutilated, panting wreck which the warders took back to the prison.

On May 9 the warders took Jeanne to the castle's large tower, where Cauchon and nine assessors were waiting for her. In a corner of the room beside the fireplace where a big fire was burning stood Maugier Leparmentier, executioner of Rouen, and his assistants with their frightening instruments of torture.

"Jeanne," said the bishop, "you did not tell us the truth on several points. We know that from divers information we received, to which are joined other proofs, and strong presumptive evidence. The time has come to make amends, for you see here before you the executors of our orders and the instruments of torture which they are ready to use so as to make you return to the true road and force you to tell the truth."

In spite of Cauchon's assurance given in private that she would not be tortured, Jeanne could hardly control the feeling of horror that filled her by the sight of the instruments of torture which took up half of the room. She regained possession of herself and answered, "Truly, even if you tear me from limb to limb and make my soul come out of my body, I will not say anything different. And if I said something afterwards I would say that I said that under duress." Then she told them that she had the reassurance of her Voices, whom she had asked whether she ought to submit to the Church Militant, and they answered her that "she should refer it to Our Lord." And she added, "I asked my Voices whether I would be burnt, and they answered that I should trust Our Lord and He would help me."

Cauchon would have preferred not to hear the end of her declaration. He hastened to cut her short and ask her if "on the sign of the crown she would submit to the Archbishop of Reims."

"Make him come," said Jeanne, "and then I will answer you."

Cauchon stopped insisting. He ordered her to be taken back to her room, and after pretending to consult the assessors he put in the records that "given the stubbornness of the accused and the kind of answers she gave, and fearing that punishment by torture would be but of little advantage to her," he had decided "to suspend their application till the matter was more amply deliberated . . ."

Three days later he assembled at his domicile fourteen of the assessors, carefully chosen by him, to sound them on the question of torturing the accused with the aim of obtaining a confession from her. With eleven voices against three the assessors found, as Cauchon wanted, that this was a case where an exception could be made to the usual rule, and that it was unnecessary to subject her to it. Thus with his cunning manoeuvring Cauchon achieved his aim, which was to save Jeanne from the awful pains of torture. Besides, he could not be sure that under the terrible treatment of the executioners she would at the end of her resistance not have revealed the secret of her birth, and at the same time blurt out the secret of the double game he had started playing even before the trial began.

The protracted procedure made Jeanne's enemies impatient, whereas those of the Burgundians, who had not ceased taking an interest in her fate, were beginning to worry. Both sides went to complain to Warwick.

Warwick on Sunday May 13 invited to dinner Cauchon, Jean de Luxembourg, his brother Louis, Chancellor of France under Henry VI, the Bishop of Noyon and several English captains. Cauchon assured the English that Jeanne would not escape the stake. Drawing the Luxembourgs aside he gave them a formal assurance that Jeanne would be saved. He promised everybody present that the trial would soon be over.

On May 18 the University's reply reached Rouen. On the following day Cauchon summoned fifty-one assessors to a solemn session in the chapel of the archbishop's palace and the reply of the doctors of Paris was read out. The Faculty of Theology declared Jeanne "violently suspected of heresy," and was convinced that her visions were "lies, seduction and perniciousness," and if they were true they could only have come from "the demons Belial, Satan and Behemoth." The Faculty of Canon Law expressed the same opinion, adding that the accused should be "charitably exhorted" and if she still refused to abjure her error "given to the secular arm to be punished in proportion to her crime."

The Paris reply was debated. Some of the assessors were all for ending the trial then and there and passing sentence at once. The majority was, however, in favour of a last exhortation to be delivered to the accused, and Cauchon sided with them.

On Wednesday May 23, accompanied by the deputy of the Inquisition, the Bishops of Thérouanne and Noyon, the prosecutor d'Estivet and seven assessors Cauchon held a session in a room in the castle of Rouen. Jeanne was brought before them and Cauchon said to her, "According to the deliberations of the Faculty of Theology and the Faculty of Canon Law of the University of Paris you will hear . . ." He waited for a second or so, then called her "My dear Jeanne" before continuing the sentence, ". . . that on several points you erred and failed." He asked her to "retract, correct and amend," and to submit to the Church.

Jeanne made no reply.

One of the assessors, Pierre Maurice, translating from the Latin read out the long text which he held up and which contained the answer of the University to the twelve propositions that had been carefully examined. Then he delivered a long exhortation "for the salvation of her soul and body," warning her that if she refused "her soul will be flung into damnation and her body broken."

"As to my speech and my acts," Jeanne answered simply, "to which I adhered at the trial, I still adhere to them and intend to maintain them."

Jean de Chatillon considered it his duty to insist, "So you believe that you are not bound to submit your words and acts to the Church Militant, or anybody else except God Himself?"

Jeanne repeated what she already had said. "What I always said and maintained at the trial I still maintain. If I were in judgment and saw the hot flames, the faggots alight and the executioner ready to stoke the fire, even if I were at the stake, I could say nothing else! I would maintain what I said at the trial till death!"

Cauchon asked her whether she had anything else to say. "No," she answered. Then he put the same question to the prosecutor who replied in the negative. Cauchon read out the formula he had prepared and which finally closed the proceedings, then he summoned the accused for "tomorrow to hear us render justice and pronounce our sentence in this case."

With the proceedings declared closed and the case heard, all that remained for the judge to do, in accordance with the canon law of the period, was to pass sentence; and if found guilty to hand the condemned over to the secular arm.

On the morning of Thursday, May 24, Jeanne was taken in a

cart surrounded by vigilant warders to the cemetery beside the Abbey of Saint-Ouen, where the sentence was to be read out in public. During the night two wooden platforms were hastily knocked together. On the first, which was covered with rich tapestries and carpets, sat the Cardinal of Winchester, Cauchon, the Bishops of Thérouanne, Noyon and Norwich and a number of assessors. To the second, which was bare of hangings and carpets, Jeanne was led followed by the court officers Massieu and Nicolas Loyseleur. Guillaume Erard, who was appointed by Cauchon to exhort her for the last time on the obedience all Christians owe the Church, was waiting for her. Martin Ladvenu and several other assessors with Isambert de la Pierre among them, remained at the foot of the platform beside the executioner and his assistants who stood in a cart. The cemetery was filled by a large crowd which the English soldiers could hardly control and the curious were thick in the windows of the church and the neighbouring houses.

When Jeanne appeared on the platform, her features relaxed in spite of the emotion within her, straight and proud in her male clothes, her head uncovered and her hair reaching to her shoulders, a long murmur rose from the crowd.

The preacher began his sermon based on a sentence from the Gospel according to St John, "The vine-shoot cannot bear fruit if it is not tied to the vine." Embroidering for a long time on that theme he explained that a Christian cannot detach himself from the Church if he wants to bear "fruits of virtue and piety." During the sermon Jeanne meditated, though not on what the preacher was saying but on the urgent advice to submit to the Church Jean Beaupère had given her that very morning. Evrard became aware that she was not listening. He raised his voice, and speaking straight to her he thus apostrophied her, "Jeanne! Do you hear me? I am speaking to you! I tell you that your king is a heretic and a schismatic."

Torn so brusquely from her meditation Jeanne protested in a voice vibrating with indignation. "On my faith, your reverence, I dare to tell you and swear on the pain of death that he is the most noble Christian of all Christians, and who loves best the Faith and the Church."

Cauchon could not help showing his displeasure, and Evrard

realised that he had spoiled the effect of his sermon. "Make her hold her tongue!" he shouted to Massieu, then unabashed he continued with the sermon. When he approached the end he spoke direct to Jeanne again, pointing at Cauchon, sitting on the other platform surrounded by most of the assessors. "There are your judges who on numerous occasions have requested you to submit to Holy Mother Church, showing and revealing to you that in your words and acts there were matters which according to the opinion of churchmen, could not be upheld and which were mistaken."

Jeanne refused to listen to more. She interrupted him, saying, "I will answer you!"

On her past declarations she simply observed, "As to my submission to the Church, I already gave my answer." Then she appealed to the Pope: "As to my acts, let those be known in Rome by our Holy Father to whom as well as to God I first appeal." Having taken this precaution she declared, "For my words and acts I assign the responsibility to nobody else, neither to the king or another. If there were misdeeds they were mine and nobody else's!"

"Your acts and words are rejected, so will you retract them?" asked Guillaume Evrard. Jeanne avoided answering that question. "I appeal to God and our Holy Father the Pope."

Evrard explained that her appeal would not be received because "bishops were the judges, each one in his diocese," then said, "appeal to the Holy Mother Church."

Jeanne did not answer.

Conforming to canonical procedure Evrard three times admonished her but could not obtain a retraction. He did not speak to her again.

Cauchon rose. Silence was complete. In a grave voice he began to read out the sentence.

Jeanne was again plunged in deep meditation and seemed unaware of her surroundings. She saw neither the swelling crowd in the cemetery which contained a number of secret partisans of the Armagnacs and declared champions of the Burgundians; nor the tribunal sitting on the official platform; not even the executioner only a few steps away from her, ready to take her to the stake. She did not hear Massieu who beseeched her to recant,

Loyseleur who implored her in the same sense, or the hundred people or so in the crowd who shouted she should save her life.

Facing her, Cauchon continued reading out the sentence. The seconds went by and as Jeanne persisted in her silence, Cauchon became petrified by the thought that the edifice he had with so much effort built during several months now would suddenly collapse. He read as slowly as he could so as to give Jeanne time to save herself. That did not go unnoticed and several Englishmen protested against his attitude. One of them called to him, "You betray the king, you favour this woman!"

Though he was infinitely relieved to be able to interrupt the reading of the sentence Cauchon pretended to be furious. "You lie," he said. "I act according to my conscience. You will have to apologise!"

Meanwhile Loyseleur and Massieu did not cease beseeching Jeanne, pointing at the executioner standing upright in his cart. All of a sudden Jeanne perceived that she was lost if she did not give in. Shaking off her lethargy she began to shout with all her strength so that the crowd should hear her. "I will do all the judges of the Church want! I want to obey them in everything. Since the churchmen say that my apparitions and revelations should not be sustained I will not sustain them! I appeal to the judges and to Our Holy Mother Church."

Massieu quickly pulled out the short formula of abjuration he had prepared, and which he read in the midst of the general clamour her submission had caused. She repeated after him, "I, Jehanne, declare that I will in the future abstain from carrying arms, wearing men's clothes and having short hair. I submit to the rules, judgment and commandments of the Church and of our Holy Father the Pope. And I swear this on Almighty God and the Holy Gospels. In proof of this I sign this."

At the bottom of the declaration she wrote the name "Jehanne" with a quill handed her by Jean Callot, one of the secretaries of the Duke of Bedford. Fully aware now that she had escaped the stake Jeanne laughed as she signed her name. In the crowd some began to murmur that it was undoubtedly a comedy arranged in advance by Cauchon. He read out as quickly as possible a new sentence that condemned the accused to perpetual incarceration, bread of pain and water of anguish "in order that she weep over her misdeeds and commit no more that could be deplored."

On leaving the platform Jeanne said to Loyseleur, "Do not take me back to the castle of the English. Take me to the ecclesiastical prison." For she imagined that it would be easier to escape if she were transferred to some convent. As detention in an ecclesiastical prison was the formal rule in a case like hers several assessors inquired from Cauchon in which place he intended to lock her up. But Cauchon knew perfectly well that if he let Jeanne go, either the University or the English would soon claim her, so he swiftly said, "Take her back to the place you brought her from." Massieu at once took her back.

In the crowd the tumult was now at its loudest. In the vociferating mob one could hear shouts of "Treason!" and the assessors were stoned. Only with considerable difficulty did Massieu succeed in opening a passage for the cart which took Jeanne back to the royal castle through the ranks of the English soldiers who had drawn their swords and shouted for her death.

Reaching her room Jeanne obediently took off her male clothes and put on the female attire the Duchess of Bedford had got ready for her. She submitted to her hair being cut short all round her head as if she were a man of the lower orders without trying to understand the reason why she was forced to wear her hair like a man when she was equally forced to dress like a woman. Anyhow, the hair-cut was in flagrant violation of the submission she had signed only two hours before.

Early in the afternoon Jean Lemaître, the deputy inquisitor, accompanied by several assessors, came to see her in her room. He did not breathe a word about an ecclesiastical prison where the condemned would expiate her crimes, but as guardian of the Faith he warned her that if she fell into error again the Church would be constrained to abandon her to secular justice.

In the town the fury of Warwick's soldiers because the Maid had escaped the stake was given full rein. Their fury was given added strength by the news that troops of Charles VII had infiltrated the whole of Normandy, and Xaintrailles had just attempted an audacious attack on Rouen which, though unsuccessful, still showed the English that the situation was becoming worse each day. The population of Rouen, worked on by Armagnac propaganda, was preparing to rise, and the local authorities were truly worried by this change of attitude. In the absence of a military victory over the French it was absolutely necessary to make some gesture to raise the badly hit prestige of the English.

Cauchon was acquainted with the mentality of the occupiers; and dreading that overexcited by fear and hatred Warwick's soldiers might invade the royal castle, seize the Maid and put her to death, he resolved to act swiftly and save Jeanne while there was time.

For the condemned, Thursday afternoon and the day of Friday went by without incident. She received several visitors, including Nicolas Loyseleur who said to her, "You passed a pleasant day, Jeanne" and of Massieu who told her of his satisfaction with her for the decision she had taken. In the middle of Friday night an English nobleman whose name remains unknown succeeded in entering Jeanne's room and tried to rape her while she slept. Jeanne fought with all her strength and called for help. She tore the skin off his face with her nails, and in any case he could not have achieved his end as the prisoner's legs were tied tightly every night to "a large wooden stump" with iron chains by a new order of Cauchon, who had always feared that in an attempt to escape she would fall victim to her enemies. The worthless creature took his revenge by kicking the hapless girl and made off before the watch arrived.

That painful incident gave Cauchon the excuse he was looking for. On the morning of Sunday, May 27, Jeanne, wanting to rise, asked the warders to take off the chains. They opened the large padlock which held the chains. She saw that during the night her dress had been taken away and was replaced by the man's clothes she had promised never to wear again. In spite of her loud protestations the warders refused to give her back the dress which the Duchess of Bedford had presented her with. Probably it was no longer in their possession.

Tired out by asking for the dress in vain Jeanne, who could have wrapped the blankets of her bed round her body and waited for the arrival of some visitor through whom she could have complained either to Warwick or Cauchon, towards noon donned her old suit and threadbare doublet. Acting on the instructions they received the warders immediately let Cauchon know of it, and early in the afternoon Cauchon sent for several assessors, also for the law officers, and informed them that Jeanne was again wearing man's clothes. They were unanimous in their opinion that they should all go to her room and establish the facts for themselves. As they crossed the courtyard in the castle Cauchon and his companions were seen by about a hundred English soldiers who booed them, calling them "Traitors" and "False Armagnacs," and there would have been trouble if Warwick's personal guard had not intervened.

The members of the tribunal entered Jeanne's room and saw for themselves that she was wearing man's clothes. They withdrew without putting a single question to her. As Cauchon left Jeanne said to him in a half whisper, "Wicked Bishop, you betrayed me!" Cauchon replied in so low a voice that she alone could hear it, "Hold your tongue, imbecile!"

On Monday May 28 Cauchon, accompanied by the deputy inquisitor, Massieu and Mauchon and eight assessors returned to Jeanne's room. Cauchon asked her why she again wore male attire.

"I put them on again," she answered, "because the promises made me were not kept, namely that I could go to Mass to receive the Saviour, and would not be put in chains again. After my abjuration and renunciation I was tormented, molested and beaten. And an English lord attempted to rape me. That is why I took back my man's clothes."

The judges changed the subject which much embarrassed them and spoke of her Voices. "On the platform you said that you lied when you boasted that they were the voices of SS Catherine and Marguerite."

"I do not mean it like that," replied Jeanne. "I did not hear myself retracting my apparitions." And she went on to explain, "I never did anything against God and the Faith even though you forced me to retract. I did not understand a word of what was written in the submission. If you want me to I will dress again as a woman, but as regards the rest I am not going to change!"

"Very well," said Cauchon before he and his assessors withdrew. "We will draw our own conclusions."

In the yard Cauchon met Warwick who was on his way to dine. For some time already Warwick had not hidden his fear from Cauchon that some complication in procedure or some other obstacle might at the last minute upset the plan they had so carefully worked out together. Now Cauchon said to him, "Eat well! It is done! "

Next day, May 29, Cauchon assembled forty-eight assessors in the chapel of the archbishop's palace of Rouen. He told them that Jeanne, who on May 24 in the cemetery of Saint-Ouen had admitted her errors and promised not to repeat them, was again wearing man's clothes. He asked the members of the tribunal to deliberate on her attitude. One after the other the assessors expressed their views. Unanimously they declared that she had relapsed, but most of them pronounced themselves in favour of the formula of abjuration which she signed be read out to her and explain to her the full significance of the promise she made, and to hand her over to secular justice only in case she continued to persist in her errors.

That condition greatly embarrassed Cauchon since it carried the risk of ruining the plan he had conceived. In the same way as he had done before he decided to ignore the advice he was given and at once sent Jeanne the following summons:

"We Pierre, by Divine mercy Bishop of Beauvais, and Jean Lemaître, deputy of the Doctor Master Jean Graverent, Inquisitor of the Faith and of heretic perversity, deputy of the Apostolic Holy See in the Kingdom of France,

"Given that the woman Jeanne, commonly called the Maid, a heretic with several errors against orthodoxy, had abjured in public her errors against the Church, and has now relapsed according to her own avowal, we summon her to appear in person tomorrow morning at eight o'clock in the Place du Vieux-Marché in Rouen to be declared a heretic, and excommunicated by us with the usual notice."

On Wednesday May 30, 1431 at seven o'clock in the morning Massieu came to Jeanne's room and read out Cauchon's summons. He was accompanied by Martin Ladvenu and a young preacher brother Jean Toutmouillé. Already the first sentence made her realise the fate in store for her, and she began to shake with fear. When the law officer finished reading her strength failed her for a moment.

"Alas! How can one treat me so cruelly? And is it necessary that my body so clean and complete and never sullied should today be consumed by flames and reduced to ashes?" Then she burst into tears, hid her face in her hands, then she tore out her hair in handfuls and added, "I should prefer to be seven times beheaded than burnt." But soon her strength returned, and in a voice which had become firm she declared the purity of her intentions. "I call to God, the Great Judge, to behold the great torts and injustice with which I am crushed!"

Then she confessed to Martin Ladvenu and asked to be allowed to take communion. Massieu hurried to Cauchon who gave permission. At eight o'clock Cauchon entered Jeanne's room accompanied by five assessors whom he had told that he would try for the last time to persuade the Maid again to abjure her errors. When she saw him she could not resist saying, "Bishop, I am dying because of you!"

Thoroughly pleased by those words that showed her personal feelings for him in front of witnesses, Cauchon said to her in a low voice, the true meaning of which she alone could understand, "Ah, Jeanne, accept your sufferings patiently . . ." Then he raised his voice for the assessors' benefit. "You will die because you did not keep the promise you made, and fell back into your errors."

He gave the assessors a signal and as prearranged they withdrew to the next room, taking Massieu, Martin Ladvenu and Toutmouillé with them. Left alone with Jeanne, Cauchon went to knock lightly on the door of the room at the end of the suite. At once the door opened and the two of them entered the third room, where Cauchon handed her over to two men who soundlessly led her through a maze of passages till they reached the entrance to the underground passage by which they left the castle in secret in front of the tower called Devant Les Champs.*

Without wasting time the Maid and her escort mounted the

* *This underground passage, which still exists, was used by the Gestapo in July 1944 to escape the soldiers of the Resistance who had surrounded the building. It ends nowadays at 102 rue Jeanne-d'Arc.*

horses that were waiting for them and rode fast out of the town in a northerly direction.

As soon as Cauchon was told that the escape had succeeded he hastened, according to the plan, to have a sorceress, who a little time before had been condemned to be burnt, taken into Jeanne's room. The prisoner wore a long grey-black dress which had been coated with sulphur and pitch up to the neck. On her shaven head was put a sort of mitre which hid her face down to the nose, and she wore a veil to hide the rest of her face. On the back of the dress was an enormous placard on which was written a long sentence containing in large letters the words, "Sorceress, heretic, apostate, idolater, schismatic." She had been drugged and was completely unconscious.

On the excuse that the hour fixed for the execution was long past Cauchon had her immediately taken from Jeanne's room, and before any of the assistants could speak to her she was lifted into a cart which set out at once for the Place du Vieux-Marché, where the executioner had been waiting for over an hour. During the journey about a hundred soldiers surrounded the cart and nobody was allowed to approach the condemned woman. In the square about eight hundred of Warwick's men guarded the entrance to the streets converging on the market place. The condemned woman mounted a wooden platform in the company of Massieu and Martin Ladvenu. Cauchon took his seat on a tribune beside the civil, religious and military authorities of the town. Nicolas Midi preached a sermon based on St Paul's Epistle to the Corinthians "If one limb suffers all the limbs suffer." The Bishop of Lisieux then read out the sentence: "We, sitting here as a tribunal, declare that you shall be, like a gangrenous member, rejected from the unity of the Church so as not to infect the other members, and abandoned to the secular arm."

Normally the condemned woman should have been handed over to the magistrate of Rouen, Raoul Bouteilles, who was on the official platform. But once again ignoring the usual procedure Cauchon had her delivered straight to the executioner after giving the magistrate a look which stopped him from protesting, and caused him to nod his consent. The silent crowd which filled the square was waiting for the last words of the condemned woman, but were disappointed because all she did was to recite prayers. The English soldiers became impatient, and murmurs expressing astonishment rose from the crowd. They urged the executioner to do his job.

The executioner's assistants seized the woman. With the movements of a sleepwalker she obediently mounted the immense stake which was built much higher than was usual, with a chimney in the middle. Tied to a pole, the woman murmured some words which nobody heard distinctly, and seemed to be waiting for something to happen.

Suddenly the executioner set fire to the straw, part of which had been sprinkled with water, inside the pyre. A huge flame rose up to the woman whose dress immediately caught fire, releasing acrid, dark smoke. Asphyxiated the woman died at once.

A few minutes later the executioner and his assistants reduced the fire, and the soldiers received the order to break ranks. Then the crowd was authorised to approach the stake and saw the half charred body of a woman whose face was unrecognisable. Then the corpse was put on burning coals and the fire finished the job.

In accordance with the saying that *Ecclesia aborret a sanguine* which forbade ecclesiastical judges to be present at executions the tribunal withdrew the moment the condemned woman was handed to the executioner. The assessors hurried back to their homes to meditate on what had taken place. Cauchon strolled back to the archbishop's palace, went to his room, lay down and slept the sleep of the just.

Fourteen

Though thanks to the Bishop of Beauvais, who had conducted the case marvellously, Jeanne escaped the stake, she did not regain her freedom, for on the Duke of Bedford's orders she was taken to a fortified castle in the North of France, probably the castle of Crotoy in Picardy, which the English had for a long time used for prisoners of state. She spent five long years there.

During that half-decade many events took place. Young Henry VI was crowned in Paris King of France and England, by his uncle the Cardinal Bishop of Winchester on December 2, 1431; but the ceremony was only an imitation of the anointing in Reims of Charles VII, and the people were not fooled. The French and the English had embarked again on military operations with varying gains and losses, and generally achieved only more devastation wherever men-at-arms of whichever side passed.

At the Court of Charles VII the insolence, incapability and greed of de La Trémouille drove all his adversaries into the same camp. In the month of June 1433 the favourite was kidnapped by conspirators from the castle of Chinon and taken to Montrésor, where, to save his life, he had to give up all his earthly goods. First the King was indignant since he lost a man he was deeply attached to, but then he soon agreed to his being replaced in the Royal Council by the Comte de Maine, the youngest son of the Queen of Anjou.

On November 14, 1432 the Duchess of Bedford died suddenly, and with her death snapped the last link of the alliance between the Regent of France and the Duke of Burgundy. A few months later the Duke of Bedford married Jacqueline de Luxembourg, who did not bother to ask Philippe le Bon her suzerain for his consent, which he certainly would have refused.

Infuriated, the Duke of Burgundy withdrew from the alliance

with the English, and after thirty years of fratricidal wars the Treaty of Arras (September 20, 1435) sealed the reconciliation between Armagnacs and Burgundians. The union of all Frenchmen put an end to English ambitions. Bedford died of a broken heart twelve days before the treaty was signed. On the 29th of the same month Isabeau of Bavaria followed him to the grave. Suspected by everybody for a long time—she was not even invited to the coronation of Henry VI her grandson—eaten away by remorse, she died after easing her conscience by publicly thanking Heaven for the reconciliation of all the French.

In the new circumstances there was no more need to keep Jeanne in prison. Officially she had died in Rouen on May 30, 1431, and Henry VI's Council did not forget to let that be known by letters sent on June 8 "to the Emperor, the Kings, Dukes and Princes of Christendom" that after her trial "the wretch was handed over to secular justice which decided to burn her body." In the same document Cauchon mentioned the pretended abjurations of the accused though the law officers refused to sign the record presented to them, saying they were not present at the meeting. But Cauchon, who was not worried by one or more forgeries in this matter, took no notice of their objections. So that nobody should be ignorant of it a circular letter narrating the execution of the condemned girl was sent on June 28 to the "Ducs, Comtes, Seigneurs and all the Cities of France"; for it was necessary to counteract the propaganda of those, particularly of the preaching brothers, who spread the rumour that Jeanne was not burnt in Rouen. To set an example one of the preachers, Brother Pierre Bosquier, was sentenced by Cauchon, on the pretext that he had spoken ill of the judges, to nine months of prison, water of anguish and bread of pain.

In the spring of the year 1436 Jeanne wrote to Pierre d'Arc, who lived in the Barrois since his liberation in September 1435, and to Jacques d'Arc who was at the Court of Charles VII in Loches, to prepare themselves to join her in Lorraine during the month of May. Their meeting place was a small village near Metz called La Grange-aux-Hommes. When the brothers d'Arc arrived on May 20 they recognised her at once. Jeanne was in a sorry state. The allowance which permitted her jailers to look after her decently had not been paid for a long time, probably not since the death of the Duke of Bedford, for doublet and breeches were threadbare, her only mount was a sorry steed, and she completely lacked funds.

As soon as the brothers d'Arc, whom the King had given the privilege of changing their name to du Lys, recognised their foster-sister they did all they could quickly to spread the news of her arrival among the important folk of the neighbourhood so that they should come to her help. One of the first to come to aid her was Nicolas Louve, who had assisted at the coronation in Rheims, where at Jeanne's request, the King had knighted him. He generously opened his purse for her, gave her a fine horse that cost thirty francs and a pair of boots, and offered her hospitality in his house. The Sire de Boulay made her a present of a felt hat and Nicolas Groingnan, Governor of Metz, gave her a good sword. Thus equipped the Maid, accompanied by the brothers du Lys and a small escort, stayed successively in several places in the district, first at Bacquillon, then at Marieulles, where she remained for three weeks, before going on a pilgrimage to Notre-Dame-de-Liesse.

From there she returned to Arlon, where her aunt, Elisabeth de Luxembourg, widow of Antoine de Bourgogne, lived, with whom she remained for over five months, leaving her only for a few days' stay near Cologne in the castle of Count Warnenburg who invited her there, together with the brothers du Lys. At the end of her stay her host, who believed that she would soon be engaged again in military exploits, presented her with a handsome breast-plate. At Arlon she met many important people of the neighbourhood, including Jean de Luxembourg who had paid ransom for her to the English according to his promise to do so at Rouen, and thanks to whom she was set free.

Listening to the different people she had met in Lorraine since her liberation Jeanne reached the disappointing conclusion that nobody cared any more for her at the Court of France. Now that the situation had evolved in his favour the King had no desire whatever for Jeanne to serve with his forces, the more so because during her absence the military leaders, who became very jealous of their prerogatives since they had won some battles, had reoccupied several places held by the English, and the

Constable de Richemont had entered Paris on April 13, 1436.

In the Royal Council, in spite of de La Trémouille's departure, she still had a constant enemy, namely Régnault de Chartres. Among the newcomers the Comte de Bourbon, who inherited a vast fortune, or the Comte de Maine, who hoped some day to regain at least part of his vast possessions lost by the House of Anjou in Italy, were also against Jeanne's return to the scene, for the programme of reforms upheld by the majority of the preaching brothers appeared frightening to them; and the Bastard of Orléans, who now held one of the highest positions in the kingdom, made common cause with them, and seemed altogether to have forgotten the immense services his sister rendered him some years before.

Aware of all that enmity, the Queen of Anjou, who in any case was preoccupied with her own personal troubles, remained neutral in the matter. After having in the past done so much for the Maid she now refused to do more, and she too had more or less reached the conclusion that Jeanne's day was over.

Reflecting on everything that had changed in France since her capture at Compiègne Jeanne could not help asking herself whether her rôle were not finished. Magnificently she had fulfilled the first aim of her mission, the lifting of the siege of Orléans and the coronation in Reims. They were sufficient for her glory. It had become, however, impossible to fulfil the rest of her mission: the liberation of Charles d'Orléans and the crusade to the Holy Land to take the Tomb of Christ from the Infidel. The head of her family showed no desire whatever to return to France; dividing his time between poetry and pleasure he recognised Henry VI as King of France and England on August 14, 1433. And Pope Eugène IV, who in 1431 had replaced Martin V on the throne of St Peter, struggled in great difficulties with the Council of Basel, and was more attached to the idea of bringing back into the Catholic fold the Christians of the East, which took up most of his time, than to entertain the project of a crusade in Palestine.

As nobody at Court seemed to have bothered about her since she had regained her liberty six months ago Jeanne decided to write to Charles VII to offer her services to him. At the beginning of August she sent Jean du Lys with a letter to Loches, where for the moment the King was in residence. The messenger passed through Orléans on August 5, and when he presented himself before the municipal council he was eagerly received since the rumour that the Maid was in Lorraine already had reached the banks of the Loire, and the municipal council sent there one of their heralds, called Fleur de Lys, who knew Jeanne well during the siege, to find out whether the news was true.

On the morning of August 6 Jean du Lys, accompanied by several horsemen, left the town for Loches. The King received him straightaway on his arrival. After spending a fortnight in consulting his advisers the King gave Jean du Lys his reply for his sister. To show in what high esteem he held the messenger, and probably also because he could thus be of some help to Jeanne who was not to return to France, the King named him Provost of Vaucouleurs, promising him for a later date the post of Magistrate of Vermandois, and ordered that he be given a hundred francs as travelling expenses. But, in fact, the treasurer could give him only twenty livres on account, for the royal finances were in a worse plight than ever.

Passing through Orléans again on August 21 Jean du Lys was obliged to ask the municipal council to make him a grant big enough to enable him to continue on his way. The councillors at once handed him the twelve livres he needed. Meantime Fleur de Lys had returned from Arlon on August 9, bringing back letters from Jeanne. The delighted municipal council presented him with two gold reals.

On September 2 another municipal herald, Coeur de Lys, who was sent to Luxembourg in case the first could not fulfil his mission, returned from Arlon to Orléans after calling at Loches, where he delivered to the King, Jeanne's answer to the royal letter.

The King's reply left Jeanne in no illusions: her rôle was finished. All that was left was to resign herself to it, to stay in the shadows—for the moment at any rate—in the hope that perhaps in the not too distant future, the situation would change enough for the King and the Court to modify their attitude. In any case her position was most singular. Daughter of Isabeau of Bavaria she could not be recognised officially as Dunois, her brother, had been, by their father the Duc d'Orléans, because of the moral outlook of the time; yet hers was the coat of arms of the House of France, given her by the King, her half-brother on their mother's side. As liberator of Orléans she had galvanised the energy of the French and led their armies to victory. But the programme of reforms which she supported and which brought her on the one hand the wholehearted support of the ordinary clergy, the burghers in the cities and of the great masses, and on the other brought on her the implacable hatred of the aristocracy, the Court and the high dignitaries of the Church, for they refused to let their privileges be attacked. Officially dead in Rouen at the stake in 1431, five years later she stayed openly in Arlon close to the Duchess of Luxembourg and corresponded with municipalities, private persons and even the King of France.

Ever since she received the King's negative answer to her request to serve in his army Jeanne considered herself free of all obligations to him. As her military career was over—or so it seemed to her—she thought that she had the right to think of her own future. Till then she systematically refused all idea of marriage, from the young peasant who wanted to marry her in Domrémy to the Comte de Macy who in Rouen had asked to take her as his wife, not to mention Gilles de Rais and many others. Though she wanted to retain her purity she never took the vow of celibacy as she herself declared at her trial in Rouen, when she said she promised to remain a virgin "as long as it pleased God."

During her stay with Count de Warnenburg she renewed her acquaintance with Robert des Armoises, a cousin of Robert de Baudricourt, whom she had occasionally met at the time when she requested the Governor of Vaucouleurs to send her to Chinon. They were pleased to meet each other again and felt mutual sympathy. Rapidly the young knight fell in love with Jeanne, and on her leaving for Arlon he hastened to the Duchess of Luxembourg and revealed his feelings to her. She invited him to stay in her castle.

Jeanne was far from indifferent to the charm, courteous manner and firm attitude of the young nobleman, and far from avoiding him it gave her pleasure to have long talks with him. Very soon she began to feel passionately attracted to him and accepted to become his wife.

Their marriage was no misalliance. Though she was of the blood royal she could not be recognised as such since she was born as a result of her mother's adultery with her brother-in-law; whereas the des Armoises family were of ancient Bavarian lineage and could trace their origin back to early feudal times.

The wedding was celebrated in Arlon towards the end of September of the year 1436.

The young couple spent the whole month of October with the Duchess of Luxembourg, probably because Robert des Armoises wished to make improvements in his two principal residences: his house in Metz, where he lived mostly during the winter months, and his castle of Jaulny, where he stayed for the rest of the year. However, the time to lead a peaceful conjugal existence had not yet arrived for Jeanne; for hardly a day passed without bringing her proof that even if the King and the Court refused to make use of her services, many private persons remembered her exploits in the years of 1429 and 1430. From every quarter she was encouraged again to take command of an army. One of her most eager correspondents was Gilles de Rais who ceaselessly begged her to join him in his castle of Tiffauges, where he was assembling a troop of warriors to purge the region of the disbanded mercenaries who devastated the countryside. Pierre du Lys, who remained with Jeanne, was doubtless acquainted with Gilles de Rais's plan, for he had met him during his last journey through Orléans.

Jeanne could not resist the desire to take up arms. Her husband, who was not involved in matters concerning the kingdom of France, since as a Lorrain by birth he belonged to the Holy Roman Empire, did not oppose her wish. Moreover, he at once sold one of his estates, the manor of Haraucourt, so that she should be able to recruit a company of men-at-arms. In the sale contract signed on November 7, 1436 at Marville it was mentioned that "Robert des Armoises and Jehanne du Lys, Maid of France, our wife" sold that manor for the sum of "350 francs and 12 gros" to Collard de Failly.

At the end of November, followed by Jacques du Lys and a small escort, Jeanne took the road to the castle of Tiffauges, where Gilles de Rais was waiting for her; and while the recruiters got together the troops needed for the expedition

Gilles de Rais ordered to be performed before her "The Mystery," which she now saw for the first time, but which was yearly played in Orléans, and which represented the principal events of the siege of the city and other events whose heroine she was.

Early in 1437 Jeanne and Gilles de Rais took the field with about five hundred well equipped men-at-arms. For two years, ignored by King and Court, the two of them fought the bands of the *routiers* (disbanded mercenaries) whom they tracked down mercilessly, and did not fail to attack the small English detachments they met on the road. In 1437 they campaigned particularly in the region of La Rochelle. There Jeanne wrote to Juan II, King of Castile, to send part of his fleet to La Rochelle to protect it from a probable English landing. As her fear was not realised—the Court of France probably thwarted her initiative— she and Gilles de Rais made a descent on the South of France, and fought the *routiers* in the neighbourhood of Bordeaux and Bayonne. Jeanne was so seriously wounded in a fight that the rumour of her death spread as far as Orléans, where in June 1439 the Town Council had eight Masses offered up for the eternal rest of her soul.

To dispel the rumour about her death Jeanne decided to go to Orléans in person. She arrived there on July 19 accompanied by Pierre du Lys and Gilles de Rais. The Duc d'Orléans's treasurer, Jacques Boucher, offered her hospitality in his house, which Jeanne eagerly accepted because she longed to see again her host's daughter with whom she so often shared a bed during the siege.

The town she now revisited ten years after its liberation gave her an enthusiastic reception. The Council met to receive her officially, and the crowds ceaselessly acclaimed their deliverer. One of her first calls was on her foster-mother, Isabelle-Romée, widow of Jacques d'Arc, who had lived in Orléans since 1431 and who received a pension from the municipality. A few days later took place the performance of "The Mystery of Orléans" which had become a yearly tradition, but this time the part of the heroine was played by Jeanne herself. On August 1 the Town Council offered her a sumptuous banquet, at the end of which she received the substantial sum of 210 *livres parisis* in gold, as is recorded in the account books of the town, "To Jehanne des Armoises as a present to her for the good she did for the said town during the siege."

At the end of August, coming from Lyons, Charles VII arrived in Orléans, and went to stay also with Jacques Boucher with his entire suite, including Dunois, the Bastard of Orléans. Between the King and Jeanne, with their half-brother Dunois as witness, there took place a long discussion, in the course of which Jeanne admitted that her part was over, especially as her expeditions to the South of France, though they contributed to the elimination of the hardened old mercenaries, had not had the spectacular results she had hoped for; and, on the other hand, she, who sincerely believed in consulting the nation, now heard from the King that he had taken the decision to summon the States General. Only one thing was left for her to do, namely to withdraw.

On September 4, 1439 the Town Council offered Jeanne a last reception before the arrival of the Court and the many personalities who were to assist at the meeting of the States General summoned to Orléans for the end of the month. This for Jeanne was an occasion to see once more those whom she had known so well: Queen Marie, Queen Yolande of Anjou, who had done so much for her in the past, Régnault de Chartres with whom she made her peace and many others. In Jeanne's honour there was a new performance of the "Mystery," and that, in the presence of the King and the whole Court, was her real apotheosis.

On the following day in the company of Pierre du Lys she left Orléans for ever.

At Jaulny Jeanne spent her time between recounting her feats of arms of yore to her husband and taking long rides through the countryside near Metz. For her the days went by slowly, with all the monotony of provincial life disturbed only by the unimportant incidents of existence, but also with sadness when she thought of the joys of motherhood which would never be hers. She gave all her affection to her godchildren and nephews.

Thus five years passed.

In September 1444 important news reached Jaulny: the

troops of Charles VII had laid siege to Metz. The King of France had taken the decision by force to uphold the cause of his brother-in-law René of Anjou, who was in conflict with the burghers of the city because they persisted in claiming from the Duke of Lorraine, his father-in-law, whose sole heir he was, large sums of money they had lent him and which he had not repaid. The exasperated citizens of Metz burst their bonds and declared themselves independent of their overlord.

Jeanne intervened in the dispute by asking her half-brother to save the town from the horrors of pillage since it could not hold out for long. Then she skilfully negotiated between the two parties with the result that Nicolas Louve, at the head of a delegation of citizens, obtained a guarantee of freedom on condition that Metz paid a yearly tribute to the King.

Before starting out for Chinon Charles VII stopped for a few days in the manor of Jaulny. The rooms had been redone in great haste according to the principles of a new form of art which was spreading in the West and which was to become the Renaissance. In Jaulny the King met Jeanne for the last time.

In the course of her rides in the Lorraine countryside Jeanne became keenly interested in the building of the church of Pulligny. Its new architectural style attracted her, and she contributed with donations to its construction. The church stood near the manor of Autrey, where usually the head of the elder branch of the des Armoises lived, whose son was her favourite godchild. Jeanne never failed to dismount when riding in the vicinity and pray in the church with the old fervour of her youth. The years did not blunt it.

At the end of 1449, while residing in the manor of Autrey, she fell gravely ill. Probably it was one of those malignant fevers with which the medical science of her time could not cope. She died to the grief of all who were round her. Aware of her predilection for the new church of Pulligny Robert des Armoises had her buried in the side chapel to the right; and there he joined her a few years later.

There rests France's national heroine.

Jeanne's death gave Charles VII the opportunity to make

public amends which he felt constrained to do for moral and family reasons; but he also had to consider the pressing political needs that clamoured for it: the solemn rehabilitation of the condemned woman of Rouen. On February 15, 1450 he issued the order to Master Guillaume Bouillé, former rector of the University of Paris, to open an inquiry on the "faults and abuses" of the trial "to enable us to settle this case as we consider it right."

Thus empowered the former rector questioned the witnesses he managed to find, took down their statements and sent them to the King of France. But as Jeanne had been judged by an ecclesiastical tribunal permission from the Holy See was needed to reopen her trial. Pope Nicolas V, Supreme Pontiff since 1447, refused to give the requested authority; for he was perfectly well acquainted with the truth concerning the case as the representatives of the Inquisition in France regularly sent the Vatican detailed accounts of what really went on in Rouen.

In April 1455 Calixtus III succeeded Nicolas V. The new Pope was asked to authorise the reopening of Jeanne's trial. His legate, Cardinal d'Estouteville, who was also Bishop of Rouen, let him know in order to obtain it that the trial would stay strictly within the limits of the petition: the solemn rehabilitation of the condemned woman. The Pope gave in in the end. On June 3, 1455 he addressed a rescript to Jean Juvénal des Ursins, Archbishop of Rheims, Guillaume Chartier, Bishop of Paris, and Richard Olivier de Longueil, Bishop of Coutances, instructing them to reopen the trial. In that document care was taken with real Roman discretion to speak of "Pierre and Jean known as d'Arc" and of the "late sister of Pierre and Jean, daughter of Isabelle," carefully thought out vagueness, hiding the truth without lying, since Jeanne was truly the foster-sister of Pierre and Jean "known as d'Arc," and the daughter of Isabelle—of Bavaria.

The trial was reopened in Notre-Dame-de-Paris on November 7, 1455. Jeanne's foster-mother came to make a statement, and then because of her advanced years and bad health returned to Orléans. Jean and Pierre du Lys let the tribunal know that they were too busy with their official functions to be able to come to Paris. Pierre Maugier, their lawyer, declared that the two brothers attacked only Pierre Cauchon, Jean Lemaître and d'Estivet. However, Pierre Cauchon was dead and so was d'Estivet, prosecutor at the trial. And the deputy inquisitor had long since retired to a monastery, where no summons could reach him.

The retrial lasted for eight months. Many documents were produced before the judges, who heard about a hundred witnesses whose testimony was mostly useless, and which said exactly what was required of them to say. On July 7, 1456 in the great hall of the Archbishop's Palace in Rouen the judgment was set aside and the condemned woman solemnly rehabilitated.

Found innocent of heresy and idolatry which were the two essential reasons for the Rouen sentence Jeanne's memory, instead of shining bright as one would have expected, fell into oblivion in the years that followed. A hundred years after her death her memory was completely forgotten. Besides, a number of those who lived in the days of her military exploits, to begin with Pope Pius II, had expressed doubts about the circumstances in which Jeanne was called to fulfil her mission. They spoke of her only with reticence and a certain reserve; and history books hardly mentioned the important part she played in the years 1429 and 1430. The common people alone retained their complete faith in her whom they considered the daughter of simple peasants. They saw in her a martyr, a victim of her love for her country who was abandoned by her cowardly monarch, who, thanks to her victories over the English, was able to wear the royal crown of France.

Little by little she began to be remembered. Playwrights, novelists, painters and sculptors, French or foreign, took the Maid of Orléans as their subject, and while official France continued to ignore the national heroine, writers and artists exalted her memory. The town of Orléans had not ceased solemnly celebrating the anniversary of the raising of the siege, though for several centuries the feast of May 9 was just an occasion for a sort of historical memorial service preceded by an encomium of the Maid. Yet it was precisely a bishop of Orléans, Monsignor Dupanloup, who upheld her saintliness in public, and in 1869 took steps in Rome to obtain her canonisation. Eleven bishops supported his request.

Pius IX gave the request to the Sacred Congregation of Rites who in 1874 decided on opening proceedings. In 1885 Monsignor Coullié, successor of Monsignor Dupanloup in the See of Orléans, drew up in Rome the second procedure known as "Additional Trial," and in 1888 the Congregation of Rites asked to have opened a "Complementary Trial" in order to put on record the miracles attributed to Jeanne.

The same year a vast number of petitions reached the Vatican, signed by 15 cardinals, 23 archbishops, 183 bishops and many heads of religious orders, including the Jesuits, the Dominicans and the Franciscans. Among the signatories was the Comte de Chambord, descendant of the Bourbons, and after him the Comte de Paris, sole candidate to the throne of France. In spite of the efforts of those pressure groups the Pope seemed in no hurry to grant what the Holy See had already refused to several kings of France, like Louis XIII who had dedicated France to the Virgin Mary; Louis XVI whose piety was moving; Napoleon I at the height of his power; Napoleon III who made the application for personal popularity—and others.

The decree concerning the introduction to the proceedings for the beatification was signed by Leo XIII only on January 27, 1894. In 1904 Pius X approved her virtues and five years later declared her "Blessed". At long last in 1920 Benedict XV, under pressure from the French government signed the decree of canonisation. That took place nearly five hundred years after Jeanne's death.

After refusing it for centuries the Holy See agreed at last to canonise Jeanne. The French can but rejoice at the thought that their national heroine has been raised to the rank of a saint. But there again one has to weigh the exact meaning of the decree of canonisation. Though the Vatican, knowing all the secrets of Jeanne's birth, trial and escape, inscribed her name on the list of saints, it strangely restricted the significance of its decision in taking extra care in inscribing her only in the "Propre de France." Moreover, it decided that Jeanne's feast, which takes place in the month of May, should be celebrated in white vestments—that clearly shows that she proclaimed her virginity during the trial in Rouen—and not in purple vestments, as she died eighteen years after she was supposed to have burnt at the stake in the Place du Vieux-Marché. Careful to respect historical truth, the Church answered yes to the virgin and no to the martyr.

For Rome knows the truth perfectly well. Knows it through the official proofs and indisputable documents in the Archives of the Vatican, that Jeanne was the bastard daughter of Isabeau of Bavaria and the Duc d'Orléans, was born in Paris in 1407, escaped from the prison in Rouen in 1431 and was buried in the church of Pulligny in 1449.

The political reasons and reasons of state which obliged Charles VII and his descendants to keep the secret no longer exist. From the religious point of view the judgment of Rouen was set aside and Jeanne rehabilitated. Moreover, the Church cannot be blamed for its attitude at the first trial since Jeanne was saved by the Bishop of Beauvais, working with the deputy of the Inquisition, both of them approved by the Papal Legate. There is therefore no valid reason left not to reveal the truth.

Let us hope that in the very near future the Holy Father will take the decision to put at the disposal of historians the priceless documents conserved in the Archives of the Vatican.

Only then will the children of France learn the true and marvellous story of that extraordinary woman, the glorious national heroine of France, Jeanne, Maid of Orléans.